Chapman 89-90
Meeting Ronald Stevenson

Illustrations by Maura Bissett, Victoria Crowe, Philip Hutton, John MacWilliam, Alexander Moffat, David Stephenson and Gerda Stevenson. Photograph by John Humphrys.

ISBN 0 906772 85 0   ISSN 0308-2695   © *Chapman* 1998

CHAPMAN

4 Broughton Place, Edinburgh EH1 3RX, Scotland
E-mail: chapman@compura.com.uk
Website: www.compura.com\chapman
Tel 0131–557 2207   Fax 0131–556 9565

Editor: Joy Hendry   **Assistant Editor: Gerry Stewart**

Volunteers: Valerie Brotherton, Marie Carter, John Edwards, Alan Jones, C J Lindsay, Colin Mackay, Emma Pitcairn and Suzanne Runbalk.

Submissions:

Chapman welcomes submissions of poetry, fiction and articles provided they are accompanied by a stamped addressed envelope or International Reply Coupons

Subscriptions:

	Personal		Institutional	
	1 year	2 years	1 year	2 years
UK	£15	£28	£20	£37
Overseas	£20/$34	£37/$62	£25/$42	£45/$74

THE SCOTTISH ARTS COUNCIL

Printed by Inglis Allen, Middlefield Road, Falkirk FK2 9AG

Editorial

Prophets are all too rarely honoured in their own land; polymaths and geniuses are rarely hugely popular. Their dedication and purpose makes them awesome and singular, because of their unique mission they may be (but often are not) difficult individuals, and too often they inspire rank jealousy rather than admiration. Often their ideas are years ahead of the rest of us, and are quite simply misunderstood in their import and significance for the future.

Ronald Stevenson celebrated his 70th birthday earlier this year, and a large part of this double issue of *Chapman* has been commissioned in his honour: not as a *Festschrift*, but rather an attempt to describe and analyse his unique and many-faceted contribution to modern life, both here in Scotland – and internationally. Prophet he is, musically, combining the earthy vigour of traditional music with a full mastery of the classical canon and adding an abiding love and understanding of the *avant garde* frontiers of music. Polymath he certainly is, having made it business to be *au fait* not only with music in all its spheres, but also literature worldwide, the visual arts, science, you name it, sharing the belief, possible or not (and increasingly impossible today) that "the 'poet' must know everything", a tenet dear to the likes of Hugh MacDiarmid and William Soutar, both writers he greatly admired and whose he work he has set.

He has also made it his business to befriend and encourage many other, often younger talented Scots (but not just Scots), pushing them to develop whatever gifts they have as far as they can, introducing them to influences they themselves might not otherwise have encountered. But this is not just a cosy coterie of talent: he has always taken deep interest in their personal lives, and his body of friends is by no means restricted to the intelligentsia. The intensity of his passion for the fortunes of others is truly remarkable, and this has not a little to do with the fact that so many contributors here have felt impelled to include an anecdote of the "I met Ronald Stevenson at . . . and he did . . . and he said . . . and I did" variety. His enemies, or detractors, no doubt exist, but we have found it hard to find them, and even harder to get them to contribute to this 'not-a-*festschrift*'.

Unwilling to be left out of this exercise: I encountered Ronald at the tender age of 19 at a bus stop in Hanover Street, Edinburgh. He was wearing his hat at the time, and a dark burbury coat. It was raining, and I was flogging *Chapman* in the street. He was amazed and delighted at this bedraggled spectacle hawking a magazine devoted to ancient Chinese art and literature, bought one and immediately subscribed, sending me one of his famous encouraging letters penned in his own fair hand. (As his own piece on Busoni shows, he has a thing about individual script, in more ways than one.) I'm especially pleased that the interview with Ronald by his grandson makes Rob the youngest *Chapman* contributor ever, showing the writing talent continuing on into the future. I hope this feature does justice to his multifarious talent.

Our thanks to Michael Lister who helped conceive and bring to fruition this issue. Without his help and patience this celebration would not exist.

One sad postscript: the death of Alan Bold, one of Stevenson's most ardent admirers. We send our condolences to his wife, Alice. No doubt that Stevenson's influence was strong in Bold's masterpiece, *MacDiarmid*. We are all the richer for that extraordinary piece of research, and poorer that his biography of Burns remains unfinished.

And a happy one: on April 15th I shared a BBC studio with Aonghas Macneacail, Stevenson's son-in-law, in a discussion on the Colin Bell programme about whether it was proper for poets to review their own work. Aonghas arrived slightly late, extremely high, and full of energy. That morning, at 6.30, his wife, Gerda, Ronald's daughter, had given birth to a baby girl, to be named Galena. May she long be a delight to her parents, to her grandparents, and continue the extraordinary seam of talent that flows in the Stevenson genes.

The rest of the issue contains much outstanding material. *Chapman* plays a part in the Robert Louis Stevenson award administered jointly by the National Library of Scotland and the Scottish Arts Council, which annually sends a Scottish writer to the Hotel Chevillon near Paris, by publishing a selection of work by the prize winners, either written during their spell there or inspired by the experience. Here we have new writing by the two most recent incumbents, Angus Dunn and Dilys Rose, and their very different accounts of their two months there.

Aonghas Macneacail features prominently here, not only in his article on Ronald. As readers will know, his winning of the Stakis Award last November caused a minor furore in the press, with people objecting that judges who had themselves no Gaelic were incompetent to award such a prize to a Gaelic writer. In a nice bit of Serendipity, an unsolicited article by Wilson McLeod tackles this issue on a broader basis, outlining a trend over the years which gives increasing prominence to English translations and less to the original Gaelic. We thought it would be interesting to have a response from Aonghas, and to bring an international perspective to bear on it by inviting comment from Peter France, an eminent translator. It is then appropriate that this issue features translation work, from Arseny Tarkovsky, Louis Aragon and George Vafopoulos. There is also a remarkable poetry sequence from Ven Bagamudré, the Scottish Arts Council Canadian fellow two years ago. We also hope you enjoy our naughty shorties.

Also here, we pay tribute to the life's work of Allen Wright, for many years arts editor of *The Scotsman* and hear from Robert Dawson Scott some of the issues facing him as the new incumbent of that post.

To conclude on a celebratory note: Gael Turnbull who appears here is 70 this year. *A Gathering for Gael Turnbull* containing poetic tributes has been published by Au Quai containing work by long time friends and admirers. We would like to wish both Gael and Ronald many happy returns. Long may they both enrich the quality and diversity of our community, especially as it moves into a new, exciting, if perhaps difficult phase, in which their inspiration and insight will be needed to build the Scotland we want and counter the more philistine idiocies of politicians.

Interview

Rob MacNeacail

Somhairle Rob Stevenson MacNeacail (age 10) interviewed his grandfather Ronald James Stevenson, for a Tollcross Primary School project on family.

Q: Where and when were you born? How heavy were you?
A: Blackburn, Lancashire, in 1928. I was 8 pounds.
Q: How old were your parents when you were born?
A: My mother and father were both 30 years old.
Q: Who did you get your names from?
A: Ronald: my parents' choice; James: my grandfather on my father's side; Stevenson: my father's family.
Q: What work did your parents do and where did you live?
A: We lived in Mill Hill, Blackburn. My dad worked on the railways – he was a fireman, stoking the engine with coal; and my mother was a cotton mill weaver. She worked in the mills from the age of 12.
Q: What sort of house did you live in? How many rooms did you have?
A: A terraced house with a small garden at the front in which my mother grew roses. We had five rooms: kitchen, livingroom, parlour, two bedrooms and an outside toilet in the back yard. We didn't have a bathroom – we bathed in a tin tub in front of the fire every Friday night.
Q: Did you have a room of your own?
A: No. I shared with my brother.
Q: What's the first thing you can remember?
A: My father singing.
Q: What toys did you have?
A: I don't remember having any, but possibly a teddy.
Q: What games did you play at home. Any hobbies?
A: Dominoes, cards and shove-halfpenny. My hobbies were cycling and boxing!
Q: Did you get pocket money each week, and if so, how much?
A: I got no pocket money.
Q: Did you have parties on your birthday?
A: No, never.
Q: What did you do at Christmas?
A: Nothing. We didn't celebrate Christmas.
Q: Did you go anywhere on holiday, or on trips, when you were young?
A: We had three holidays, one day each time. We went to Llandudno, Southport and Blackpool by train. Llandudno was my favourite place.
Q: Do you have any other memories of when you were a boy?
A: I remember when I was very small, standing on a bridge over the railway line, holding a bunch of Forget-Me-Not flowers, waiting to see my Dad go by on the train. My aunt was holding my other hand. I was so excited when I saw my Dad that I waved to him and dropped my flowers onto the track, and cried bitterly. I also remember that during the war I

played piano for Blackburn Ballet Club from when I was about 12 or so.

Q: Tell me about your first school? How old were you when you started primary school? What do you remember about the place, and the teachers?

A: I started when I was five. I had an exceptionally good teacher, who taught me a poem, by William Blake, about a lamb. The school itself was a big Victorian building.

Q: What did you like best about school?

A: Music and poetry. And I loved drawing. I was good at drawing.

Q: Where did you go to secondary school?

A: Blakey Moor Secondary School and then Darwin Grammar School. My parents saved up to pay for me to go to Darwin Grammar School.

Q: How did you get to school?

A: I walked.

Q: Which subjects did you not like?

A: Mathematics and science. Maths was very difficult for me. My father paid for me to have lessons in maths.

Q: Which subjects did you prefer, and which were you best at?

A: Music and poetry. I played piano, of course – and liked dancing!

Q: How much homework did you get?

A: Two to three hours.

Q: Were you good at sports?

A: Yes, boxing.

Q: Did you have close friends at school?

A: Yes – and I kept in touch with them after school.

Q: How old were you when you left school?

A: I was seventeen.

Q: Did you know what you wanted to do?

A: Yes, I wanted to be a musician. So I went to college to study music. I studied at the Royal Northern College of Music in Manchester.

Q: What was your first job?

A: I had been in prison for six months as a conscientious objector (this was after the war when you still had to serve in the army), and after that I had to do a job in place of national service. I worked with a squad of Irishmen, doing ditching and draining on a farm. I was paid just over £4 per week. Then I got a job as a music teacher in County Durham.

Q: How much were you paid? How much had you left after paying for food and lodging?

A: I was paid £8.00 per week as a music teacher. After I'd paid for necessities there was nothing left. I stayed in the job for two years.

Q: How did you go to work?

A: I walked.

Q: How many hours did you work?

A: Eight hours, five days a week.

Q: What work have you done for most of your life?

A: I taught in various schools and colleges for about 12 years, but I have been a composer and concert pianist for most of my life – and I've enjoyed it very much – very much indeed.

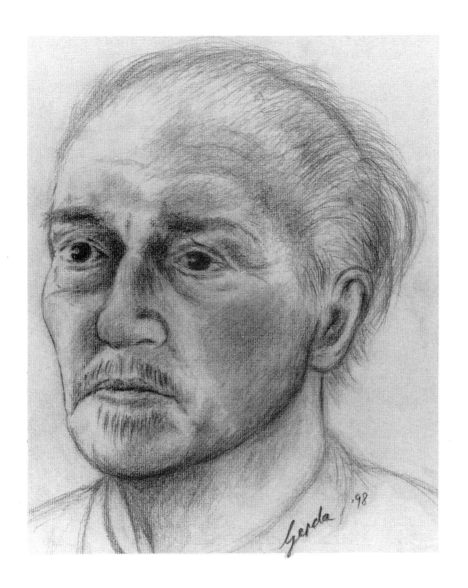

Illustration by Gerda Stevenson

Q: Have you enjoyed good health, or have you had any major illnesses?

A: I've enjoyed good health until recently. Once, I had appendicitis and I've had three minor strokes.

Q: Have you ever had to go to hospital because of an accident? Or have you ever broken any bones?

A: No

Q: Where did you first meet granny, how old were you and what were you doing at the time?

A: We met at my parent's house, and I was 19 and Marjorie (your granny) was nearly 15. I was practising the piano at the time. Marjorie came visiting with her mother – Marjorie and I are second cousins. I thought she was very beautiful.

Q: When and where did you get married?

A: 18th August, 1952, in a registry office in Edinburgh. We came to Scotland because Marjorie's parents wouldn't give their consent to our marriage, but in Scotland you could get married at the age of 16, whether your parents agreed or not. Marjorie was 20.

Q: Were you still staying at home? What did your parents think about it?

A: Yes, I was still at home. They thought I was too young to get married.

Q: What did you wear on your wedding day? Who else was there?

A: A suit. My brother was there and my landlord.

Q: Have you ever met anyone famous in your life?

A: Yes: Yehudi Menuhin, Benjamin Britten, Dimitri Shostakovich.

Q: What would you most like to do in the coming year?

A: I'd like most to compose music and play the piano.

Q: What has given you the greatest pleasure in your life?

A: My marriage and my piano.

Q: What's the funniest thing that ever happened to you?

A: My brother's false teeth fell out when we were on the roller-coaster at the fair in Blackpool.

Q: If you could live anywhere else in the world, where would it be?

A: Switzerland.

Q: Which country would you like to visit that you've never been to before and why?

A: Portugal, because of its ancient culture.

Q: What's the best advice anyone has ever given you?

A: Hugh MacDiarmid told me: "Be as good as you can be, and no better."

Q: What's the best present you've ever been given?

A: My father bought me a pair of boxing gloves, shorts and a punch bag, when I was a boy, to bribe me to practise the piano. It worked! But the best present ever was a grand piano from my parents. Dad was very good at saving. He saved £1 per week for years and years to be able to buy it for me.

Q: If you were able to have an impossible wish, what would it be?

A: I would love to be able to hear Paderewski play the piano, 100 years ago.

Meeting Ronald

Aonghas MacNeacail

Years before I met Ronald Stevenson in person, I had met him through the pages of *The Listener*, that distinguished and now much lamented house journal of the serious radio listener, when there were only three wavelengths to listen to; the Home Service, the Light Programme and the Third Programme. Ronald contributed regular articles on the kind of music then heard primarily on the Third Programme in an auto-didactic quest for understanding of the widest possible range of musics.

I can't pretend to remember the specific subject-matter of any of Ronald's essays. What I do recall is that his columns were always required reading. His fluent, vivid style gave a strictly non-musically-literate reader, such as I was (and remain), a sense of the shape of the pieces he described, so that what had previously seemed altogether remote became more accessible. He took a delight in making pictures in words, as, I would later discover, he also did in his own music.

My first encounter with Ronald Stevenson in person was entirely accidental – if such moments ever can be entirely anything. I'd gone along to a local hotel with a friend who was collecting stocks for the bar at a wedding ceilidh at the Gaelic College in Skye where I was Writer in Residence. I'd no intention of going to the event. I'd only made this lunchtime trip with Davie to help him load his van with crates of drink. Because it was lunchtime, and midweek, the bar was empty, apart from a lively group at one table who were obviously in party mood. Trying not to eavesdrop, but eavesdropping, I heard fragments of an anecdote in which Ronald's name came up on more than one occasion. When, eventually, a dapper gent with a fine head of grey hair came up to the bar to replenish his friends' glasses, I diffidently asked whether he might be Ronald Stevenson.

Quickly recovering from his surprise at being recognised at such an hour in such a place, he set about finding out who I was. A Gaelic poet? I must meet his daughter who was at that moment in Portree, being witness at her best friend's wedding. Gerda, he informed me, was an actress with a deep interest in poetry and in Gaelic. He'd introduce us at the wedding ceilidh later that evening. I hadn't planned to go to the wedding ceilidh, but curiosity about this ebullient man's daughter persuaded me.

My next meeting with Ronald was at his and Marjorie's home in West Linton, when some time later Gerda took me to meet her parents properly. My abiding memory of that occasion, and many subsequent visits, is that I was inundated with books from Ronald's extensive library which he insisted would be of essential or compelling interest to me. As yet another book descended on my lap before I'd proceeded beyond the fly-leaf of the one previous, I was soon overwhelmed, physically and emotionally. While books slid off the growing literary mountain on my lap, I had to deal with feelings of guilt that I had not the speed-reading capacity to offer informed comment on their contents. Meanwhile some aspect of our conversation had sent Ronald off in search of another key text.

I later discovered that I was not the only victim of his enthusiasm for sharing knowledge, and that his propensity to bury guests under Gutenberg mountains was shared by a dear friend and former colleague of his, Charlie King. When I first met Charlie, he was the English Adviser in the Education Department at Grampian Regional Council, but many years before he taught English at Broughton Senior Secondary School in Edinburgh where one of his colleagues in the music department was Ronald Stevenson. As Charlie's great passion was music, while Ronald's was literature, with each at times finding it hard to separate personal enthusiasm from professional obligation, it's hardly surprising that they should have become such close friends. I have often imagined a scenario where pupils discovered their music in the English class, while learning all about literature in the music room. One contemporary Scottish writer, and in his time a very reluctant scholar, Alan Bold, certainly credits Ronald's literary enthusiasms with firing his own interest in writing.

By the time I met Ronald he had long since parted company with the formal education system, although the pedagogic impetus remained strong. He still gives regular piano lessons to children from the West Linton area, including his own grandson, while older students from various corners of the world make frequent pilgrimages to obtain personal tutorials from a master. And such is his passion for ideas that few can have left his study without some item of knowledge that may have little obvious connection with music, but which fits into the totality of life as Ronald lives it.

I have inevitably had many discussions with him about music, and I am sure I'm much wiser on the subject than before, although the only specific musical fact that I can acknowledge learning from him is that the precentor-led Presbyterian Gaelic form of psalm singing, with its wonderfully wild improvisatory qualities, is known as heterophony. Such an admission implies no failure on his part, but on mine. The languages of music and mathematics are as accessible to me as ancient Sumerian.

I did learn from him that my own interest in the folk song of the Gael as a potential motor for cultural revival was paralleled by the instincts which led composers like Kodaly and Bartok to collect the folk songs of their native Hungary. Their perception that song was central to the soul of a culture led them to recognise the importance of the language in which the songs were sung. This in turn brought them to play a central part in the revival of the national language of Hungary, Magyar, which, in their time had become a very fragile language indeed, having languished under the homogenising Teutonic pressures of the Austro-Hungarian Empire.

Another cultural territory I had tentatively begun to explore was that of the Native American peoples. Dee Brown's *Bury My Heart at Wounded Knee* made me aware of a number of striking echoes between the experiences and attitudes of American Indians and my own people. Removal from their lands was one factor: their feelings for the lands they inhabited, their sense of belonging to it rather than it to them, inevitably struck a chord. Ronald drew my attention to chords, in a more literal sense, when he showed me Natalie Curtis's collection of traditional songs of the North American Indian. It was a short step from that to her brother Edward's extensive collection of photographs which spanned life-styles, linguistic families and generations of Native American communities. Farmers, fishers and hunter-gatherers, wise ones and warriors, are all portrayed. It quickly became clear to me from the Curtis family's work and the wide range of summaries and studies I now sought out, that those people I had previously only seen representations of as destructive savages were actually a heterogeneous social medley of great cultural and linguistic diversity. Their histories I would probably have sought out anyway: Ronald's particular enthusiasms steered me naturally toward the deeper and more essential aspects of their nature, to seek out what they sang, and how, and why.

Among other visitors to any conversation with Ronald, one is liable to encounter Keats, Goethe, Whitman, Marx, Morgenstern or Dante Alighieri, in quotation or biographical anecdote. He had a long correspondence with the noted theatre designer, Gordon Craig, whose work he greatly admires. Ronald likes to make an annual pilgrimage to the Scottish National Gallery's Turner exhibition which can only be brought to the surface in the weak light of January. Other artists, particularly the great Italian Renaissance masters, are tremendously important to him. This concern for the verbal and the visual may offer a significant key to the way he approaches his own music. He frequently talks about his compositions in terms of narrative and a sense of almost visible physical structures.

Having maintained contact with his former pupil Alan Bold long after Broughton school was a memory to both, he would meet and befriend artist friends of Alan's including John Bellany and Sandy Moffat. Many years earlier a chance meeting with the great thistle head of Scottish poetry, on the last evening bus from Edinburgh to Biggar (which passes through West Linton) began a friendship with Hugh MacDiarmid which would endure till the end of the older man's life. Through MacDiarmid he met Sidney Goodsir Smith, whom he remembers with great warmth, Norman MacCaig and Sorley MacLean, among other denizens of Edinburgh's literary howffs.

My own bridge to that legendary coterie was MacLean, which is not to suggest that I thought less of the others, as poets or as people. But with Sorley I had direct kinship in terms both of language and of history. That Ronald recognised on our first meeting, and the understanding remains an important part of our relationship as artists, as members of the same family and as friends. I remember that the works of John Lorne Campbell and Francis Collinson on Gaelic music and song were among the books that descended like a volcanic lava of knowledge into my lap in those early days. F G Scott has also mattered to him, as an adopted Borderer perhaps, because of the MacDiarmid connection certainly, but particularly because of what Scott had done with and for Scotland's own music.

If I suggested that Ronald taught me little about music, it should be clear that that is only true within the realms of possibility and at the level of technicalities, the finer nuances of which will remain forever beyond my comprehension. I have gained much knowledge and appreciation of his own music and of many others', particularly of the composers that have mattered most to himself such as Shostakovich, Busoni, Percy Grainger, Paderewski (who was both pianist and head of state), all the MacCrimmons and the innumerable makers of songs whose only identifying characteristic was the melody which endured and defined their urge to sing.

My earliest experience of that urge manifesting itself in Ronald occurred one Christmas day – it was either the first or second I spent among the Stevenson family. I'd given Gerda a copy of Flora MacNeil's album *Craobh nan Ubhal (The Apple Tree)* for Christmas. When all gifts had been exchanged, the album was played and listened to with obvious pleasure. Later, I heard Ronald at his piano. There was something familiar, yet not fully formed, about what he was playing. Before evening a new work had taken shape. Ronald had been particularly taken by Flora's singing of 'A Bhradag Dhubh', the Barra version of a musical duel between two women from neighbouring islands. She described it as a "boasting song": inevitably, in her version, the Barra woman has the edge over her Uist rival. In Ronald's piece, which he called the "Barra Flyting Toccata", right hand and left take the place of the opposing voices in the song, in a wonderfully exuberant piano transposition which remains totally respectful of the tradition, while being new and different.

And that's how meetings with Ronald continue to be, even if a succession of illnesses has drained something of his natural ebullience. Ideas, in their historical place, in their present relevance, and in their potential to make the world new and different, still remain an animating factor in his personal and creative life. Then when the circumstances are right, and the company congenial, he can be observed forgetting how well he's supposed not to be, as the old ebullience spreads through his bones and overflows into great gusts of laughter and music.

A Plaited Music: Ronald Stevenson at 70

Malcolm MacDonald

(Towards a literature-aesthetic of music)
Come, follow me into the realm of music. Here is the gate
Which separates the earthly from the eternal.
It is not like stepping into a strange country
As we once did. We soon learn to know everything there
And nothing surprises us any more. Here
Our wonderment will have no end, and yet
From the very beginning we feel at home.

So Hugh MacDiarmid writes, beginning his poem 'Plaited Like the Generations of Men'. Or rather he transcribes, into poetry, the prose of Ferruccio Busoni (1866-1924), the composer-pianist whose music and thinking profoundly infuse the art of Ronald Stevenson. It was Busoni – condemned for most concert-goers to a half-life under the rubric 'Bach-Busoni' through his transcriptions for the modern piano of the music of J S Bach – who observed that notation of any kind is already a transcription, one possible realisation, of the ideas present to the composer's mind.

MacDiarmid's, then, is the latest act in a chain of transcriptions. Busoni's visionary essay 'The Realm of Music', cogitated (presumably) in Italian, was formulated in German in 1910 in a letter to his wife and first published in 1935. In 'Plaited Like the Generations of Men', issued in 1955 as part of *In Memoriam James Joyce*, MacDiarmid (with footnoted 'acknowledgments to Ferruccio Busoni') translates the essay into English, selects and versifies it – and, as the poem opens out, he combines it with other ideas, other voices, including his own. Ronald Stevenson – like Busoni a musician who writes better than many full-time authors – has analysed this process in detail in one of the most penetrating of his numerous literary essays.[1]

In his music, Stevenson reveals a mastery of polyphony, the contrapuntal combination of voices and the transcriber's art of re-casting music from one medium to another. The European art-music tradition seems totally present to his mind, as it was to Busoni's; yet, composing on its Scottish edge, he responds equally to the power of folksong and landscape, sharing the hills of MacDiarmid's Border country. (His West Linton home was close enough to Brownsbank to allow a firm, mutually enriching friendship over 20 years.) His output, like MacDiarmid's, encompasses the epic and the lyric, and in it, too, many voices speak, sometimes with direct, unmediated simplicity, as in the irresistible melodic upwelling of his little MacDiarmid song 'Ae Gowden Lyric'; sometimes with such freight of meaning, in works of such scope they seem themselves to embody a kind of cultural nexus.

Such a work, by common consent, is the *Passacaglia on DSCH*, still perhaps Stevenson's most celebrated creation. At around 80 minutes' duration it is not only a gruelling test of stamina for any pianist, but perhaps the long-

---

1. 'MacDiarmid, Joyce and Busoni: Towards a Music-Aesthetic of Literature', in *Hugh MacDiarmid: a Festschrift*, ed. K G Duval and Sydney Goodsir Smith (Edinburgh, 1962.)

est continuous movement in the repertoire of the piano, a prodigious essay in an ancient and strict variation form. Derived ultimately from a seductive Spanish dance (in Spanish *pasar calle* means 'to walk the streets'), it weaves continuous variations above an unvarying 'ground', a repeating pattern in the bass. Stevenson forms his 7-bar ground from three permutations of the notes D, E-flat, C, B: the musical monogram[1], 'D.Sch', of the Soviet composer Dmitri Shostakovich. By basing his *Passacaglia* on these four notes, Stevenson testified to his admiration for this contemporary master who received a preliminary version of the piece during the 1962 Edinburgh Festival at a ceremony presided over by Hugh MacDiarmid.

This tiny kernel engenders music on a titanic scale. The *Passacaglia on DSCH* extends the tradition of Bach's *Goldberg* and Beethoven's *Diabelli* Variations, and of Busoni's *Fantasia Contrappuntistica,* a polyphonic masterpiece whose starting-point is a completion of Bach's last, unfinished fugue from *The Art of Fugue.* These works present a kaleidoscope of musical characters by exhaustive variation of a theme, worked into a powerful architectural design whose intellectual and expressive apex is a fugue, or series of fugues, where the imitations and combinations of voices, episodes, inversions and foreshortenings crown the structure like the tower of a cathedral. By accomplishing all this over a constant and unifying bass, while accommodating a far wider range of musical reference and idiom, Stevenson has dramatically enlarged the genre. He shapes his continuum of variations into a Baroque suite, virtuoso etudes, a Russian march, a Polonaise, a Spanish fandango, reminiscences of Chopin, Shostakovich and Bach, a pulverising evocation of African drumming played directly on the piano strings, a pibroch based on Patrick Mòr MacCrimmon's *Cumha na Cloinne* (Lament for the Children) and a huge triple fugue over the ground bass. This fugue, whose three subjects include the *Dies Irae* plainchant and the musical monogram Bach (B-flat, A, C, B natural) which J S Bach used 200 years before Shostakovich adopted DSCH, ought to be the work's climax – yet the most intense and impressive music occurs after this, in the final *Adagissimo* (extremely slow) variations. These build remorselessly from a sculptured simplicity by way of music marked 'with a Gagarinesque sense of space' (the *Passacaglia* coincided with the dawn of the Space Age) to a vast agglomerative climax that is truly the crown of all that has preceded it.

80-odd minutes sounds a long time, but like Beethoven's Choral Symphony or Wagner's *Ring,* Stevenson's *Passacaglia* simply imposes its own time-scale. As Paul Rapoport has remarked,

> when you experience it clock time is unreal. Real musical time, intense and immanent in such an undertaking, is very different. It is quite possible to feel, after hearing the *Passacaglia,* that it is much shorter than its stated duration, and, after hearing it a few times and thinking about it for a while, that it is much longer.[2]

---

1. In German (which calls E-flat 'Es', and B-natural 'H', reserving the letter 'B' for B-flat).
2. Notes to the composer's recording on Altarus Records AIR-CD-9091 (2).

Nevertheless Stevenson himself, with 20 years' experience of performing the work, senses a deeper relation between the *Passacaglia* and 'clock time'. He has suggested that it seems to map a lifetime, one minute to one year, with a physical climax about 35 minutes in (this marks the start of the sequence of central variations, symphonic march, fandango and African drumming), as there is in human life around 35. The climax begins about 70 (where the triple fugue comes to an end and the *Adagissimo* variations begin), and is not physical but "psychical in the Greek sense – of the mind, not the body". It remains to add that when he completed the *Passacaglia* Stevenson was just short of 35 – like MacDiarmid when he finished *The Drunk Man looks at the Thistle,* to which in some sense the *Passacaglia* is cognate, with its unwavering, universalising gaze upon a single symbol over a similarly epic span.

By now it should be plain that you cannot pigeonhole Ronald Stevenson. No doocot was ever built vast enough. To speak of him is to describe a 'man o' pairts' indeed – composer, pianist, scholar, transcriber, editor, teacher, author of books, essays, criticism and (occasional) poet, broadcaster, raconteur, speculator in pasts and futures, in the history and potentialities of his art. And, inevitably, speaking of him we invoke many others: those *magistri in absentia* from whom he learned the lessons he most values, whose traditions he embodies and sustains, the poets and painters and writers to whom he has responded in his works and the friends pictured within what one of them recently and vividly termed his 'peopled music'.

Stevenson's birth in Blackburn Lancashire made him a native of MacDiarmid's "Old Brythonic Kingdom" bestriding the Forth/Clyde and Humber/Mersey lines. His maternal grandmother could speak Welsh; as a child labourer she pushed trucks in the Welsh coalmines. Her daughter who worked in the Lancashire woollen mills married a railway fireman of Scots descent. Ronald was the younger of their two sons. It was a purely working-class environment, the only bath a tin one before the fire, yet Ronald's pianistic talent manifested early and his father patiently saved enough for a grand piano. Stevenson senior had a good tenor voice and loved to sing the songs of John McCormack and Richard Tauber; his son became his domestic accompanist almost as soon as he could play. Ronald's love of song, of melody, his conviction that music should always sing or dance, began here. In his teens he was already writing songs (Byron, Tom Moore, Walter Scott) as well as music for the Blackburn Ballet Company.

Winning an open scholarship to the Royal Manchester College of Music, he studied piano with Iso Ellinson and began a lifelong friendship with the young John Ogdon. While at the RMCM he discovered the music of Busoni, which gave meaning and direction to his burgeoning compositional talents far beyond anything he was taught at the college. Avid to discover everything about this renaissance man of music – pianist, composer, transcriber, writer, conductor, teacher, keyboard philosopher – Stevenson embarked on a decades-long programme of original research into Busoni which amounted to a musical self-education at the highest level.

Busoni, a convinced pacifist, had spent World War I in self-imposed exile in neutral Switzerland. Stevenson's pacifism took root in boyhood during World War II, a blend of religious and socialist impulses and more particularly his reading of Albert Schweitzer and William Blake. At 19, after graduating with distinction from the RMCM, he refused call-up for National Service as a Conscientious Objector. Though a minor in law, he was imprisoned for a year alongside hardened criminals in Preston, Liverpool, Winston Green and Wormwood Scrubs. It was a searing experience. The Appellate Tribunal eventually allowed him to finish his sentence working on the land. For a time he worked at a farm run by the poet J H Watson at Freighting Hall, near Colchester and ended digging ditches and drains in the company of Irish navvies.

His prison sentence immeasurably increased Stevenson's difficulty in securing employment. Finally he gained a job at Boldon Colliery School in County Durham where his conscientious objection was approved of rather than the reverse; he taught music and directed the school brass band from 1950 to 1952. For several years he had been courting a distant cousin, Marjorie Spedding; in 1951 she had moved to Edinburgh where she found work in a factory. Ronald left Boldon to follow her there, and his story becomes a Scottish one.

Already he had composed works far more than merely promising, such as a major song-cycle on Blake's *Songs of Innocence,* drafted while working on the land. As early as 1947 Stevenson had written *War,* an astonishingly powerful 'dramatic scene' setting a little-known Blake text – a passionate denunciation of war and the politicians and clerics who support it. Even now this seems one of his finest achievements in song. Discovering Busoni led him back to the 19th-century tradition of keyboard invention on operatic themes. In 1949 he wrote a *Fantasy on Busoni's 'Doktor Faust'* for piano, evoking the visionary world of the opera which was Busoni's masterpiece. From the same source he took the theme Busoni gives to the title of a magic book, *Clavis Astartis Magica (The Key to Stellar Magic),* and produced a magnificent piano fugue. Some years later, at John Ogdon's suggestion, Stevenson would combine the 'Clavis' Fugue and the Fantasy with an introductory movement, creating the large-scale *Prelude, Fugue and Fantasy on Busoni's 'Faust',* now one of his best-known works; later still he enlarged and re-cast this for piano and orchestra as his First Piano Concerto, *A Faust Triptych.*[1]

During the 1950s Ronald taught music in a variety of Edinburgh schools. He married Marjorie in 1952 and in 1956 they settled in West Linton, their home ever since, to raise a multi-talented family: the violin-maker and photographer Gordon, the actress Gerda (delivered by her father in the absence of a midwife), and the harper and composer Savourna. Stevenson's return to his ancestral Scotland produced an epiphany to rival the discovery of Busoni: his growing awareness of the range and beauties of

---

1. A later example of 'operatic reminiscence' for the piano is the compelling *Peter Grimes Fantasy,* in which Stevenson encapsulates the dramatic essence of Britten's opera in a single virtuoso fugal structure.

Scottish folksong, both Lowland and Gaelic. Thus in the 1950s he began – significantly with a piece entitled 'Lang Hae We Pairted Been' – a substantial series of *Scottish Folk-Music Settings*. Many of his arrangements achieve a timeless quality as in the 'Sailing Song' and 'Christ-child's Lullaby' from the *South Uist Folksong Suite*.

His inspiration in this endeavour was the music of Percy Grainger, with whom Stevenson had been corresponding since the early 1950s. Grainger proved a powerful counter-influence to Busoni, advocating a music altogether more democratic and demotic, enriched by the folksongs and popular music of many lands. In this his effect was comparable to that of Hugh MacDiarmid, whom Stevenson befriended in 1956. From MacDiarmid Stevenson learned of Francis George Scott, the master song-composer whose signal achievements included his brilliant settings of MacDiarmid's lyrics of the 1920s and 30s. Stevenson never met Scott, but the latter's death in 1958 prompted one of the finest of Stevenson's shorter piano works, the 'Keening Song for a Makar'. Combined with two later, equally impressive musical tributes, the 'Heroic Song for Hugh MacDiarmid' and the Chorale-Pibroch for Sorley MacLean', this now forms the *Modern Scottish Triptych*.

During 1963-65 Stevenson sojourned in South Africa as senior lecturer in composition at the University of Cape Town, where he completed and premièred the *Passacaglia*, and began his long series of settings of Mac-Diarmid's poetry concentrating (unlike F G Scott) on the poet's later work.

On his return to Scotland, Stevenson devoted himself to composition, piano-playing and teaching, writing and frequent BBC broadcasts as lecturer and performer. His centenary radio programmes on Busoni earned a Harriet Cohen International Music Award in 1967, and in 1974 he devised, scripted and presented a television documentary on Busoni entitled *Harlequin and Faust*. (Subsequently, for BBC Radio Scotland, he devised and presented three major series on Scots fiddle music, the Highland bagpipe and the Celtic harp.) His involvement with MacDiarmid's work culminated in the early 1970s in two massive song-cycles: *Border Boyhood*, largely setting MacDiarmid's autobiographical prose and *The Infernal City*, where MacDiarmid's apocalyptic vision of Glasgow is counterpointed with 'Calbharaigh', Sorley MacLean's lament for the children of the slums. But this focus on Scottish music and literature was balanced by an exploration of many other national traditions. Partly inspired by Percy Grainger, Stevenson thought long and hard, before the present age of total availability of every musical experience, about a 'World Music' that would synthesise what all the different cultures had to contribute. As he wrote in his challenging book *Western Music, An Introduction*:

> African music is primarily rhythmic and physical; Asian is primarily melodic and spiritual; and European music is primarily harmonic and polyphonic, emotional and intellectual. The sum of the physical, the spiritual, the emotional and the intellectual, is the whole being of an individual's life. So the sum of world music is the complete music of mankind.[1]

---

1. *Western Music, An Introduction* (London: Kahn and Averill, 1971), p 208.

Three major works stand as Stevenson's most ambitions realisations of this ideal. The *Passacaglia on DSCH* has already been described. His Second Piano Concerto, *The Continents* (1970-72), is a globe-spanning trek, emerging from a purely percussive opening of African drumming to take in Chinese pentatony, Vietnamese song, Hindu raga, Hebridean pibroch, Bulgarian dance, European fugue, American jazz and South American rhythms, but all tautly structured into a series of variations on a double theme deriving simultaneously from *DSCH* and Busoni's 'Clavis Astartis Magica'. Finally Stevenson's Violin Concerto, *The Gypsy* (1973-9) – one of the largest works in its repertoire and one of his greatest – arises with an Indian raga of the dawn in a spellbinding opening aubade. Its broad three-movement design traces a westward-moving history of the violin through Rumanian gypsy fiddle-tunes, solo writing of Bachian eloquence, a homage to the Norwegian Hardanger fiddle and a main finale theme that Stevenson terms a 'strath-reel-jig' because it combines the rhythms of all three characteristic Scottish and Irish fiddle dances. These three tremendous works are much more than the sum of their disparate parts: the many musical characters enlarge the expressive range and aspire to a humane synthesis rare in Western music.

Stevenson has studied many of these national traditions first hand. He has travelled worldwide as pianist and lecturer, as advocate not just of his own music but of Busoni, Grainger and Paderewski in particular. He has advocated many other less familiar figures from the post-Lisztian piano traditions, such as Nikolai Medtner and the Swiss-domiciled Pole, Czeslaw Marek, as well as British friends and colleagues like Alan Bush, Bernard Stevens, Edmund Rubbra and William Wordsworth and the neglected Aberdonian master, Ronald Center. He visited the USSR in 1968 as guest speaker at the 4th Congress of Soviet Composers: subsequent concert tours have taken him as far afield as the USA, Canada, Australia, China, Eastern Europe, and many times to Switzerland for whose mountains and lakes he has an enduring affection.

Through the years he has added steadily to a compositional output as remarkable for its scope as for its fecundity. The decade following the Violin Concerto saw the creation of several important piano works – the *Symphonic Elegy for Liszt*, the scarifying toccata for the atomic age *Motus perpetuus (?) temporibus fatalibus,* whose query is integral to its title; and the bravura test-piece for the 1990 Scottish International Piano Competition, *Beltane Bonfire,* to name three. His output of chamber music and instrumental music was significantly expanded by the virtuoso guitar duo *Don Quixote and Sancho Panza* (a tone poem after Cervantes in the guise of a set of variations), the *Scots Suite* for solo violin (a work to rank beside Bartók's solo sonata for the instrument), the Fantasy Piano Quartet *Alma Alba,* and the String Quartet, *Voces Vagabundae,* with its fleet, fantastic scherzo 'The Bird Path' in homage to the poetry of Kenneth White.

And many, many songs. Stevenson has become one of the century's most prolific song composers, responding to poets as diverse as Burns, Morgenstern, Sydney Goodsir Smith and Ho Chi Minh. Besides his body of work on MacDiarmid he has enriched Scottish literature with many settings of William Soutar, *Songs of Quest* on poems of John Davidson and a setting of R L Stevenson's *Child's Garden of Verses* for tenor and/or soprano with optional boy treble. (Music *about* childhood, not for children: but he has long been concerned to make music accessible to children, and has written many pieces involving young and even handicapped performers.) There are also songs to words by James Joyce, and among others Stevenson has set Yeats, Masefield, Wordsworth, Tagore, Sacheverell Sitwell, Kathleen Raine and Alan Bold; German and Italian poets in their own tongue, Scots Gaelic, Lancashire dialect and Aberdonian Doric. And those are just the solo songs. His choral music includes *Songs into Space*, after Walt Whitman, a triptych on medieval Scottish texts, a Gaelic cycle *Anns an Airdre, as an Doimhe* on poems of Sorley MacLean, the biblical *Peace Motets* and the magnificent 12-part motet *In Memoriam Robert Carver* setting James Reid Baxter's modern recreation of aureate Scots.

In the past five years the output has slowed because of the serious health problems he has suffered since 1992. And yet these recent years have seen the completion of the Cello Concerto *The Solitary Singer* in memory of Jacqueline du Pré and two major piano works: *A Carlyle Suite* and *Le Festin d'Alkan*. The latter, lasting over an hour in performance, is perhaps his biggest conception for solo piano since the *Passacaglia*.

In the *Carlyle Suite*, commissioned to celebrate Thomas Carlyle's bicentenary, he remembers Caryle's biography of Frederick the Great, the King-composer who propounded the noble 'Royal Theme' on which J S Bach based his *Musical Offering*. The bulk of the *Carlyle Suite* is a series of variations on that same theme, presenting a miniature history of music as they evolve from the idioms of the baroque to those of the modern era. One variation is entitled 'Chopin plays for Jane Carlyle' (as, in fact, he did) and combines original dances (by Stevenson) in Scottish and Polish style with an old Scots Psalm tune. *Le Festin d'Alkan*, a homage to one of Chopin's closest friends, the remarkable pianist-composer Alkan, is in three movements: the first original composition by Stevenson, the second a free transcription of a Barcarolle by Alkan and the third a set of bravura variations on the theme of Alkan's famous Étude *Le Festin d'Aesope*.

Thus Stevenson is still exploring the continuum between the musics of different traditions and between 'original' composition and music founded on pre-existing ideas, ideas strong enough to be considered the common property of humanity. He has been known to quote, with approval, Goethe's lines from *Faust:* "Who can think wise or foolish things at all/ That were not thought already in the Past?" – and despite his command of modern composition techniques, the sometimes uncompromisingly contemporary sound of his music and the impossibility that any of it could have been written save in our troubled and uncertain times, the inspiration he has drawn from previous masters has sometimes been criticised as reactionary, or perhaps mere conservatism.

This is fundamentally to misunderstand the kind of composer Steven-

20

son is. Despite the largeness of his personality his music has less to do with himself, individuality, than with human traditions and how they endure and change. He may be brim-ful of ideas, but he does not simply express those ideas in music: insofar as they have been shaped through history, the ideas express themselves through him. But music is not a set of propositional statements. "Cares the nightingale/ who hears it sing?" as MacDiarmid wrote in the poem Stevenson set as 'The Song of the Nightingale', and whose music he quotes at the close of the Cello Concerto, *The Solitary Singer*. As in poetry, everything comes down to the singing voice and how it affects us. Thus it all depends *what* one instinctively reacts against ("Better ae gowden lyric/ Than Insurance, Banking and Law"), and *what* one works to conserve ("Civilisation, culture, all the good in the world").

Transcription, of words or music, is one powerful means of conservation, giving ideas new life in new contexts. Stevenson has been one of its most tenacious masters in an age when musical transcription was downgraded in the quest for 'authenticity' – the belief (a bastard form of Platonism, related to the modern passion for 'originality') that each art-work has only one possible valid form, an academically-recoverable *Urtext*. Among his multitudinous and always superbly effective piano arrangements are Elizabethan music, pieces by Purcell, a whole series of keyboard reworkings of Victorian and Edwardian songs entitled (in homage to Thalberg) *L'Art nouveau de chant appliqué au piano*), towering virtuoso transformations of Mahler's Tenth Symphony Adagio, Nielsen's organ work *Commotio* and the six solo violin sonatas of Ysaÿe realised as piano sonatas.

This latter feat recalls Godowsky's recomposition of Bach's Sonatas and Partitas for solo violin as piano sonatas, and also Busoni's encyclopedic array of 'Bach-Busoni' arrangements, long scorned but now coming back into fashion for their sovereign pianism. Bach himself arranged Vivaldi concertos for solo keyboard. The most famous movement in his solo violin works, and a direct ancestor of *Passacaglia on DSCH*, is the Chaconne from the D minor Violin Partita, a gruelling test of any violinist and a challenge to the transcriber. Brahms arranged it for piano, left hand only. Busoni's famous version uses the full resources of the modern piano. Leopold Stokowski arranged Busoni's transcription for orchestra and gave it a new ending of his own, based on Bach's material. When Ronald Stevenson recorded his own stirring performance of the Bach-Busoni *Chaconne* for CD[1], he transcribed Stokowski's orchestral ending for the piano, to create a version that can justly be labelled 'Bach-Busoni-Stokowski-Stevenson'.

Truly potent art simultaneously endures and renews itself, whether in development, variation or transcription. World literature shows us the like. In archaic Greece, in a purely oral tradition, poets whose names we do not know fashioned the *Nekuia*, the tale of a hero visiting the underworld

1. On 'Cathedrals in Sound' Altarus Records AIR-CD-9043.

to seek counsel from the prophetic dead: about the future and how he can get there. Somewhere in the 8th century BC a genius who spoke and recited in Ionic dialect wove the *Nekuia* into his epic of the sea-voyager Odysseus, seeking to return home from Troy. That blind, retentive poet did not write his epic, but as literacy spread a vulgate was variously recorded by men who heard it recited by bards two or three generations on. The text was standardised centuries later by Alexandrian librarians who, not without their own talents, divided it into 24 books. We call this process 'Homer'. Then it bifurcates. On one fork, recomposition: Virgil reworking the *Nekuia* into his own epic of Aeneas, Homeric in form and incident but in Augustan Latin, redirected to create a foundation myth for the new-found peace – beneficent, murderous – of Imperial Rome. Dante making his *Divina Commedia* a vast Christian *Nekuia*, with Virgil himself, a shade like the rest, as his guide. James Joyce transposing the entire *Odyssey* to 24 hours of a severely realist yet mythical 1900s Dublin, creating a new kind of novel: *Ulysses*.

On the other fork, transcription. In the early 1500s Andreas Divus issued a modest, serviceable Latin translation of the *Odyssey*, one Latin word for each Greek one. Four centuries on, Ezra Pound translated Divus' version of the *Nekuia* into a purely Saxon, un-Latinised English vocabulary he'd developed for his version of the Anglo-Saxon *Seafarer*, one Saxon word for each Latin one. The tale intact, Pound breaks off to say "Lie quiet Divus. I mean, that is Andreas Divus/ In officina Wecheli, 1538, out of Homer" – numbering Divus and Homer in their turn among the shades from whom we seek counsel. And a new kind of epic poem sets its keel to the waves: the *Cantos*. That "poem including history" – quoting documents from many cultures, moving between different languages and alphabets, sometimes phonetically recording voices the poet heard – profoundly influenced MacDiarmid, notably in *In Memoriam James Joyce*. Thus (for example) his use of Busoni.

In like fashion has Stevenson created a music including history, plaited from many sources, in which ancient, potent, fundamental ideas are renewed and launched on fresh voyages. These musico-literary parallels remind us that all art – verbal, visual, auditory – is patterned energy, or the appearance of it: a mimesis of kinesis. What distinguishes Ronald Stevenson is his paramount awareness of that fact and his rare ability to renew such patterned energies in artistic communion with like minds from the past and present; so that he, and they, and we, are participants in a continuing poetic act.

The Man in the Fedora

Ruzena Wood

My first sight of Ronald Stevenson was during the Edinburgh Festival, 1962. I had taken a day's leave from being music archivist in the National Library of Scotland to go to an orchestral rehearsal in the Usher Hall. Dmitri Shostakovich was present at this rehearsal for a concert of his works. Short and stocky, with pebble glasses, he seemed dwarfed by the little group of Russians huddling round him in the unlit auditorium. His wife, his children, his interpreter? Had he got a political minder? And if so, which one was the minder?

In the dark behind me a door creaked open. A tall man in a fedora paused on the threshold, clutching a bulky music case like a concertina. His face, outlined by the corridor lights behind him, was lean, intense, with high cheekbones, his eyes penetrating. "That's Ronald Stevenson," whispered my companion. Next day the newspapers described the presentation of the score of Ronald Stevenson's *Passacaglia on DSCH* to the visiting Russian composer. This eighty-minute piano solo is dedicated to Shostakovich, the theme carved out of his name. I had witnessed a historic occasion.

That fedora lingered in my memory. The wide-brimmed dark velour framed his face perfectly. It expressed style, confident awareness of design. Extrovert East European flair had found traditional British understatement wanting. If the great Russian bass, Chaliapin, could have had the opportunity to try on that fedora, he would have sung a few arias from *Boris* to be allowed to keep it. Years later I asked Ronald Stevenson about the origins of his famous fedora. "It was a present from my father," he answered simply. I looked at the photograph of Ronald's father on the mantelpiece. All those years ago in Blackburn, Lancashire. He looked a quiet railwayman. But perhaps, like his composer son, he was not always quiet, for he held up his railway lantern like a beacon.

It was Ronald I turned to for technical advice when my music theory teacher died. Having studied by correspondence, I was afraid that a surfeit of exercises in 1880's four-part harmony would leave me stuck in a stylistic groove. Following a chance meeting at a performance of Gershwin's *Oh, Kay*, I found myself in a bus heading for West Linton with a draft of my arrangement of the Scots tune, *The Rowan Tree*. Ronald met the bus. We detoured on the walk down to Townfoot House to stop and look and touch real rowan trees, hung with rich clusters of red berries. The front door of Townfoot House was guarded, almost obstructed, by a giant hydrangea. I was reminded of *The Sleeping Beauty*, when, with a flourishing virtuosic sweep, Ronald pushed the bush aside and we went in. When, eventually, that hydrangea had to be hacked down, I missed it.

After lunch I asked Ronald about his own work. Did he think of composing in terms of colour? "Yes. This is red." (Hard, quartal counterpoint on the piano). "And this is light grey. An illustration of an angel's wing. From a very beautiful Christmas card." He fetched the card to show me.

From about 1979 I had two or three lessons a year – not systematic study. I usually chose what I wanted to learn next. In Ronald's studio, which I nicknamed his 'den of musiquity', I worked through Bach chorales, pentatonic harmony, and how to score for strings. Ronald demonstrated how to make my continuo for a Hebden concerto blend, as well as support the concerto grosso players. The studio, usually warmed by a real coal fire, was lined with Ronald's favourite books and scores. Perhaps a thousand books, the tools of his trade. Treasured autographed first editions of the poet, Hugh MacDiarmid. A shelf of Walt Whitman with a paragraph added at random in the poet's hand, like a message in a bottle, tossed into the sea.

More than the spines of books on shelves, I liked looking at the photographs on the wall. Beside the Steinway, intense creative faces gazed down: Ignaz Paderwski, Percy Grainger, Yehudi Menuhin – who conducted the première of Stevenson's *Violin Concerto*. And Ferruccio Busoni, who knew all about emergence from poverty and continual striving for education. These influences orchestrated the solitude of the studio so that no student need ever feel they struggled alone. Ronald placed his entire range of scholarship: musical, literary and linguistic – at a student's disposal. His approach was holistic. He did not simply answer a question, he would outline the context, so that one could recognise a similar situation next time round and learn to deal with it.

Some highlights stand out. One morning when I arrived, Ronald admitted he had stayed up till two, composing a song which is now part of his song cycle *A Child's Garden of Verses*. He immediately played it for me from his pencil draft.

News of Ronald's stroke came as a shock to all. Ronald's wife, Marjorie, used her skills as a qualified nurse when, in recovery mode, he was forced to relearn the use of his fingers at the keyboard. Ronald's successes and survival owe much to the qualities of this remarkable woman and their long happy marriage. Friends rallied. I remember I hit on the idea of photocopying pages of Saint-Säens études for the left hand alone, sending it to West Linton as a matter of urgency. To survive as a pianist Ronald refingered his piano repertoire – a mammoth task if he had been well.

Over lunch in their farmhouse kitchen the Stevensons told me that Ronald was due to play a piano recital in Dunblane Cathedral – his first foray into the recital arena since the stroke. I recount this story because facing a series of painful challenges is very much part of normal human experience, yet rarely discussed. Ronald said, "What if something goes wrong?" I hesitated. "I would not dare say this if you were a young pianist starting out. We all know what youngsters go through. But you are a mature performer. If you have to stop – you'll carry on. And your audience will be mature enough to share everything with you. That's the way life is."

The Dunblane recital was a triumph over adversity. A friend told me that the *Moonlight Sonata* had been deeply moving and unforgettably beautiful. Beethoven, who fought alone against the pain and isolation of deafness, would have rejoiced every step of the way.

Now Ronald and Marjorie are producing an edition of his work under the auspices of the Ronald Stevenson Society. What is interesting and encouraging here is the amount of interest shown by a new, young generation of performers who do not want to be fobbed off with music without meaning. Ronald Stevenson's music has turned out to be something they can relate to. With their friends, the Stevenson's hold a weekend summer school every year. An enterprise like this helps to dispel some of the myths about compositional processes and composers. The Victorians, while apparently admiring creative talent, were secretly afraid of it. They cherished the notion that composers were not really creatures of this world, inhabiting instead, some alternative loftier realm. This attitude has led to misunderstandings which linger to this day. Real men of vision have their feet firmly planted on this earth even though they can touch stars. At the age of seventy, this is certainly true of Ronald Stevenson. Once he told me how much he disliked half-baked attempts to categorise him and his music. "Pigeonholes," he smiled, "are only appropriate for pigeons."

Ronald Stevenson

Twa Sangs Frae the German o Christian Morgenstern (1871-1914)

Dinna Stir

Dinna stir the sleep o the darlin lass, ma aa!
Stir her tender, tender sloomran no avaa.

Hoo far awaa she's noo. An yet sae near.
Yin flichter – an agen she wad be here.

Och, wheesht, ma hert, an wheesht yet mair, ma mou:
Wi angels spaks her speerit, ilka oor an nou.

Hairst

The warld hes gane tae gowd;
for ower lang
the skinklan sun caresst
the leaf, the boucht.
Sink noo
o warld, sink doon
in wintersleep.

Soon wull it faa tae ye
in flaws an flachts the fleece
that smuirs the muirs –
an hansels Peace,
o warld,
tae ye, lued Lyfe, be luve garred gowden,
Peace.

The Princess of Scotland

Ballad for unaccompanied medium voice
or may be sung by a questioning male voice and an answering female voice.

Poem: Rachel Annand Taylor

Music: Ronald Stevenson

Moderato rubato

"Who are you that so strangely woke, And raised a fine hand?"

Po-ver-ty wears a scar-let cloke __ In my __ land.

"Du-chies of dream-land, __ e-me-rald, __ rose Lie __ at your com-mand?"

Po-ver-ty like a prin-cess goes ___ In my __ land.

"Where-fore the mask __ of sil--ken lace Tied ___ with a gol--den band?"

(1)

Po-ver-ty walks with wan-ton grace ___ In my ___ land

"Why do you soft-ly,___ rich-ly___ speak Rhy - - -thm so sweet-ly___ scanned?"

Po-ver-ty hath the___ Gæ-lic and the Greek ___ In my___ land.

"There's a far-off___scent a- -bout you___ seems Born in___ Sa-mar-kand."

Po-ver-ty hath lu-xu-ri-ous dreams ___ In my___ land.

(11)

"You have wounds that like pas-sion flowers you hide: I can-not un-der-stand."

Po-ver-ty hath one name with pride ___ In my ___ land.

"Oh! Will you draw your last sad breath 'Mid bit-ter bent and sand?" ___

Po-ver-ty begs from none ___ but ___ Death ___ In my ___ land. ___

Composer's note: Hugh MacDiarmid included this poem and another by the same poet in The Golden Treasury of Scottish Poetry MacMillan, London 1948 He also wrote an enthusiastic article on Rachel Annand Taylor in the organ of the E.I.S. reprinted in his Contemporary Scottish Studies. 'Scottish Educational Journal, Edinburgh; 1976.
— R. S.

Stevenson, Music and Marxism

Eddie McGuire

The invitation, when it came in September 1977, filled me with awe; polit-ical ideas raced, kicked off by the starting pistol of Ronald's sentence "The three of us could have a useful discussion about music and Marxism". I had first made the acquaintance of Ronald Stevenson in 1974 when we began periodically talking of current political struggles, debating the mer-its and contradictions of China's (then cooling) Cultural Revolution and, of course, many aspects of music-making. In the summer of 1974 my attention had been grabbed for the first time by a piece of his. In reviewing his Second Piano Concerto (*The Continents*) for *Music and Musicians* I had been struck by its world-music power, political boldness and, unu-sually for the time, adherence to a strongly melodic, romantic tradition.

However, it was the third participant in "the useful discussion" who nearly tipped the scales of awe – the late Alan Bush, veteran of the Com-munist Party (the one now defunct), founder of the Workers Educational Association in 1936 and prodigious composer. He was unique in being the only composer to receive the honour of an official ban from the BBC (over his vigorous support for the Soviet Union and the setting up of the Peo-ple's Convention early in the Second World War.)

The weekend of October 15-17 in West Linton proved affable and mem-orable – the contentious issues such as revisionism (a too-convenient accu-sation of the period), formalism (many a good Soviet composer fell foul of that one), petty nationalism (Scottish separatism or a strong, united Brit-ish Labour movement?) having been set aside for later debate! Musical memories include my learning what the oft-repeated phrase "transcen-dental pianism" might mean when we all heard Louis Kentner playing Liszt at Haddington, and hearing Alan and Ronald practising for a concert organ-ised by Ronald pursuing Pablo Casal's idea of "Music for All." (These "peo-ple's music" concerts were to continue into 1978, mixing folk with classical. They included my own flute playing, and clarsach playing by his daughter Savourna who has herself become a composer of note.)

Encapsulated in that weekend is what I see as the key to understanding Stevenson's political outlook and role. I was convinced by the empathy that existed, of their deep conviction that as artists we were "of the peo-ple" and should play a full part in common struggles; by their acceptance of their position as worker-intellectuals who by their art transcend petty differences and present the platform of the class on a higher and more united level. Angus Calder, in his 'Revolting Culture', draws support from Gramsci in advocating a moral and intellectual leadership role for such individuals – but not in isolation from the wider labour movement.

(However, although it may have been apt in that decade for Colin Scott-Sutherland to emphasise of Ronald that, since Havergal Brian, he was "the only nationally known composer of industrial proletarian parentage". Comprehensive schooling, free music tuition and the welfare state with its socialist aspects nurtured new composers of both sexes from similar backgrounds during the 1950s, 60s and 70s. More importantly, a convincing two-class line has evolved among the Labour movement, Marxist and Communist thinkers which points to the majority of the population – who do not own the means of production – being of the same, modern working class which would naturally encompass all ages, the unemployed and those with illusions!)

Ronald would later – in 1995 – give the oration at Alan Bush's funeral, but much earlier, in the *Music Review* of November 1965, he portrays Bush's achievements in vivid terms. He ranks him with the best of the "laconic, pungent and utterly unsentimental" anti-Nazi creations of the Brecht/Eisler song writing partnership and gives strong advocacy for Bush's operas *The Sugar Reapers*, *Wat Tyler* and *Men of Blackmoor*. Almost ignored in Britain, this operatic output was given due recognition and staging in the socialist German Democratic Republic. Ronald often spoke to me in the 1970s of his ambition (now abandoned) to write an opera on the subject of the anti-Nazi defiance and trial of Dmitrov (falsely accused of causing the Reichstag fire). I believe his inspiration was the operatic path laid by Alan Bush. Described by Ronald as "almost unique in Britain as the expression of a politically committed composer", he was a strong exponent of Marxism and the struggle for a better, socialist way of life. His encouragement opened the door that helped lead to the great cornerstone of Ronald's output, the *Passacaglia on DSCH*, presented to the bearer of those initials, Shostakovich, at the 1962 Edinburgh International Festival.

The music and its great performances (Ronald's own, John Ogden's and Raymond Clarke's, for example) will be recalled and analysed elsewhere. However, moral and political ideas nurtured the roots of the *Passacaglia* and the world-view therein is laid out on a vast canvas. Rooted in turn in his own very personal opposition to the exploitation of a class or oppression of a people, these ideas are strongly anti-imperialist in tone, Marxist-Leninist in their analysis. Music, of course, adds depths of emotion and universality that mere political polemics can never plumb! So it is with this piano piece. Truly prophetic has been his section marked "to emergent Africa"; now marking the end of an epoch, the section intoning the Bolshevik demand of 1917 for Peace, Bread and Land; the epic struggle marked by the idea of hammering the swastika into a sickle; peace is celebrated by uniting the musical symbols for Bach and Shostakovich; and, most tellingly the memorial section for the millions of Jewish people who died at the hands of Nazism. Another visionary allusion – to the first cosmonaut – ends the piece. Gagarin's timing was impeccable, rocketing up just as Ronald was completing the piece in 1961! And the 'oneness' experienced in orbiting this world of music is encompassed by influences such as Scottish Piobaireachd and African Drumming.

This openness to world influences and his generous sense of solidarity is demonstrated amply in his vast output of over 300 songs. From another orbital experience – setting Alan Bold's poem of a Soviet satellite twinkling over an Edinburgh slum – he descends with Sorley MacLean into the decay of inner city Glasgow. Extending his solidarity worldwide led him to the struggle for Vietnamese national liberation and his setting of poems by Ho Chi Minh. I am amazed to have just realised that these songs were composed in 1966 – well before it became a *cause célèbre* and the focus of the massive student-led anti-Vietnam War demonstrations of the late 1960s.

The range of inspirations for his songs is impressive; from the dialects of Lancashire and Scotland, from classic poets to those of the present, a purposeful humanity shines through. A large portion of the energy and impetus that lies behind his song writing emanates from his productive decades of dialogue with Hugh MacDiarmid. Significantly, his 'Heroic Song For Hugh MacDiarmid' was commissioned from him by the BBC in 1967 to honour MacDiarmid's 75th birthday.

However, there are elements in the MacDiarmid canon that I find unpalatable. Perhaps further debate would iron out these quandaries: for example, his proximity on some levels to Ezra Pound (whose anti-semitism and support for Fascism are alleged), recent writings (in *Cencrastus*) on Mac-Diarmid's own early play with ideas that seem to be of fascist origin and an erratic fluctuation between Marxist thoughts and extreme nationalism. Now I think one of the biggest factors stabilising his outlook in his final decades was artistic interaction with such deeply humanitarian creators as Ronald Stevenson and, earlier, Francis George Scott. His commitment to Leninist thought grew, although sometimes he seems to despair unnecessarily of the people doing anything for themselves, citing their "mindlessness". Rejoining the Communist Party in 1957, he seems to have mended his fences with the veteran Scottish communist Willie Gallagher ("a great humanist, true comrade and friend") – writing a warm tribute on his 80th birthday. I would have liked to have known his thoughts on Britain-wide solidarity at that time (a concept close to Gallagher). MacDiarmid had, of course, nailed his socialist colours to the mast much earlier in his poems 'Fascists, you have killed my comrades' and 'In Memoriam Garcia Lorca'.

It fell to Scott – and ultimately to Ronald Stevenson – to add further, deep, universal, emotional extensions through the power of music to many of MacDiarmid's utterances. A little gem of a song, to Ronald's music, as one example, is 'The Skeleton of the Future' (subtitled 'At Lenin's Tomb') – a synthesis of past and present, of music and Marxism.

Recent years have seen Ronald mining ever deeper veins of emotion with, for example, his moving cello concerto in memory of Jacqueline du Pré, and the philosophical and even spiritual traditions of Scotland under the influence of James Reid Baxter. In other works nuclear arms are condemned and pacifism strongly propounded, giving rise to the thought that his approach to national liberation struggles is an area I would ask him more about.

Perhaps a longer weekend that October, 21 years ago, would have answered my questions; no, it's probably time to have another one!

Now, on returning to my first thoughts on encountering Ronald Stevenson's music, I feel my enthusiasm rising to its 1974 level and stand by what

Photograph by John Humphrys

I wrote then:

> ... the last night possessed the SNO's traditional spree of light and national items, but this time, in tune with the ambitious programming of the whole series, there was the addition of the Scottish (public) premiere of Ronald Stevenson's *Second Piano Concerto* with the composer performing. I think its placing in this context was quite apt. Stevenson has asserted that the composer should not despise popularisation in art, and indeed in every layer of the work some use of folk or folk-like material – from the five continents – was made and in 'seeking to voice humanity' it was essentially popular.
>
> The concerto, subtitled *The Continents*, is almost a speech outlining a world view, in musical terms, to the United Nations; the driving optimism of the music, optimistic despite the origin of its inspiration being a poem on the Sharpeville massacre, is a virtual celebration of the Third World standing on its feet shaking off the yoke of colonialism. Yet not just that: the trek through the continents ranges through the bustle of Europe too, described, as the composer says, by a 'dialectic' fugue, no doubt pointing to it as the birthplace of dialectics and materialism.
>
> Long resident in Scotland he is well known there and to London audiences, but what is not common knowledge is his almost two-year honorary presidency of the Scotland-China Association. His interest in this field explains much about the concerto. Influences range wide from the sound of the Chinese silk-string orchestra, the also silken tones of the bamboo flute and the close connection between the pentatonic scales of Chinese and Gaelic folk music which he uses to spell out the 'unity' of peoples.
>
> Perhaps more significant is Stevenson's active study of Mao's *Talks at the Yenan Forum on Literature and Art*, which he regards as a great advance in socialist-realist thinking and which he points to as having been recognised as such by Brecht.
>
> The stormy, but triumphant Asian themes, notably the references to the Vietnamese liberation anthem, clearly indicated which 'view of struggling humanity' was being referred to.
>
> Given the popular intention of the piece, the many adventuresome harmonies and textures (including playing directly on the piano strings), a brilliant rendering by the composer-soloist and understanding of its tradition albeit at present 'going against the tide', it was hard to accept the hostility and controversy aroused in local reviews.[1]

---

1. From *Music and Musicians*, November 1974.

Composing A Song-Cycle

Ronald Stevenson

As a composer, I find that ideas for a new work come unawares, and sometimes in unexpected places. From my music sketch-books I see that one night in September 1968 I couldn't get to sleep for a theme that kept jolting my subconscious into consciousness. Finally, there was nothing for it but to don my dressing-gown, go down to my desk and put the thing on paper – and my mind at rest. Being interested in the psychic mechanism of composing, a little reflection told me what sparked it off on this occasion. That afternoon, I'd been romping in the autumn woods with my children near our home in the Borders. We'd returned to hot buttered toast and piping-hot tea by a fire that blazed even brighter than the conflagration of colour we'd seen in the woods. Then I read the youngsters a bedtime chapter of *Huckleberry Finn*. In the middle of the night, I knew the musical idea that had been tied like a cracker to the tail of my dreams was an evocation of childhood. I headed the manuscript *allegro con nuovo ardore* (quick with young ardour). It was my childhood calling to me across forty years.

Now, that page of manuscript lay in my sketch-book till the next summer, June 1969, when one morning I received a letter from Peter Pears commissioning a song-cycle from me to be dedicated to our mutual friend, Miss Tertia Liebenthal of Edinburgh. To me, Tertia was the last *grande dame* of the Scottish capital, an old-world patroness of music who organised seven hundred lunch-hour concerts in Edinburgh's National Gallery. She even died at one of these concerts, surrounded by music and her friends.

I remember her enthusiasm, shortly before her death, about some childhood memories of the Borders broadcast by Hugh MacDiarmid. So, when Peter Pears asked me to compose a song-cycle, I immediately thought of the childhood memories of MacDiarmid and began setting them. And I realised that I'd already written the first page of the song-cycle on that sleepless night in the autumn of 1968. Tertia Liebenthal died before the work was completed, so it is dedicated: "In memory of Tertia, who loved the Border Country". I gave it my own title: *Border Boyhood*.

Five of the six songs are settings of MacDiarmid's prose, the other song a setting of his free verse. I find prose rhythm nearer to the flow of music than are the more regular patterned rhythms of rhymed verse. Except in 'patter-songs' (à la Gilbert and Sullivan) or in four-square musical phrases, the free flow of music tends to minimise or even obliterate the regularity of rhymed verse.

Another problem of setting words to music is this: every musical motif or theme contains the germ of its own development; set words to it, and the development of the *musical* idea has to be subjugated to the development of the *verbal* idea. The music has to yield to the words: like a creeping plant, it has to be trained to a trellis. This problem can be overcome partially by careful selection of the text. In the case of the MacDiarmid words I chose, I didn't use the complete original text but selected from it what suited my purpose. In particular, I selected passages containing recurrent poetic motifs, so that I might allow my *musical* motifs to recur also and be developed. This thematic cross-reference made the form of my song-cycle cyclic in the symphonic sense.

Here are some examples of what I mean. There are recurrent references to the *wood* throughout the cycle. Can you remember the first time you entered a wood as a child? I can. Suddenly to be encircled by shadows and to see the shadows become luminous with blue-bells – this was *magic!* I've tried to evoke the suddenness of this experience by a single chord in the opening song. Later, this chord bears a melody associated with bird-song in the wood. Later still, this melody is treated in variation-form in a piano interlude, like a meditation in the woods. Another recurrent motif is the *river.* It meanders in and out of the music of my song-cycle as it does in the Border landscape.

Looking through my sketches again, I remember how I worked at the song which is a celebration of colour: the Scottish Borders in the pageant of autumn. First I copied out MacDiarmid's poem. Here's how it opens:

> The birch tremulously pendulous in jewels of cairngorm,
> The sauch, the osier, and the crack-willow
> Of the beaten gold of Australia;
> The sycamore in rich straw-gold;
> The elm bowered in saffron;
> The oak in flecks of salmon gold;
> The beeches huge torches of living orange.

When I'd copied out the whole poem, I took coloured crayons and heavily underlined each colour mentioned with the appropriate crayon. Then I saw at a glance that the poet's colour scheme presented a kind of life-cycle of colours – yellow, green, gold, orange, sienna, purple. This immediately suggested a harmonic scheme which determined the form of the whole song. To give only one example; take these words:

> Beyond the willow a young beech
> Blazes almost blood-red,
> Vying in intensity with the glowing cloud of crimson
> That hangs about the purple bole of a gean
> Higher up the brae face.

My brightest crayon underlined the words 'blood-red' and I drew a crimson cloud in outline around the phrase "the glowing cloud of crimson that hangs about the purple bole of a gean". (The gean is the wild cherry.) I also underlined the word 'purple' in its own colour. Then I sat back and saw that the words and colours were already clothing themselves in music.

At the end of the song, the poem closes with two masterly lines: "Even the robin hushes his song/ In these gold pavilions." The *robin,* mark you. The most prosaic of birds. None of your skylarks or nightingales. And the robin doesn't stop singing: he *hushes* his song. This suggested to me the idea of inserting, at this point in the cycle, a nocturne for piano, subtitled 'The Hushed Song', played *sotto voce* throughout. This nocturne reminisces on themes already heard and anticipates a theme to be heard later.

Illustration by Philip Hutton

The *main* theme of the cycle is presented at the opening – that call of childhood that I wrote first of all. Throughout the cycle, this theme is developed. For instance, when MacDiarmid in one of his unexpected metaphors writes, "Memories of a clump of mimulis shining like a dog's eyes, with all the world a bone", the theme is treated in progressive augmentations of the rhythmic values, dilating like the dog's eyes.

In the penultimate song, which is a kind of scherzo/march/jig, only the spiky outline – a sharp profile – of the cycle's main theme is adumbrated. This is a punchy characterisation of Border people. It is meant to be sung relentlessly, a spate of words:

> Border life was raw, vigorous, rich, bawdy, a thing of unquenchable humour, biting satire, profound wisdom cloaked in bantering gaiety, and the mad wealth of humour, with not a trace of whimsy, in the general leaping, light-hearted reckless assault upon the conventions of dull respectability.

The final song takes the main theme as the subject of a fugue. This form was suggested by MacDiarmid's memories of a place in his birthplace, Langholm, called 'The Curly Snake'. That very name suggested the serpentine contours of the fugal subject. And the poet's train of thought pursues in itself a fugal development in its twining, twisting movement, occasionally arrested by episode-like impressions of nature, like camera 'stills'. You'll see what I mean from this quotation: "There is a place called the Curly Snake, where a winding path coils up through a copse; whence, after passing a field or two, it runs into the splendid woods of the Langfall." Then MacDiarmid tells us that this place has always haunted his imagination. At this point I composed a fugal episode like the haunting of the imagination; treating the solo voice as two parts in *stretto*, the voice answering itself by vocalising the theme in low chest-voice notes, answered by the theme's inversion, hummed in head-voice tone – one note of each part at a time. MacDiarmid tells us that the Curly Snake was for him what the Nook of the Night Paths was for Kierkegaard, the Danish philosopher. In his book *Stages on Life's Way*, Kierkegaard writes of the place in Grib Forest in North Zealand: "It is found only by one who seeks worthily, for no map shows it. The name 'The Nook of the Night Paths' is itself contradictory – for how can a meeting point of eight paths form a nook? – how can the public and frequented be reconciled with the solitary and concealed?" Perhaps the intimate yet public form of music-making which the song-cycle is may be one way of reconciling – in musical terms – the public and frequented with the solitary and concealed.

"But," you may ask, "is it still valid in the age of technology and electronics to write 'nature' music?" My reply to that couldn't be more affirmative. Where I live in Scotland, nature – even in an age of pollution – is still very much with us. Believing as I do that the artist's work reflects reality – a reflection as quick-changing as the sky's in the river – how can I *not* celebrate nature, when I have chosen to live among it? Remembering Thoreau, I went to the woods, not as an escape, but because I "wished to live deliberately, to front only the essential facts of life." And I want my music to talk straight about life.

Stevenson and the Child

Colin Scott-Sutherland

The eternal dawn, beyond a doubt,
Shall break on hill and plain,
And put all stars and candles out,
Ere we be young again.

Robert Louis Stevenson, *A Child's Garden of Verses*

When Ronald Stevenson was asked what he would wish to do on his sixtieth birthday his immediate response was "spend it with the children of course!" And spend it with the children he did – under the auspices of EPTA (the European Piano Teachers' Association) in an upper room in St Mary's Music College, Edinburgh in the company of a number of young players, pupils of Edinburgh teachers, with whom he conducted a master class of enchanting warmth and sympathy. Concerned as much with approach, preparation and posture as with technique, he managed to enlarge Adam Carse's and Hilda Capp's little pieces – to say nothing of his own 'A Wheen Tunes for Bairns to Spiel' – into a series of object lessons that ranged far beyond the purely technical, interspersing his comments with hectic, excited and quite unpractised passages from Chopin, Bach and Grainger!

The inspiration of the young, indeed of the ever young, has the most profound effect upon him:

His particular concern for the child, in the laments of the *Passacaglia* and the programme of the Second Piano Concerto, is expressed with the keen contrast of size and medium in the short pieces such as 'A Wheen Tunes for Bairns to Spiel', 'Three Scots Fairytales', and in the Soutar song 'Day is Düne'. There are, too, the simple transcriptions of Delius, the careful editing and transcribing of 'The Young Pianist's Grainger', and the volume of harp arrangements 'Sounding Strings' (composed for his younger daughter and published by United Music Publishers) which convey to the child, with all the skill and touch of a born teacher, his own infectious delight in all that is music.[1]

His love of the child is exemplified in his connection with the Steiner-inspired Garvald School for the handicapped child at Dolphinton, near his home. In 1965, he set for unison children's voices, descant recorder, violin, cello and guitar, the words of the Christian Morgenstern poem 'One and All' which became the school song and which he later transcribed as a 'Meditation' for piano solo. In 1961 he was teaching at Broughton School in Edinburgh: "It bore no resemblance to being a musician, but I was in contact with the raw material of life"[2]. This kind of realism he evoked in the massive 80 minute long *Passacaglia on DSCH*: "On the afternoon of the premiere I composed a new section of two pages based on the 17th century Scottish pibroch 'Lament for the Children', composed by Patrick Mòr MacCrimmon as a lament for seven of his eight sons who died within a year. I recast his melody, thinking of the child victims of Nazism."[3] It is no coincidence that this was sparked off in South Africa. And, in Australia

---

1. C Scott-Sutherland: 'Ronald Stevenson' in *British Music Now* (ed Foreman) Elek 1975 p36.
2. *The Daily Mail* 3.10.66.
3. '*Passacaglia on DSCH*': *The Listener* Vol 82 No 2115, 9.10.69, p 494.

in September 1982, Stevenson wrote: "In Dandenong, Victoria, I composed, taught, recorded and broadcast (from Sydney) all within a week, a little song for the mentally handicapped (over one hundred of them between two and sixty years of age) – title, 'Adam was a Gardener'."

Nowhere is this insight more poignantly reflected than in the 17 songs of *A Child's Garden of Verses*, a song-cycle to the words of his namesake Robert Louis Stevenson. For all its apparently unpretentious nature, this cycle is one of Stevenson's deepest creative expressions, enshrining a unique understanding of childhood experience. It can be compared with the most evocative pages of literature such as the richly imagined introduction to de la Mare's famed anthology *Come Hither* and limns the poetry with the artistry of an illustrator, including decorative touches of acute perception, probing to the heart of the poet's vision. These are not in the true sense poems for children (no more than de la Mare's 'Nod' would, except superficially, be a fit subject for a nursery wallpaper – his subject of course is Death). Stevenson has wisely chosen the alternative, setting the verses as a *Kinderszenen*, rather than as an Album for the Young.

Set for tenor, soprano and treble (the latter voices ideally those of children) and commissioned by the BBC to mark the centenary of the first publication of RLS's volume in 1885, the cycle incorporates the dark element from which Ronald Stevenson's original expression sprung: the dark feverish fears of the sick child, a prey to his vivid imaginings; the mysterious, even terrifying 'Shadow March'; and 'All Around the House is the Jet Black Night', a setting made for his children some twenty-three years earlier and now central to the cycle.

This is the reflection of a strange indefinable terror that must be a part of every child's experience, perhaps in later life rationalised or even forcibly buried. It is of considerable relevance in an analysis of Stevenson's setting of the verses of RLS's "little ragged regiment".[1] For he does not set

1. RLS's description in a letter of 12.3.1885 to Edmund Gosse.

all the poems – to do so would result in a burdensome, over-long composition. What is revealing is not what the composer chose to set but what he chose to omit. Discarding lines that could be considered naive, even those which have become perennially popular, he sets aside also lines dealing with games, toys, picture books or pious thoughts. He chooses lines which, almost without exception, are concerned with experience, not simply visual but noticeably sensual – feelings of bed, rain, sunshine, darkness, the act of swinging, rail travel and woodsmoke! He omits all verses in which the child evokes companions, choosing only those lines in which the child alone is engrossed in solitary play, his only companion the shadow.

Other considerations too have drawn Ronald Stevenson to the poet. RLS's best poetry is perhaps to be found in his quasi-autobiographical 'Songs of Travel'. Ronald Stevenson, too, is a voyager – underlined in his large scale concertos (for piano – No 2, subtitled *The Continents*: and for Violin subtitled *The Gypsy*). Living as he does on the south flank of the Pentland Hills on the other side of RLS's beloved Swanston village, he had already set, in 1976, the poem sequence 'The Hills of Home'.[1] And in this sequence both poet and composer look nostalgically back to childhood "to mount again where erst I haunted" the red bird-enchanted hills and hear "the pee-wees a-crying". This earlier setting of RLS's 'Blows the Wind Today' firmly establishes the key of D major – in the context of this later cycle providing the necessary contrast with the Shadow. (Both Rimsky-Korsakov and Scriabin equated the key of D major with the colour yellow and with the adjective 'sunny').

There is yet a further interesting relationship between poet and composer. Of the *Verses,* Frank Swinnerton makes this profound observation: "*The Child's Garden of Verses* alone then of the four volumes of children's verse, exhibits a strict harmony of design with performance." And from the contrasts of the sunny D major and the A flat minor of the Shadow, Stevenson constructs a cycle whose formal strength is developed from the opening juxtaposition of two chords – a minor 9th and major 7th – and in the matter of formal construction it is not too fanciful to see, in the selecting and re-arranging of the poet's verses, an imaginative programme that delineates not only the hours of the day but the progression of the seasons, amply justified in both verse and music.

At the centre of the cycle the Shadow with its subtle and imaginative combination of the voices of child and adult casts its own baleful shadow into the very first song. From the tenor's opening exhortation (by the sick child "now well and old") to the faithful nanny (Alison Cunningham or 'Cummy') to "take, nurse, this little book you hold", to the wistful child's appeal "and I would like so much to play" ('Bed in Summer') and the poignancy of his plea "Leerie, see a little child, and nod to him tonight", there are many wonderful felicities. The cycle is indeed one of the most beautiful and moving pieces of imaginative writing from the 20th century.

---

1. 'Blows the Wind Today': 'In the Highlands': 'I Saw Rain Falling': 'Requiem'.

Ronald Stevenson and the Choral Voice

Jamie Reid Baxter

Before we can have a choral voice, we must have voices. Ronald Stevenson's music springs from the human voice. In a radio interview, he
answered the question "Why did you become a musician?" with the simple
words: "It was my father's singing". His father, a railway worker who loved
to sing, persuaded his son to learn the piano so he could accompany him,
and even bought him a grand piano. We tend to think of Stevenson as a
performer on and composer for the piano, but the fact is that his earliest
compositions, written when he was fourteen, were songs, settings of Walter Scott and Byron. And during a long and productive creative life this
composer-pianist has written hundreds of songs for solo voice, setting not
only lyrics by MacDiarmid, William Soutar, R L Stevenson, John Davidson,
aonghas macneacail, Alan Bold and many other Scottish poets, but also
Tagore, Busoni, Morgenstern, the Australian master A D Hope – and ump-
teen others. This essay however surveys Stevenson's music for many
voices, his choral music. Specifically, it seeks to understand why a man so
sensitive to words (he has written fine poetry in Scots himself) should make
choral settings of verse which uses the first person singular. Both of the two
recorded Stevenson choral works do so. The first of these sprang directly
from the sound of a human voice – that of Sorley MacLean reading his
extraordinary poem 'Calbharaigh'. Stevenson's 'Calvary' forms the middle
movement of a Gaelic choral triptych; all three texts are by MacLean. In
'Calbharaigh', Stevenson certainly makes use of a solo soprano. Yet the
work begins with wordless humming from the full choir, before the solo
voice sings "Chan eil mo shuil air Calbharaigh" – my eyes are not on Calvary, nor Bethlehem the blest. The solo voice then gives way to the full
choir. And the presence of that murmuring choir, that multiplicity of individual voices speaking 'as one', seems essential to Stevenson's conception.

'Calbharaigh' is not set as a howl of protest or anger. It is music of pellucid beauty. In a long poem about Stevenson, I tried to capture some tiny
echo of this work, writing of Stevenson's friendship with MacLean, whose

> . . . human heart saw Calvary in no strange land,
> Nor in the distant past, but here, in all the slums
> And tenements of Scottish towns, where growing life
> Decays, a Bethlehem of pain and infant death.
> Mac Ille Eathain's searing song of sorrow over how
> Humanity has made a hell of Eden here
> Inspired his comrade Stevenson to write no howls
> Of anger; for the music to this poem of pain
> Must count as Stevenson's most perfect utterance.
> Its euphony and glowing loveliness are what
> Life could be here on earth, but we will not allow;
> And so this setting of such beauty grieves for us,
> For what we could be, and for all we fail to be.

The key word is "we". It is a 'we', a sense of community, that so many
of us have learned from Stevenson. His vision of music as a language

capable of breaking down all barriers is an inspiration in a world increasingly fragmented by the lie of the 'information society' and the 'age of communication'. Stevenson's socialism is a belief in the 'we' of the collective identity of human individuals, and it is not an adjunct to his music: this sense of 'we' is of the essence of all his work. There is nothing more 'individual' than being a solo virtuoso by profession, although all the great virtuosi of course want to take their listeners with them as they make available to us the genius of the composers they are performing. Stevenson likes to break down the barrier between performer and audience in his lecture recitals; but to me, the deepest expression of his desire to realise all-embracing solidarity is his choral music. These works are relatively few in number compared with his huge output of solo song and piano music; but if we look at the texts, we find that without exception they are all concerned with solidarity, with 'us' – the 'usness' of all creation, the awareness that "hearts and stars are one with another" spoken of by Busoni in the essay turned into verse by MacDiarmid in the final section of *In Memoriam James Joyce*.

Busoni and MacDiarmid are widely thought of as Stevenson's principal spiritual mentors. But there is one whose presence is even more fundamental. When jailed at 18 for refusing to do national service out of pacifist conviction, the young Stevenson drew strength from the smiling compassion and wisdom of William Blake, and in prison he set many Blake songs including a four-voice chorale version of 'On another's sorrow', which voices solidarity with all creatures. "Can I see another's woe, And not be in sorrow too? Can I see another's grief/ And not seek for kind relief?" Over forty years later, we find Stevenson in his sixties setting Psalm 23 – a text about the trust without which there can be no solidarity. Even in death's dark vale the 'I', the individual, is not alone. A Blakean, cosmic solidarity is expressed in Stevenson's joyous (and simple) setting of St Francis of Assisi's hymn of praise to all creation, *Frate sole*, and that feeling of cosmic harmony finds overwhelming expression in his largest work of all, the choral symphony *The Praise of Beinn Dobhrain*. This hymn of praise for double chorus and large orchestra is the work Stevenson regards as his *summa artistica*. It sets MacDiarmid's verse paraphrase of the great 18th century Gaelic poem in praise of the mountain and all the natural life it sustains. The *fons et origo* of the whole huge musical fabric is the *urlar* or ground on which it is all founded, setting the opening words:

> Over mountains, pride of place to Ben Dorain!
> I've nowhere espied a finer to reign;
> In her moorbacks wide, hosts of shy deer bide,
> While light comes pouring diamond-wise from her side!

Essential to the whole concept, then, is the idea that "light comes pouring" – 'Brother Sun' indeed. Light that drives out darkness also drives out fear, because it lets us see. It gives the unknown a face. In the mood of Blake, William Soutar wrote: "When no man fears his brother's face/ Truth walks about the market place". Stevenson, who loves Soutar's work, brings light literally blazing out of darkness and fearful mystery in the choral recitative which forms the prelude to his setting of Ps 23. While the psalm is sung in a 16th century Scots translation probably by Alexander Montgomerie, the prelude sets Lorimer's translation of the opening of St John's Gospel, including the words "Aathing that hes come tae be, he wis the life in it, an that life wis the licht o man; an ey the licht shines in the mirk". The bringing together of Montgomerie and Lorimer makes this a remarkable tribute from an agnostic composer to the vernacular religious tradition which Lowland Scotland was denied by the linguistic Unionism of the post-1560 establishment, both kirk and state. Ps 23 is a fascinating work using a variety of techniques including the genuinely Scottish one of "psalms in reports", and it even includes spatial effects a la Gabrieli, but what abides most vividly in the memory is that explosion of light. Of course, it's when it's *dark* that we most need a sense of trust, but in fact solidarity is most easily perceived when light is pouring forth. As Blake wrote:

> God appears, and God is light
> To those who dwell in darkest night,
> But doth a human form display
> To those who dwell in realms of day.

Solidarity with all humankind is, of course, inherently and ineluctably pacifist; and so Stevenson's music eschews sonata form and tonal conflict, and draws instead on variation forms like passacaglia: circular forms, the basic element of Celtic art. Conflict is impossible within a circle. The richness of Stevenson's pacifist vision of the great circle of being can be appreciated if we think of Busoni's reference to the round dance at the end of his opera *Doktor Faust:* "So that in the act of striding onward, soul is heaped upon soul – This gives meaning to the continued climbing; in full circle thus the round dance closes". We might paraphrase this as "so that in the act of singing its own identity, each voice is added to other voices".

Stevenson's pacifism is stated with simplicity in another luminous choral work, the four *Peace Motets,* premiered in a 'concert for peace' to mark his 60th birthday. The short Biblical texts are "Thou shalt not kill – Put up again thy sword into his place, for all they that take the sword shall perish by the sword – They shall beat their swords into ploughshares, nation shall not lift sword against nation, neither shall they learn war any more . . ." The appropriateness of setting these words for chorus is evident. The aspirations are universal and need a multiplicity of voices, but not one that will obscure the clear message of the words, and this is a work Stevenson envisaged being sung by amateur groups as well as professional singers. It is a message from the depths of our collective consciousness, and Stevenson places his music at the service of that message. In a radio talk years ago, he spoke movingly about "peace – man's greatest need", referring to his own wish for a "music of many musics, a music of oneness – it's like the desire for universal peace, really". And he went on to quote Paul Robeson: "There are many nations, but there's only one race – the human race".

But we should not misunderstand this Stevensonian view of the oneness of humankind. The essential "Einheit" of reality is not faceless and abstract. On the contrary, like St Francis in *Frate sole,* Stevenson seeks to express a specific solidarity with every specific thing. It's a oneness of endless 'uniquenesses'. William Blake with his heaven in a wild flower, universe in a grain of sand and eternity in an hour. Yet our own smaller identities as individuals, groups, cities, nations are also unique: they are part of the diversity of Stevenson's Oneness. So the same man who wrote the *Peace Motets* is also the composer of the *Mediaeval Scottish Triptych* which sets patriotic words from the most violent period in Scotland's history.

The *Triptych* begins with dark lamentations with the oldest surviving Scots poetic text, "Quhen Alexander oor king wes dede", and it ends with Barbour's great cry of "Fredome", the word thundered "like bells" in a choral ostinato. Between these two famous texts comes part of the epic poem *The Wallace*, the eponymous hero's 'Lament for the Graham' —another text in the first person singular, the words set to heart-shaking melodies of clearly Celtic inflection as an expression of collective fellow-feeling. Part of a serious pacifism is a love of justice. The suffering of a tiny free nation at the hands of a huge invading power utterly bent on destroying its identity is something familiar to us in the wake of Grozny and the Chechen struggle; and was it not the suffering of "gallant little Belgium" that made MacDiarmid and others start to think about their own small country? The heroic and victorious struggle of mediaeval Scotland to retain its right to be itself – what Barbour calls "fre liking", i.e. self-determination – are seen by Stevenson as an inspiration to all minorities and individuals everywhere in their fight against oppression which would deny them the right to exist – and thereby, of course, diminish the diversity of oneness.

This great work from 1967 shows the range of Stevenson's handling of choral sonorities. Singers love Stevenson because he always writes gratefully for the voice. He likes to point out that Rossini was one of very few modern composers who was a singer, and though Stevenson claims he can't sing himself his vocal lines are always utterly singable. The choral harmonies, however, are often fiendishly complex: he does not limit himself to the pellucid, diatonic harmonies of 'Calbharaigh', the 'Christ Child's Lullaby' (another Gaelic work) or the 'Peace Motets'. The singers who premiered *Ballatis of Lufe*, a chamber work for four solo voices and lute, spent many long hours on getting the extraordinary harmony right. But when it did come right, there was no mistaking it: utterly personal and luminous. *The Herald* music critic Michael Tumelty has twice written about Stevenson's ability to capture the quality of light in his choral writing. The *Ballatis of Lufe,* setting five lyrics by the 16th century Alexander Scott, are another example of writing 'plural' music for first person singular – as well as another instance of Stevenson's extraordinary knowledge of Scottish culture. One of the most perfect of all his compositions, this work has yet to be heard complete in Scotland. Written in 1971, it was premiered in Luxembourg in March 1993 to mark Stevenson's 65th birthday.

The commercial recording of Stevenson's setting of Maclean's 'Calbharaigh', too, was made in Luxembourg. The only other Stevenson choral work recorded is very different. Perhaps the most complex of all, the 15 minute long motet for twelve part choir, *In Memoriam Robert Carver,* was premiered by Cappella Nova to mark Stevenson's 60th birthday. But the complexity of this music has never proved any sort of barrier to audiences whom I have witnessed applauding it with more enthusiasm than that beloved classic, Fauré's *Requiem,* with which it has shared a programme. This is to me the most startling of Stevenson's plural settings of the first person singular; the text is a poem which I wrote as an individual state-ment, indeed, as a cry from the depths of individual alienation and lone-liness, even if it was a cry of gratitude. In the concert programme I wrote:

> The poem *Domino Roberto Carwor* describes a specific event and my reac-tions to it. My words were a spontaneous expression of gratitude for the mir-acle of music, or rather, for the miraculous generosity of one creative artist – an individual who had the courage to share his personal gifts and visions with the rest of us less articulate folk, in what ultimately amounts to an act of solidarity with the future, an act of trust. No artist can know whether his or her work will survive.
>
> Robert Carver's music very nearly did not. The Abbey of Scone was burnt down by the 'rascal multitude' in 1559, quite probably before Carver's very eyes, for he lived on into his eighties, at least until 1568 – long enough to real-ise that his life's work had been rendered meaningless. It had no place in the new Reformed Scotland, and indeed there were no choirs to sing it. Even the choir stalls had been smashed along with the statues and altars. Yet all this destruction had happened before. In the 1540s the armies of Henry VIII of England had annihilated all in their path, towns, villages, men, women and children, churches, castles and abbeys. Yet in 1546, amid these horrors and intimations of the uselessness of all endeavour, Carver had composed his mass *Pater creator omnium.*
>
> This commitment to meaningfulness and to hope, this refusal to reject a sense of trust in those yet unborn In was something that over the years I had found exemplified in Ronald Stevenson's life and work. And so I sent him a copy of my "meditation in winter", in gratitude for all he had taught me about music and its power to heal and reconcile. The persistence of the evil mad-ness of war is no reason to abandon a pacifist creed; lack of present recog-nition for work achieved is no reason to abandon the generous activity of artistic creation, and Stevenson has never ceased to create and to share. I was nonetheless taken by surprise at Stevenson's reaction to my poem – a twelve part setting of my text for three choral groups conceived as a monument to Scotland's greatest composer.

Why was I surprised? Because I'm a smaller person than Stevenson who had understood far better than I did the deeper meaning of my spontane-ous words (the poem was written in two hours). I had thought it as a highly subjective monologue, restricted to the first person singular. The poem is certainly about a 'me' – but it's a 'me' who is singing the anonymous Gre-gorian *cantus firmus* on which Robert Carver based his mass, while others are singing around that *cantus firmus.* The poem is about choral singing – communal music making. Stevenson understood, as I had not, that what breaks down the barriers of alienation in the poem is quite as much the shared experience of singing *with others* as the music itself. Busoni once wrote that music acknowledges no border posts; music also transcends the barriers of space and time; the crux of the Carver poem is literally a cross which comes at its centre: "*Roberte, frater mi,* in thir derk day is noo/ I think

on you, *o faber optime*". The modern individual breaks through the barriers
of the alienated ego and addresses the "best of craftsmen" across the centuries as Latin and Scots criss-cross in the rhetorical figure of *chiasmus*, and
an echo of the youthful Carver's contemporary, the poet William Dunbar.

Stevenson invariably puts deep thought into his setting of words; he's
not one of those all too many composers who just 'set' whatever is put in
front of them. It has been my dispiriting experience that music lovers and
even practising musicians can be rather oblivious to words, just as literary
minded people are often surprisingly content to be musically uninformed.
Stevenson, like Busoni and MacDiarmid, seeks a synthesis of all aspects
of the human spirit as expressed in what we call the arts. Stevenson's
Carver Motet quotes Busoni's *Doktor Faust* (the music being on the word
"*pax*"). The poem itself quotes from St John's Gospel, the text of Carver's
mass and Dunbar's, 'Meditation in Winter'. So too Stevenson in his musical
setting also half-quotes from that musical statement of alienation and lone-
liness, Allegri's *Miserere*, which sets Ps.50, a psalm of the winter of the
soul. And inspired by the medieval practice of 'troping' which features in
Carver's mass *Pater creator omnium*, Stevenson added words in Latin to
the text, tropes glossing the poem and creating a vision in sound of a literal 'family of man' – or even of God and man: *pater creator, mater creatrix, filius creator, filia creatrix OMNIS VITAE*. In such a vision, the fear
and alienation of the individual vanish. The work concludes with a rain-
bow-like chord spanning three and a half octaves on the words "the soon-
din colours o eternitie": the male choir sings in fifths, the mixed choir in
fourths, and the female choir in thirds, as the music shimmers up from "the
depths of all depths to the dome of all domes in the heights", to quote
MacDiarmid's translation of Busoni. Stevenson's choral music is truly a
choral voice, and its message is one of reassurance. Harmony is possible.
The braids are bound together in the light that comes pouring from the
recognition that the one and the many need each other in order to be
whole. There is no need to fear our brother's face.

> A mind that looks upon the undivided truth
> That life is one, can only weep at how mankind
> Betrays itself at every turn, mankind that soars
> In every little, nameless, unremembered act
> Of kindness and of love, and plunges down to hell
> Each time the least of all its little ones is hurt
> Through human selfishness and pride and greed – and fear,
> Of all emotions far the deepest, ever-present
> In thinking minds that will not take the inner road
> Less-travelled, undercutting thought and petty self,
> And hence, unmasking fear as no more than the ghost
> Of bogles from the nursery that fleggit bairns,
> And that we could have left behind us long ago.

Singing together in the first person singular is perfectly possible and by
so doing we will not merely not lose our individual identity, but infinitely
enhance it. All we need to do, of course, is to grow up and be oorsells –
and nae haurder task tae mortals hes been gien. Stevenson's light-filled
choral music seeks to help us exorcise that ghost.

Ronald Stevenson and the Early Borders Festivals

Judy Steel

In the mid-1980s I was setting up the first of the Borders Arts Festivals. They came under various names – the Ettrick Shepherd's Festival, the Festival of Ballads and Legends. In trying to establish a festival that would speak for the area, I was concentrating on approaching practising artists in different disciplines who lived in the Borders or who came from here.

Most of them were young, at the start of their careers. It was with some trepidation that I approached the distinguished and established Ronald Stevenson and asked if he would take part. He had, he told me, wanted to set up a festival in the Borders years before, along with Ronald Mavor who lived near the Stevenson home in West Linton. It had never come about, but he transferred all his enthusiasm and support to my initiative. He could so easily have doubted my flimsy credentials for such an enterprise.

Key to his support was the work that was being done on James Hogg, for whom he had long had an admiration. He didn't only keep track of what I was doing: he was informed and interested in the work of Douglas Mack and the Canadian Hogg scholar David Groves. By a happy coincidence, it was his son Gordon who restored Hogg's violin to playing condition for that first Festival. Ronald's friend the late Leonard Friedman played it, and at the following festival the two of them along with Gerda and Savourna took part in a memorable concert in Yarrow Kirk. Despite the location, half a dozen miles out of Selkirk up the Yarrow Valley, it was packed. I remember a local musician stalwart saying: "This is the most significant concert I've ever attended in the Borders".

He could well have been right: there were after all two premieres. One was two movements from a piece on which Ronald was currently working, his *Solo Suite for Scots Fiddle*, as demanding of a player as all his works, but accessible to an audience unused to contemporary music. A year later, in that wonderful attic performance space at the top of Ricky Demarco's gallery in St Mary Street we heard the full suite which he dedicated to the memory of his friend Hugh MacDiarmid.

The other piece that was premiered on that October Sunday afternoon *A Year Owre Young* was inspired by James Hogg. Its story is unusual: not for Ronald the easy route of using a song in one of James Hogg's published editions. Instead, the reference came from Alexander Campbell's *Journal of a Tour in the Scottish Border in 1816*. Hogg had told Campbell that he has learned it from "The female maniac Billy", a "poor thing" who wandered about the Borders. ". . . the first half only is mine – the latter very old . . . I got both verses and tune from her, and I never heard anyone else sing them". In his setting of the verses, for voice and violin, Ronald captures all the pathos and imbalance of poor Billy. It is a work of the highest dramatic content. Subsequent to that first performance by Leonard

Friedman and Gerda Stevenson, it has been taken up and performed in concert from time to time by Lucy Cowan and Hilary Bell.

The Yarrow Kirk concert was also the first time I heard Savourna Stevenson play which led to the commissioning of her historic piece for clarsach and band, *Tweed Journey*.

A few years ago, after I had established the Hogg exhibition at Aikwood, Ronald presented me with the manuscript of *A Year Ower Young*. By coincidence and to my delight, this happened when the Hogg Society was having its biennial conference here, so the occasion was provided with the ceremony it deserved.

I am glad to have this chance to express my appreciation to Ronald for all the encouragement he gave me those long years ago, and for the friendship that has developed between us since. The Borders Festivals have provided a crucible for much of the new work that has come out of the Borders in recent years: without Ronald's support and direct involvement, the pattern would never have been established on such sound foundations.

Tribute to Ronald Stevenson

Victoria Crowe

During the seventies and eighties we lived in the small hamlet of Kittley-knowe near Carlops, just a few miles away from Ronald's home in West Linton. My husband, Mike Walton, and I were both artists, working between the Art College in Edinburgh and my studio at home. Our children, Ben and Gemma, went to the local primary school in West Linton and the overlapping circles of the art world, the community in Carlops (with its orchestra and pantomime) and school concerts and music groups, soon brought us into contact with Ronald and Marjorie.

We knew of Ronald as a composer and pianist, but by the beginning of the eighties we began to know him as a friend and teacher of our son. To say he taught the piano is, I think, incorrect – he taught *music* – in its entire creative and thought-provoking spectrum. After his first lesson with Ben, Ronald said my son " . . . had music in him . . ." and would " . . . be playing Beethoven before the year is out . . . " – that proved to be true, but more importantly Ronald gave Ben a life-long enthusiasm for music – for composing, playing and enjoying.

Around the same time I had a big exhibition at the Scottish Gallery in Edinburgh and two of the paintings – portraits and tributes to Dr Winifred Rushforth and her work, were purchased by the Scottish National Portrait Gallery and the City Art Centre. I hadn't worked with portraiture very much at that time, but I began to think of painting Ronald as I watched him in the music room at West Linton and enjoyed the happy and creative relationship he and my son had. So, the portrait of Ronald Stevenson (which was purchased by the Scottish National Portrait Gallery for their 20th century collection of eminent Scots) began as a tribute to the composer, the musicologist, the teacher and friend.

Looking back among the first notes and drawings in my sketch book, the image of that room was always present, with Ronald " . . . possibly profile . . ." or " . . . moving in room . . ." or " . . . right on picture plane". The next drawings have the composition much as it is in the finished piece, with Ronald, hands on hips, three-quarter view, and right to the foreground of the painting, the room somewhat telescoped behind him and the curtained window onto the street providing the main light source.

The positioning and back-lighting of the figure gave it qualities of monumentality, a certain strength and constancy – rather a heroic, uncompromising quality I suppose. I have always felt Ronald to be someone who more than stood his ground in an argument and who held passionately to values and concerns he felt to be important – in life and politics as well as music – despite contrary or current fashionable thinking.

The colour in the painting has its starting point in the opposing crimson and green of the tartan shirt, which, muted by the back-light, provided a slightly off-key kind of harmony – remember, this is *not* a musician talking! – which continued throughout the painting. To me, that colour range

Illustration by Victoria Crowe

echoed the musical nuances of his *Passacaglia* which I listened to during the time I was painting him.

I kept coming back to the view outside the window, beyond the "wild duck" curtains; outside, life in the Borders village continued much as it always had done, local fairs were held, church services went on, horses were ridden, children passed on their way to school or the sweet shop, people gossiped, – but inside, well, the music spanned time, place and culture, pushing one's mind into new areas. Photos of Busoni, Percy Grainger, John Ogden, images of Liszt and Shostakovich, books and papers covering a wide range of interests in painters, poets, literature, politics, – sheaves of compositions and teaching notes added to the atmosphere of divergent and creative thinking. Two other images stood out for me – a photo of Ronald with Marjorie – the loving, long-supporting wife, smiling together in a garden – and W Gordon-Smith's striking photograph of Hugh MacDiarmid, Ronald's close friend, from further down the bus-route to Biggar, and a giant of Scottish literary life.

I wanted to use all these aspects of the room in juxtaposition with the strong, back-lit figure of Ronald right in the foreground of the work. (For those of you with a historical interest, this painting was completed a year or so before Ronald's music room was completely altered and turned around. The grand piano was moved away from the window and now bookcases take up the space it once occupied.) A last and very personal note, looking into the detail of the painting you will find, on the music stand, just discernable in the original, a sheet of music written by Ronald and called 'A Duet on the Names Ben and Gemma'.

When the portrait was presented we had a marvellous musical evening in the Scottish National Portrait Gallery. Ben and Gemma unveiled the painting, Ronald played for us and then his great friend John Ogden, who had travelled up from London especially for the ceremony, played for us and the invited audience.

Sadly, the person that brought Ronald and I and the painting together, my son Ben, died in 1995. However, a measure of the affectionate and lasting friendship he and Ronald shared came to fruition in a little requiem Ronald wrote for him. There is also a proposed piece on clarion which we all hope will one day ring out in Aberdeen, where Ben was a student.

Seven years ago we moved – to West Linton, to a big old house opposite Ronald and Marjorie. Now my studio windows overlook the same village street referred to in Ronald's portrait. It's a good feeling to be working in my studio and to see the light across the road in Townfoot House and to know Ronald is at work too.

The Contrapuntal Muse

Derek Watson

To walk with you, Sir, is for me
a real experience for the mind . . .
(Wagner to Faust in Robert David Macdonald's translation of Goethe)

Ronald Stevenson once showed me an unpublished letter. Dated 5 July 1920 it was from Ferruccio Busoni to the young William Walton, and contained this pertinent sentence: "You have a happy inclination to polyphonic lines; this will lead you safely through the Waters and Fires which stand between you and the Parnassus". The observation could equally be applied to Stevenson. As composer and player and, to stretch the metaphor, as thinker, writer and teacher he is a remarkably contrapuntal man.

Yet this in no way detracts from his warm directness of appeal. The academic 'Ebenezer Prout' image of polyphony or many-voiced music *alias* counterpoint may remain a popular perception. (Stevenson, characteristically, admires Prout.) Fugues are not perhaps an obvious musical species to possess mass appeal. There are reasons for this. First, ignorance is bliss: if you don't know what's happening you are content. But if you think you *should* know and consequently don't follow every entry, every countersubject, inversion, augmentation or whatever, you may feel upset, inadequate to the music. I cannot imagine the latter response being a general one to the works of Stevenson, even at their most richly contrapuntal.

Just as transcendental technique in playing disguises both effort and the accumulation of details that add up to the sum total of the performance, so too in composition the vision or final goal can embrace an panorama of individual details without strain on the listener. Stevenson possesses this 'art that conceals art' in abundance, however virtuosic the thought or dexterity required in its interpretation. His closeness to the very essence of music is akin to that of another great contrapuntist, Donald Francis Tovey. Stevenson's embrace of music is an enlightened continuance of the Toveyan concept of the 'mainstream of music'. But *contra*-Tovey, Stevenson would convince us most reasonably that we should include leagues more than the '3 Bs' of Tovey – Bach, Beethoven, Brahms. 'B' in the Stevensonian Alphabet would find places for at least Bartók, Berlioz, Bellini, Bourgault-Ducoudray, Buddy Bolden and, needless to add, Busoni.

Yet I wish Tovey and Stevenson had met. My piano teacher, Jessie Dick, told me of a great *Passacaglia* (I nodded knowledgeably and ran home to look up the term in a dictionary) about to be presented to Dmitri Shostakovich at the 1962 Edinburgh Festival. Wilfrid Mellers has called this *Passacaglia on DSCH* "one of the greatest works for solo piano, not merely in our own time". My own teacher also spoke with enthusiasm of its composer's recent researches in Italy into the life and music of Busoni – a virtually unknown name to me then (not one of Tovey's '3 Bs'). Further lexicographical rummagings informed me about the composer of the *Fantasia Contrappuntistica*, and bit by bit over the next few years Stevenson's own works too became known to me.

At later concerts in the 1960s I heard the Piano Concerto No. 1, *A Faust Triptych*, performed both by the composer and by John Ogdon and was bowled over by the latter's Empyrean playing of the Busoni Piano Concerto. At the end of the decade it was in fact the subject of Tovey that brought me my first personal contact with Ronald Stevenson. I heard a Third Programme talk by Stevenson on Tovey (later reprinted in *The Listener,* 22 May 1969) and was struck by its fresh approach and the not uncritical understanding of another great exponent of the difficult skill of talking and writing about music. Stevenson on Tovey's writing:

> His prose style contains parentheses as labyrinthine as De Quincey's, whimsy as fantastic as Lamb's and as nonsensical as Edward Lear's; but it also contains common sense expressed with precision. He is too ingenuous a man to turn a Wildean epigram, as Ernest Newman could, and too open to emulate a Shavian paradox as Edward Dent did. Perhaps we do wrong to consider Tovey 'literary' at all, for most of his published writings were made to be read as lectures . . . Tovey must have been one of the most brilliant talkers since Coleridge.

Anyone who has enjoyed a long talk with Stevenson or listened to his flights of oratory will at once recognise what I mean by his personal brand of parentheses. There is an illuminatory diffuseness in his range of references, more often visual, literary, theatrical or political than musical, that bespeaks the contrapuntal mind. (Ronald and I jokingly call them Toveyan footnotes – those sort of footnotes that might almost crowd out the text from the page!) The gift for apt allusion, cross-cultural, historically gauged and lit with the glow of humour is reserved for masters of the literary and oratorical arts. I certainly know of no other musician who can hold up such a mirror to his own work and to reflect the trends of his times. My letter of in response to his Tovey talk evoked a first invitation to West Linton, where I have since been lucky enough to feel one of the family, and where unforgettable hours of improvisatory insights upon a cornucopia of topics, laced with music often heard for the first time, have been my deep joy.

A full consideration of Stevenson as musical contrapuntist is fodder for a sheaf of microfiche theses. These already exist in some abundance, starting with the epic polyphonic achievements enshrined in the *Passacaglia*. For the purpose of this modest *paean* I will cite only a handful of examples which have strong personal resonance. I possess the pencil sketches for the *Peter Grimes Fantasy* which provide a fascinating insight upon the creative workings of the contrapuntal mind. I will always remember Stevenson's boyish delight when in the heat of composing this piece he found himself led into entirely new ways of combining Benjamin Britten's melodic material, i.e. ways untried by the original composer. This operatic fantasy is in the best tradition of Liszt: a personal distillation of the form and content of the original drama, which never descends into *pot-pourri.*

My love of Liszt is another spiritual bond with Ronald. His *Prelude and Fugue on a Theme by Liszt* for organ takes as its basis the 12-note theme from Liszt's *Faust Symphony* depicting Faust the *magus,* the visionary, the summoner of spirits. Stevenson's treatment of it has strong echoes of both Liszt and Busoni and the fugue in particular remains one of the most singular of his output. Malcolm MacDonald has described the whole piece as "elusive, yet on closer acquaintance deeply moving . . . perhaps the most impressively 'hermetic' of all Stevenson's creations".

Singular is perhaps the wrong epithet for that organ work. There is another *Prelude and Fugue* for organ (almost complete at the time of writing and dedicated to Will Scott and myself) which takes as fugue subject the shepherd's tune from the opening of Act III scene I of *Tristan und Isolde*. This hauntingly unusual melody, scored by Wagner for solo cor anglais, makes a subject of extraordinary fecundity for contrapuntal elaboration.

Wagner was renowned for 'sound symbols'. Liszt used fugue or fugual texture in a specifically symbolic way as recent analysts have shown. Stevenson in his occultly Lisztian and Faustian organ fugue and in the dramatic evocation of a frenzied mob in the fugato passages of the *Grimes Fantasy* shows himself part of this historical process of using counterpoint as 'sound-symbol' which stretches back to Bach, and beyond him.

Fugue played its part in a visit I made to Townfoot House early in 1971 with Peter Pears, who was to give the premiere of the song cycle *Border Boyhood* at that summer's Aldeburgh Festival. Pears was intensely involved throughout his career with new music, not just Britten's but a plethora of other composers (many of whose works he commissioned, including this cycle), that it was fascinating to hear him trying out something that was technically and stylistically entirely new to him. The final song of this MacDiarmid cycle, *The Nook of the Night Paths*, incorporates fugue and uses the voice integrally and I think uniquely. After the setting of the (prose) words:

> There is a place called the Curly Snake where the winding path coils up through a copse, whence after passing a field or two it runs into the splendid woods of the Langfauld. It has always haunted my imagination . . .

the singer performs in two-part counterpoint with himself, off-setting the normal register and the head voice.

There is a fine illustration of Stevenson's instinctive gift for counterpoint quoted by Malcolm MacDonald in his book on Stevenson, from a conversation with the composer. Stevenson is talking of his boyhood awareness of musical *lines*, and his early realisation

> that melody is the profile of music, and the bass completes its human face . . . I realised it was necessary to write a tune and to have a good bass line. And how I did that was very often to write a bass line which was an inversion of the melody, a kind of mirror inversion . . .

To Ronald I owed the introduction to my own teacher of composition, Alan Bush, another master-contrapuntist. Thinking of this sequence of teaching and tradition leads me to recall finally one of Ronald's favourite tales relating to Busoni. To the young, keen Italian working in Finland, Wegelius, the principal of the Helsinki conservatory, one day remarked, "I must say you *are* a master of punctuality Mr Busoni!" To which came the reply, "And you, Sir, are a master of contrapuntuality!" The praise may be, in all senses, retrospectively bestowed on Ronald Stevenson.

Tom Hubbard

The Aonach of West Linton

Crying up colour from the colourless,
Hidalgo, stepping high up Pentland slope;
Cascading semiquavers with largesse,
The tonal turns of a kaleidoscope:

We have struck out together on that favourite hike –
Your 'curly snake' through the woods above the village;
A map of the path would resemble of your scores,
And I striving to be the accompanist
In a sonata for two climbers. At an andante clearing,
We stopped. "It's here," you said, with your gentle chuckle,
"That I sit and read Walt Whitman." Of a sudden,
A rocky shelter of Long Island beach,
Young Walt himself, and the three of us sharing poetry,
Camerados across a century.

This more-than-university of West Linton,
This universality of your West Linton,
That from its North extends us East and South –
For have you not hammered out in your Scottish forge
This triad of the continent's archetypes:
The smokey chords of Mephistopheles,
As mocking shadow of Germanic power –
Then, as in chiaroscuro counterpoint,
Faust's other self, upon the rainbow side –
Light Latin motley, dancing Arlecchino:
Myriad facets spangling in tension:
Out of the Gothic twilight into the Mediterranean sun!

Out of the struggles of art, the assertion of peace:
The notes on the stave urgent against the twisted wire on the fence,
The orchestral crescendo bold against the camouflaged landmine,
The pibroch's eternal love for the children in their shrouds.

I remember your image of Busoni, the maestro's contempt for the war;
Artist-ocratic in his greatcoat, pacing the edge
of the Bahnhofstrasse,
Brooding towards Lake Zurich scintillant under the moon
the constellations;

Even as I have heard you, Ronald, at the townhead parapet
Questing with me our future through the witness of our dead:
– Scotland the theme, with global variations . . .

> aonach: "Scottish Gaelic, meaning 1) a solitary place, 2) a place of
> union". (Gloss by Hugh MacDiarmid)

So we'll go no more a-roving ...

Poem by Lord Byron

Andante

Music by
RONALD STEVENSON
(aet. 14 or 15
in 1943)

2. For the sword outwears its sheath,
   And the soul wears out the breast,
   And the heart must pause to breathe,
   And love itself have rest.

3. Though the night was made for loving,
   And the day returns too soon,
   Yet we'll go no more a-roving
   By the light of the moon.

A Pilgrimage to Townfoot House

John Bellany

As a very youthful and starry-eyed painter I made a pilgrimage with two fellow rebels the poet Alan Bold and the painter Sandy Moffat. We were students at Edinburgh College of Art and Alan at the University. Ronald Stevenson had been Alan's teacher at Broughton School and was already a legend in my mind because of the endless anecdotes told about him by Alan. His long friendship with John Ogdon, his introduction to Alan of a certain novel *Ulysses* by James Joyce, his friendship with Hugh MacDiarmid and his virtuosic skills on the pianoforte.

All those marvels were buzzing through the mind of the young 'Port Seton man' as we sped out to West Linton on the SMT bus in the early sixties. The bus stopped at the Gordon's Arms, so we had to wet our whistles in the usual Scottish style then toddle down the road to Townfoot House.

Waiting with a welcoming smile was the maestro himself. I was dumbfounded by the likeness to his namesake RLS. We entered the splendid stone house and were introduced to the other members of the family – his wife Marjorie and two daughters Gerda and Savourna, now wonderful talents in their own rights. His son was out playing football. The drawing room was staggering for a unsophisticated East Lothian beginner like myself. The walls were covered with paintings and photos of Ronald's heroes from Liszt and Grieg to Percy Grainger, and in pride of place in the middle of the room was the grand piano given to him by the renowned composer Alan Bush. The place just oozed creativity. My creative juices were on fire aided by the hefty dram he gave us as a refreshment of welcome.

After a lunch which was sizzling with frenzied "art talk" with some raucous interjections from our poet friend and a few bawdy tales from myself, Ronald slid onto the piano stool and fairly rattled into some Percy Grainger to fortify our mood. Then he showed us the score of his *Passacaglia*. It was fantastic to see the notes and sharps and flats by the master's hand. He played the opening passage for us which was breathtaking, then a passage from the middle of the work where he jumps from the piano stool and plays the open strings, plucking them like a cello and stroking them as if it was a harp. I had never seen anything like this in my life. Then he was back playing and singing some MacDiarmid poems set by Francis George Scott. Then some Liszt, followed by more Stevenson. I was mesmerised by such talent. It was the first time I had met a composer and the first time I had seen a musical virtuoso in action.

When I think back, remembering the many times I have seen Ronald performing, be it at the Purcell Room in London or the National Gallery in Edinburgh or when I see Alfred Brendell or John Lill playing at the Edinburgh Festival or the Queen Elizabeth Hall, I do not think I ever get that ecstatic tingle of excitement I experienced that day at Townfoot House. It was my introduction to the grandeur of the musical creativity which has brought me endless joy and spiritual uplift for my entire adult life.

The Atlantic Cantata

Kenneth White

I first met Ronald Stevenson in autumn 1990. That was at Elizabeth Lyons' place in Edinburgh. Liz had thought Ronald and I should get together. The more I got to know Ronald, the surer I was her idea was a good one.

I liked the man's manner first of all. Scottish, definitely – but with a kind of American touch. Part gentleman of the South, part Western ranger, let's say a mixture of Mark Twain and Daniel Boone: it was there in the way he held himself, it was there in his precise and elevated way of speaking, it was there in his necktie, or rather neck-string, which bore, if I remember rightly, a bit of turquoise from Arizona or thereabouts.

But it was especially the animated, wide-ranging conversation.

In no time at all, we were talking not only about why, after long years in France, I had decided to work again on Scottish ground which we both knew had, for politico-historical reasons, some pretty sterile, life-reducing patches, but also about Whitman ('Salut au monde'), MacDiarmid ('On a Raised Beach') and other elective affinities. There were parallels too, we discovered, in our itineraries. And Ronald had a project in mind for the two of us, with 1992 coming up: the year not only of the discovery of America, but of the centenary of Whitman's death and the centenary of MacDiarmid's birth. What a conjunction, what a constellation!

I had a lot of misgivings about 1992: I could imagine the load of pseudo-cultural crap that would be swilling around the world in that year and I'd more or less decided, so far as public manifestation was concerned, to put 1992 in brackets. But Ronald's plan stuck in my mind.

I was back in my Breton outpost when a letter in Ronald's beautiful hand, dated 'Yuletide 1990', arrived. I quote it in order to show the exaltation, generosity and tenacity that mark Ronald's personality:

Dear Whitmanesque camerado Kenneth!

I warm my hands at the embers of the year and they blaze up with thoughts of you.

Meeting you has been the highlight of my 1990. I never thought that after the passing of my old friend MacDiarmid another shooting-star of poetry would land on my path! [...]

I've gone on composing. You said you hoped to visit us with your wife Marie-Claude in March 1991. Be welcome! Stay with us! Then you'll hear a cassette of my String Quartet *Voces vagabundae* with its scherzo, 'The Bird Path', *en hommage à* K. W.

Have you put out antennae about our project of collaborating on a Cantata for voices and orchestra to honour the double event of the centenary of Whitman's death and the centenary of MacDiarmid's birth in 1992? I feel strongly that this should be premièred in Paris. The tradition of honouring great ones is much more in evidence in French history than in Scottish! Ideally we need a commission, at least a firm offer of performance.

It was this last point that stumped me a bit.

58

I'd been thinking around the project, and had begun to have some kind of concept. But I hadn't a clue who to contract for commissions and promises of performance. I was in France because it seemed to me the most interesting *general* field, but at the same time I was on my own, in my Scoto-cosmic atopia. The 'music world' in particular was unknown to me. I'd worked with various French musicians on poetry readings. Singers and musicians French-based had set some of my poems, that were on record here and there. Recently the France-based American jazzman Steve Lacy had got in touch, saying he wanted to set a series of poems, and later on we were to do a long jam-session programme on French radio together. About six years before, I'd worked on a cantata with the musician Jean-Yves Bosseur, a pupil of Stockhausen. On the basis of the fifteen modes of traditional Breton music, I'd worked out French lyrics. The text of the cantata was these lyrics, sung solo or by various choirs, as well as some longer poems of mine *said* by myself. But I had no connection with any musical institution. So, leaving the contractual side alone, I'd concentrated solely on the conceptual.

In answer to Ronald's letter, saying that I didn't imagine lyrics for this piece, but large prosaical sequences, I sent him a preliminary, tentative concept that went like this.

The '1992' Cantata

Twilight on Jamaica Bridge
Soundings in Glasgow, the most 'American' city in Britain, and the present state of things.

Whitmania
Celebration of Whitman – Paumanok, Brooklyn Ferry and the rest.

In Praise of the White Rose
A Salutation to MacDiarmid – from the drunk man of Rose Street to the prophet of the Raised Beach.

On Rannoch Moor
Emptiness and geopoetics.

The Atlantic Arc
Evocation of that Western littoral of Europe, from Portugal up to the Scottish archipelagoes – a wide swinging.

The idea was in the air – but Ronald must have felt keenly the absence of any firm, signature-on-the-line commission.

When we met at West Linton in June 1991, we talked about the idea, I said I'd get in touch with Jean-Yves Bosseur for advice on commissions, but the main theme of our conversation was Ronald's principal music-reference, Busoni: Ronald played his music, talking enthusiatically about his work. When I left, he made me a present of Busoni's letters to his wife, inscribing the volume so: "For Kenneth, the voyageur of *The Blue Road*, who today heard Busoni's *Bluebird Song* from the *Indianisches Tagebuch*." Those letters interested me in an extraordinary way. Elective affinities again: "Work proceeds with colossal regularity ..."; "How young our European music is, still only a few hundred years, and our culture numbers many thousand."; "It is the land which gives beauty to the sea; it is only when the coast comes into sight that the sea acquires drawing and colour and seems bigger, too, by comparison"; "What a long road the road to mastery is, even for someone who is very gifted – and often still further for him, because he sets himself bigger problems!" Busoni wasn't only a piano virtuoso, he was also a live mind at large. That's why he occupies a prominent place in the chapter devoted to music in my 'introduction to geopoetics', *Le Plateau de l'Albatros* (Paris, 1994).

Time went by. The year 1992 had come and gone and Ronald and I still hadn't done the cantata.

Simply because I had so much work on the go, I hadn't pushed the commissioning side. But mainly, the whole thing was undergoing a submarine evolution in my mind. I remember writing to Ronald at one point that commemoration was fine, but that cosmopoetic presence was better. What had been vaguely conceived as 'The 1992 Cantata' was turning in my brain vaults into 'The Atlantic Cantata', based largely, but not exclusively, on the 'Atlantic movement' section of *The Bird Path*. I was thinking not only of 'atlantic-geopoetic' composition, but of all kinds of original, land-based, sea-tuned instrumentation ...

We never did get round to it.

Well, the big things take time: tides and cycles.

The idea is still there, in the air, like a nebula, like the embryon of a cyclone.

Maybe we'll do the thing sometime yet – and in Scotland, a newly grounded, Atlantic-minded Scotland.

Ronald Stevenson the Man

Geoffrey Elborn

It was said of one of the Bourbons of France that he raised his hat forty different ways, according to whom he met. There seem to be multiple hats that could be worn by Ronald Stevenson rather than many ways of doffing just one, for to say that of RS the *man* is rather limiting. As it happens, it was Stevenson as a hat I saw first in 1971, aged 21, in the West Linton to Edinburgh bus when I boarded it at Fairmilehead. Not the sort of hat that could be easily left behind black with a large, stiff brim, slightly Spanish perhaps, and under it, Stevenson quietly reading a book as we rumbled towards St Andrew's Square. Mentioning the black hat to a relation he replied, "Oh, yes, a bit of a crank, isn't he?" something I regarded as a compliment for he did not understand my interest in Edith Sitwell either.

I had heard of Stevenson from another mutual friend, Sydney Goodsir Smith, and thought of both as key figures who were vital in shaping the Modern Renaissance of Scottish culture. It was Stevenson wearing his hat as a composer and pianist I expected to meet when I managed to be invited to West Linton. A little like meeting Tennyson on the Isle of Wight clad in a cape and "moving in classical metres", I imagined. I was not prepared for the tornado of energy that presented such a variety of delights and unexpected interests, leaving the impression of one man quickly taking on and off many different hats, with a slight touch of the satisfied and successful conjuror which was not at all embarrassing or unjustified.

That may seem a little flippant, but it took several visits and meetings before one could begin to discern that nothing in Stevenson's work or conversation was at all random or unconnected. If the early part of his creative life became informed by his search for Busoni, this quest has produced innumerable links in a remarkable way that I do not understand but have simply observed between Stevenson's friends and their own imaginative discoveries. New or old friends happen to mention something that interests them and Stevenson can show a sequence of connections which he has divined belong to a deep rooted cultural tradition. I am not thinking only of the Lisztian tradition of the virtuoso pianist composer which he had inherited. Nor of the neo-platonic tradition which began with Blake and which has descended through Yeats to Kathleen Raine and David Jones, although both *are* part of some artistic collective consciousness, and which encompasses this mysterious process which defies explanation. I think this will be understood by those who know RS well. In my case, I knew Sacheverell Sitwell who knew Busoni and heard all his recitals and concerts, and both encouraged William Walton who recommended that OUP should publish the *Passacaglia*. I discovered that RS shares my devotion to Casals, and no comment is necessary on that towering and presiding genius, Bach. Other friends will produce their lists of those who help to define their own life and understanding of it, (to which must of course be added RS) but as important as any 'name' to him, and essential to Stevenson's being is his deep concern for humanity. It is of course this which motivates all his actions, and which makes a coherent whole of his diverse interests. He is thankfully free of a curse which can affect musicians, and which anybody who has been a music student will understand, that of being what a mutual friend called 'music daft'. An obsession with music for the sake of the object that excludes life in which it was created. A blindness to the whole imaginative process, an unawareness of the disturbance in a composer's life that shaped some composition, an attitude that ultimately results in a musical performance that may be technically proficient, but emotionally worthless.

Stevenson was immensely fortunate in having parents who did not hinder or stifle his own precocious creativity, but he rewarded that trust by never having wanted to abandon or forget his roots. As a man of conscience, he was incapable of doing anything else and has always kept his principles throughout a life which has not always been financially comfortable. It would be unkind to 'name names', but I recall RS giving a broadcast performance in Glasgow University where during the rehearsal the pedal board on his piano dropped off. We were joined for lunch by a composer who was then completely unknown and who shared the programme with RS. He has since become extremely famous for producing 'music' of such astonishing mediocrity that it is nevertheless completely understandable, in an age where certain 'pop' musicians are household names, that he is considered a kind of genius.

Such a reputation, falsely acquired, easy compromise in a bid for immortality and perhaps as quickly lost, has never had any part in Stevenson's mode of behaviour. It would answer none of the questions which he as the human being he is, feels compelled to ask, which require a life time of living to come to any conclusion, and which will not allow any short cuts. RS has a restless and probably troubled spirit, one that is never satisfied and in this age of commercial obsession and instant gratification, he could hardly *be* comfortable. As composer, pianist, writer, translator, lecturer, musicologist and with his work for the young, he is teacher and learner.

It is an honour to be writing of RS on this celebratory occasion although there *is* the slight horror of Ronald reading what I have written. And if RS was in the room he would be arguing gently for a more exact phrase, a Joycean embellishment. The conversation would spin off in unpredictable directions and he would have the fortunate knack of making me feel that I had contributed a great deal while in reality I learned everything from him. Thankfully this essay is only an attempt to hint at his quality, for the elusive *essence* of Stevenson reminds me of T S Eliot's statement that "Genuine poetry communicates before it is understood".

From time to time, when RS and Marjorie plan to come to London I have a telephone call asking if they can stay. I am momentarily thrown into a panic and an unaccustomed flurry of 'good housekeeping' none of it grudged, but with the anxiety of wondering if the meals are adequate or the house warm enough. We often meet at King's Cross Station and any momentary nervousness is dismissed after a warm embrace. In fact my guests are no trouble at all and have very few demands – only the necessary and sensible insistence on arriving at a concert on time and walking with my dog. In that part of London, written of by Goldsmith, Blake (the green fields of Islington) we also stroll to small house where Charles Lamb lived with his sister and where Lamb's poet friend Dyer stepped too far forward from the front gate and fell in the bordering New River, alas now covered by a concrete path. If a revolution had taken place in 1848 in Britain it would have, it was said, started on Clerkenwell Green, later known to both Marx, and Lenin. Strange to think of a worker from London meeting Lenin in the Kremlin and to hear his carefully formed English "And how is Clerkenwell?" Musing on this, and how the world might have been, the "if" is important – but there is also the humour of friendship never far away with verbal word play – as well as serious allusions to mutual interest which could not be shared by anyone else.

A visit from RS also means the continuing setting of that extraordinary poem of Blake's' The Island and the Moon', completely mad words, which RS adds a little more music to on each visit. This is a burlesque which has references to Edith Sitwell's and Walton's *Facade*, the DSCH motif and only RS, my dog and I understand the private reference to "thumbs" and "Bears". And all sparked by a request for matches to light a pipe, a reading of the poem which will make this reference obvious, but also give an example of an ultra quick association by RS.

All one can write of is "*Aspects* of Ronald Stevenson the man" one of the few who belongs to a now dwindling tribe of the wise who are unafraid of risking strange and unpopular byways in search of the universal.

For Stevenson, the paths of exploration with a Whitmanesque expanse, have taken him through the continents to China and the former Soviet Republic, but he always takes with him Scotland and especially West Linton and the nearby hills in his heart wherever he is. Stevenson has had the loving support of his wife Marjorie and their children without whom he could not be the man he is. His family is part of that 'completeness' of his vision and hopes. Both RS and MS have suffered the threats and testing times of serious illness, and survived through a love which began and has endured from late childhood. Stalwart, resilient and yet vulnerable. RS only once caused me great upset when he heard of some revelations of mine years ago when I did not know him at all well and of which he seemed to disapprove. I stayed the night at Townfoot House and we both strode out on a beautiful summer morning for a hill walk where Ronald apologised for hurting me, explaining how he had thought of the whole matter during a disturbed night of sleep. It is with a sense of gratitude that I remember this, that RS had the courage to 'swallow his words'. Many memories of conversations and meetings which often occur at moments of discouragement have the revitalising effect of a drink at the end of a hard day. I am proud to consider Ronald and Marjorie as part of just of a few but significant friends, who matter through and beyond all the trials life dredges up, who enhance one's way of being and are a vital support to it.

A Filter in the Stream

John Purser

Ronald is the most flamboyant gentleman I know. I know only a very few gentlemen: they are mostly quiet, well-behaved people who keep the better part of their opinions to themselves, including their own self-estimation. On the other hand, I know lots of flamboyant people, but very few of them could be classed as gentlemen, either on grounds of sex or, that requirement satisfied, on grounds of manners. So Ronald stands almost alone in my estimation, even if he had never composed or played a note of music.

Besides being flamboyant and a gentleman, he has that love of art, generous in its acknowledgment of the achievements of others and generous in its intellectual curiosity which, however assertively focused upon his own opinions, is ultimately profoundly unselfish. By art I mean all the arts, including a whole lot of occupations which think they are sciences. They attempt by experimentation to differentiate themselves from the rest of us speculators in a creative matter and end up preventing us from eating our baron of beef at Yule because they insist upon being taken seriously.

Ronald insists upon being taken seriously and, mostly, I have been able to cooperate. Now and again, however, there has been a credibility gap. I recall long, long ago the dimming of lights in one of Glasgow University's fine Victorian halls – probably the Randolph Hall – and Ronald making his way, in an imposing impersonation of Franz Liszt, to a pianoforte which, had it known what it was about to undergo, would have loosened its bowels. The instrument, however, divulged no more secrets to the audience of voyeurs than it might have done had the *Passacaglia on DSCH* been a little shorter, or its dedicatory sections been confined to a less ambitious range of suffering humanity. It was at a particularly sensitive moment in this monstrously ambitious piece that the University clock, having selected the correct key, announced that it was time for brandy and cigars. I remember it all too well. My first wife and I had a fit of the giggles, thereby scandalising the rapt audience; and I believe it was on the same occasion that our first child leapt in the womb, though with what critical purpose remains undisclosed.

The damnable thing about it is that years later I have come to appreciate the power and intensity of the *Passacaglia*, both as a piece of virtuoso piano writing and as a virtuoso composition. I regard it as one of Ronald's most coherent and impressive works, and if I ever do have a fit of the giggles during it again, I shall not be embarrassed because I know my true opinion of it is one of sincere admiration. This is all the more surprising in that it is musically inspired by composers whose music I heartily detest – Liszt and Busoni. Perhaps the clean-limbed strictures of composing music largely confined by the notes D-S-C-H and B-A-C-H have filtered those muddier waters and produced a turbulent but crystalline result.

I have no memory of first meeting Ronald; but an unforgettable one of his first appearance in my household. I see him at the piano – I don't believe he either entered, exited, ate or passed down a corridor. He was at the piano and then he was not. Bartok was under discussion. I knew quite a lot of Bartok but, not being a pianist, I simply gaped in wonderment as Ronald wrestled with an old Broadwood which probably instantly turned white, but who cared. He, then, began a spontaneous discourse upon the relationship of Bartok's music and researches to pretty well everything else in the world. Tippett had the same tendency, his mind roaming over vast savannahs across which innumerable cultures have advanced and retreated. By both of them I was left excited and confused. That response I have often felt to Ronald's music. There is a splendid eclecticism which bears a close relationship to the work of MacDiarmid, but, though I have no aesthetic objections to eclecticism, I do find with both of them that the attempt to be inclusive can become distracting.

Yet Ronald has written music which, like MacDiarmid's lyrics, has reached straight to the heart of things without pretension or fancy; but with the clear beauty of the pure drop. He has also frequently honoured the music of others, particularly in his masterly piano versions of F G Scott songs. Like Scott and Chisholm, Ronald Stevenson has made his peace with Scottish music. I say "made his peace" because bringing traditional music into the classical music concert hall, whether dragged by her hair or led by the hand, tends to produce a sense of unwillingness overcome, of a struggle for attention between cultures which seem to some to be diametrically opposed. But they need not be so. Bartok demonstrated the vitality of the traditional music he leaned upon in his own compositions, without depriving us of the reality of his sources. On the contrary, he lovingly preserved those sources. The task of collecting has been carried out by others, but Scott, Chisholm and Stevenson have done for Scottish traditional music a similar service to that of Bartok for his own musical traditions. In Ronald's case, to such effect that when I had to decide how to end my radio series and book, *Scotland's Music*, it was a piece of Ronald's which came to my rescue – appropriately a setting of MacDiarmid's 'A'e Gowden Lyric'. What I wrote then remains as true in my heart today, so I will simply repeat it.

A'e Gowden Lyric claims, and what musician worthy of drawing breath would claim anything other? that one golden lyric is not only better than the castle's soaring wall, and all the achievements and history that that image implies; it is better than anything else at all. Stevenson's setting could never be mistaken as traditional, but it could not have been born without that tradition: it is both new and wholly Scottish. Its soaring vocal line demands from the singer a technical mastery and a deeply-informed expressive simplicity that has been at the heart of Scotland's lyric traditions for hundreds of years. It is a song so unaffectedly expressive of the enduring qualities of Scottish music that it feels as though we had all had a share in its making, as though it were our own private gift to ourselves.

For my son Gordon

A'e Gowden Lyric

Poem: Hugh MacDiarmid

Music: Ronald Stevenson

Poems reproduced by kind permission of Deirdre Chapman and Carcanet Press Ltd., Manchester, publishers of *Hugh MacDiarmid: Complete Poems* (edited by Michael Grieve and W R Aitken).

den   lyr-ic____   Than   o - - - ny-thin'

else   a - - - vaa.   -vaa.

If the accompaniment is played on the harp,
distribute the notes like this:

etc.

An Age of Enlightenment?

Martin Anderson

In *The Proms and Natural Justice* (my first venture into publishing as Toccata Press in 1981), Robert Simpson attacked the monopoly of taste which the BBC allows its 'Controller, Music' – the chap who plans the Proms, amongst other things. The Controller, Music, decides who plays what at the Proms and thus, for the length of his reign, decides single-handedly the fate of hundreds of composers and performers by facilitating or blocking their access to millions of ears across the globe. Simpson had no disagreement with the monopoly itself (indeed, he argued that the enthusiasms of a passionately committed individual were much to be preferred to the pallid compromises of a committee); what he objected to was that this cultural dictatorship had no term. It ended only when the incumbent was claimed by death or by the BBC pension scheme.

When *The Proms and Natural Justice* was published, the only Controllers, Music to have enjoyed the position were William Glock and Robert Ponsonby. Since then John Drummond has come and gone, replaced now by Nicholas Keynon, and the validity of Simpson's argument has faltered not a bit.

Bob Simpson was a committed socialist, and my argument that state subsidy – and the taxation necessary for other forms of subsidy – is bad for the arts made precious little sense to him (indeed, though our musical sympathies were very closely aligned, Bob and I expressed our opinions of each other's views on economics with what might be described as good-humoured contumely). But the logic is inescapable: if you allow the funding of music to be allocated through government largesse, the funds involved will flow through a select group of associations, arts councils or ministries of culture, broadcasting organisations and similar institutions. Inevitably they will become the focus of a clique and the result is, sooner rather than later, the institutionalisation of a particular set of values.

And what has constricted the Proms in microcosm is exactly what has happened on a vast scale across the western world: the monopolisation of artistic choice is a hallmark of the institutions that have governed cultural life since the Second World War. War always allows a huge enlargement of the apparatus of the state, and that particular war was no different. In the United Kingdom Keynes' lobbying brought about the transformation of the wartime Council for Encouragement of Music and the Arts into the post-war Arts Council, through which People Who Knew Best would allocate state monies to ends they saw fit – a move paralleled in country after country as the fingers of the taxpayer were gradually prized from his wallet and the state rammed its shovel into his stores.

The success of the composer had once depended on his pleasing a patron – a high functionary in the church, an aristocrat, an industrialist – a real person, a living, breathing individual with his own likes and dislikes whether he was a saint or grade-A bastard. Now, for the first time in history the composer was faced with a committee and usually one whose members felt that they must press for the immediate advancement of their art. And so the modernists captured the castle and the composer's link with his listeners was broken. Those whose voice was not loud with the *dernier cri* were locked outside the walls. Music, hitherto a thing of emotion governed by a controlling intelligence, became the pursuit of high intellects whose (sometimes avowed) purpose was the squeezing of the last vestiges of emotion from the art.

Out of the Iron Mask

That fifty-year domination by the intellect has only recently been broken and the modernists are being hounded from the temples. (Mind you, it's hardly fair of commentators like Julian Lloyd-Webber, lamenting in Davos recently, to blame the composers themselves: they are, after all, rational beings who respond to economic stimuli like the rest of us and they must feed their families. And no one is denying the composer the freedom to write what he likes. It's just that there's more than one path to salvation, Webern is not the only god and Boulez not the only true prophet.)

One of the composers consigned to the Gulag during the onward march of modernism was Ronald Stevenson, a socialist consumed by the application of socialist methods (there were plenty in the Soviet Union, too). Stevenson's socialism, though, was a far cry from the arid doctrinism of his friend Alan Bush, a man for whom theory seemed to be more important than the people it was supposed to serve. Stevenson grew up among the working poor of Blackburn, was scrubbed in the tin baths in front of the coal grate, and his music and his music-making – no matter how complex the intellectual processes that inform them – have always remembered that man is the provenance of all passion. Stevenson's music embraces tonality, even when expanding it with lessons learned from dodecaphonic practice. It dances. It rises and falls with the drawing and exhalation of human breath because, above all, it is a lyrical art. It was deeply unfashionable for reasons its composer can be proud of.

Interestingly, the scorn then reserved for tonal composers by their more advanced *confrères* was directly paralleled in economics, the discipline which has provided my bread and butter since I left university. With the ascendancy of socialist thinking, market economists of all stripes, conservative to libertarian, were held in more or less universal contempt until the failure of state institutions began to become manifest in the 1970s and erstwhile statists began to look at market solutions with grudging curiosity.

And one can take the analogy further. There are remarkable parallels between the market economy and tonality which are both 'systems' (I use the word cautiously) that work with the grain of human nature, markets by gratifying the urge for self-advancement , and tonality by using those intervals that strike the ear as more or less consonant, as the laws of physics dictate. And they share similar histories: each arose from more restrictive practices in the Middle Ages (mercantilism, modality) and passed though stages of growing sophistication until, at the end of the 19th century and beginning of the 20th, the intellectuals of both parties threw tradition out of the window. Socialism/serialism tightened its hold on academic thinking through the middle of the twentieth century, alienating the politician from the people and the composer from his audience until the 1970s when the barrenness, the sheer inhumanity of these approaches began to produce the inevitable backlash that only now is leading to a degree of economic freedom and artistic choice. Again, the parallels are striking: just as consumers are using markets to demand better standards of health care than the state has been able to provide, there is likewise a vigorous consumer backlash against the aridity of much of the 'classical' music forced on the public by the Great and Good.

There is a tendency among informed commentators to look down their noses at the unwashed public that buys something as crass as the Three Tenors. But can you blame them if the middle ground of serious music is obscured by the self-indulgent banalities and obscurities of so much modern music? It's small wonder that the unenlightened consumer makes for the safety of C major and Alberti basses when his only forays into more demanding repertoire are met head-on by total serialism. Until recently, his chances of hearing that middle ground were slight: the concert halls were full of standard classics and the more organised institutions thrust music at him that offered no handle to hang on to. The music of our middle-grounders – the Stevensons, the Rubbras, the Simpsons, Irgens Jensens, Holmboes, Brians, Goldschmidts and hundreds of others – may not walk straight up to the listener but at least it encourages the trust that will retain his attention. Yet it simply wasn't heard.

The Market to the Rescue

In view of the enthusiastic but unavailing arguments Robert Simpson and I used to have about the relative (de)merits of state and market, it is therefore no small irony (and for this libertarian no slight satisfaction) that it is the market that has come to the rescue of Bob's music, as it is likewise fetching from obscurity a large number of other neglected masters.

The decades-long indifference of the state apparatus (the Arts Council and the BBC in this instance) to Simpson's radical conservatism has fallen before the combined forces of an enlightened individual (here in the form of Ted Perry, the managing director of Hyperion Records) and ordinary listeners. Perry responded immediately to the suggestion of the Robert Simpson Society (more individuals!) that Hyperion, with some small assistance, should begin recording Simpson's string quartets, and the results were encouraging enough to lead Hyperion on to the symphonies.

Sixteen years later, though Bob himself is no longer around to enjoy the prospect, the Hyperion Simpson cycle is nearly complete and already it has completely transformed this particular corner of musical history. Robert Simpson is now recognised – by the informed public, by the people who have put their hands in their own pockets to buy his music on disc as one of the master-composers of the twentieth century. I am, for example, a member of several classical-music discussion groups on the Internet and I am constantly heartened by the fact that every time Simpson's name is mentioned, often as part of some high claim for his importance, there is not a hint of apology for views which even fifteen years ago would have been regarded, at the very least, as mildly eccentric.

I am convinced that the market will shine the same forgiving light on the music of Ronald Stevenson. Ronald's music can be immediately attractive – all those who know his music will have their own favourite lyrical high-point, from the microcosmic 'A'e Gowden Lyric', through the grippingly beautiful *Nine Haiku*, to the extended eloquence of the 'Elegy' that ends the Cello Concerto – but it also rewards repeated, extended listening. Indeed, I find that more often than not the central message of a Stevenson piece eludes me first time round. It has both outside and inside. Simpson's music tolerates fools less easily than Stevenson's, and yet it has won an enthusiastic audience among ordinary music-lovers with no particular axe to grind. Simpson's music kicks your door down and pushes past you. Stevenson's you ask in. It is certain to command a wide audience.

The striking non-musical difference between these two composers, these two friends, is that Simpson's music is now well known. CD collectors going into shops in Seattle, Singapore and Stockholm will find his music on the shelves. That is what must happen with Ronald Stevenson's. The time is right: the public is ready, tonality is back with a vengeance (rather too lustily in the case of some American minimalists). It's no good expecting concert promoters suddenly to start dropping a Stevenson *opera* into their programmes (no more conservative beast ever existed than the concert promoter). The discovery procedure must happen via the compact disc, where market conditions are such that CD buyers are actively seeking adventurous new repertoire. It is not mere chance that, whereas Claudio Abbado and the Berlin Philharmonic did not sell enough copies of a recent Mozart recording to reach triple figures, Gary Brain's disc of the *Sinfonia* by Czeslaw Marek (an unknown conductor in unknown repertoire – and a project that ultimately owes its existence to Ronald Stevenson) has sold some 10,000 copies in its first year. There has been some progress on the Stevenson front, of course: several recordings of the man himself on Altarus (not least the *Passacaglia on DSCH*), the Piano Concertos on Olympia, another *Passacaglia* on Marco Polo. But the attack must be broader. A first disc of his songs has already been recorded and should be released later this year; another such is under discussion for Hyperion with their songmaker-general, Graham Johnson. Marc-André Hamelin has declared his intention to record Stevenson's *Festin d'Alkan*, and he, forsooth, is a Hyperion artist. There is also a project underway to get some of the orchestral music onto CD with the same Gary Brain who made such a runaway success of the Marek. And by then the cat will be out of the bag.

Bit by bit, it will happen. The Simpson who was the private pride of a coterie of enthusiasts a decade and a half ago is now acknowledged as one of the century's great symphonists. In relative terms our Ronald Stevenson is still a whispered passion, shared by a ludicrously small group of initiates. But when the word gets out, borne afar by the compact disc, we shall happily see him torn from our grasp and acknowledged as one of the century's finest song-writers, a master in the lost art of writing for the piano, a contrapuntist with few equals among his contemporaries, a composer whom younger generations will be delighted and relieved to discover. It's a wonderful thing, free enterprise.

'Comrades-in-art'

Alexander Moffat

I first met Ronald Stevenson late in the summer of 1959. Alan Bold and I were walking home after a Film Festival screening of Ingmar Bergman's *The Virgin Spring*. As we made our way along Princes Street the figure of Ronald Stevenson (who was Alan's music teacher at the time) suddenly appeared before us. In a long coat and magnificent black hat he looked as if he had stepped out from one of Bergman's films. He proceeded to lead us through the shadows of Rose Street to the Abbotsford where we were introduced to the pianist John Ogdon and treated to a glass of shandy. This was my first time in a pub. Ronald brought out a copy of *Ulysses* from his music case and started to read aloud, emphasising the musicality of Joyce's prose. My life as an artist had begun . . .

We were not to meet again for several years. Amusingly, this second meeting took place in the bar of the Glasgow-Edinburgh train in the spring of 1967. On this occasion John Bellany and I were returning from the Kelvingrove Museum when we noticed Ronald entering the bar. I had made a series of drawings of Ronald performing his *Passacaglia on DSCH* at the National Gallery in Edinburgh in the autumn of 1966 and as a result plucked up the courage to introduce ourselves. Afterwards John described the meeting as 'historic'. Not only did Ronald invite us to his home in West Linton, but he immediately arranged for us to attend the Handel Festpiele in Halle in the German Democratic Republic as guests of the Scottish Composer's Guild. This act of generosity was to change our lives.

Over the next decade I made regular trips to West Linton, usually failing to catch the bus back to Edinburgh. At long last I was in contact with a working composer and someone who really believed that art mattered. (Art in Scotland in the 1960s was largely an amateurish affair.) Ronald's passion and intellectual energy created an astonishing flow of ideas. Likewise his appreciation of an artist's intentions or his analysis of individual pieces was unfailingly illuminating. It was a special privilege to visit Town-foot House and I always departed in an exhilarated state of mind. I learnt most of what I know about art and music from those all-night sessions.

Ronald Stevenson's importance for myself (and for John Bellany) sprang initially from the fact that he too seemed to be outside the system. In our student years in Edinburgh in the early 1960s, Bellany and I put together an artistic platform based on, firstly a wish to unite our painting with what we perceived as a distinctive European figurative tradition, secondly to form a synthesis of older parts of this tradition with aspects of modernism and thirdly to address the problems of producing a complex art of ideas (in the MacDiarmid mould) but which would renounce any form of obscurity or esotericism and would seek to communicate with others. We loathed fashionable posturings and pseudo-intellectual strategies. Our ideas fell on stony ground in Edinburgh and London and we came to realise our creative lives would almost certainly involve some kind of struggle against art world orthodoxy.

That Stevenson gave us hope in this struggle cannot be over-estimated. Condemned as romantic and conservative, Ronald stood in total opposition to current fashions and to the 'official' avant-garde. He appeared almost single-handedly to be carrying forward the great tradition of European music in which meaning was constructed from an imaginative fusion of form and content. His mastery of monumental design and structure had culminated in the colossal achievement of the *Passacaglia on DSCH*, and his uncompromising belief in the continuing potential of tonality and the relevance of specific traditional forms was inspiring. We could relate what we were attempting in our paintings to his compositions and see a way ahead.

It was important too that Ronald's work involved a dialogue between art and politics, between art and philosophy, between art and literature, and between music and the visual arts. Ronald showed that music could, to paraphrase Mahler, include the world. The *Passacaglia* contains passages such as the Pibroch, Lament for the Children, the Glimpse of a War Vision and the pedal-point, To Emergent Africa. Scattered throughout his manuscript score are newspaper cuttings, photographs, postcards, etc. serving to remind us how he composes, transforming so-called 'extra-musical' material into purely musical ideas of great emotional power.

Ronald's interest in painting is extraordinarily wide ranging. He introduced me to the innovative stage designs of Edward Gordon Craig, to the paintings of Giovanni Segantini, the Northern Italian symbolist, and the 19th century Russian realist, Ilya Repin. Segantini's aim, to make art an instrument of 'social illumination', seemed especially to echo Ronald's own intentions. As a humanitarian socialist his concerns were to reflect on and to transform reality, at all times seeking out the human content in music.

Up until meeting Ronald most of my ideas had come through reading and from my contacts with certain Scottish poets (Bold, MacCaig and MacDiarmid). The older Scottish painters, including my teachers in Edinburgh, simply had not been interested in ideas. Ronald was one of the first artists I got to know who had a real intellectual presence. His book on the history of Western music and the reviews he wrote for *The Listener* reveal an immense knowledge of his subject. I was to benefit greatly from his expertise. It became possible to discuss the theories of Marx and Nietzsche, the operas of Brecht and Weill, the symphonies of Nielsen and Shostakovich, the ideological positions of Lukács and Adorno, the influence of Jazz on European music, the differences between Bartok and Janácek in their use of folk melody, and so on. All of this would lead us into an ongoing debate about Scottish art and culture, past, present and future.

Looking back over the long period of our friendship (or as Ronald might put it "as comrades-in-art") certain moments leap to mind beginning with the London premiere of the *Passacaglia* in the Purcell Room in the company of Ronald's fellow composers Alan Bush and Bernard Stevens. In 1978 we both found ourselves in New York. Ronald gave an unsurpassed account of the *Bach/Busoni Chaconne* in concert in White Plains where he was staying in Percy Grainger's house as a guest of Grainger's widow.

Illustration by Alexander Moffat

I was invited to stay as well and I made some drawings of Ella Grainger who was then 97 years old. Ronald dashed off the waltzes from *Der Rosenkavalier* in Grainger's arrangement (*Rosenkavalier Ramble*) before dinner. The next day we embarked on a pilgrimage to Rachmaninov's grave in upstate New York before taking the train back to 'The Big Apple'. As the train passed through Harlem talk broke out about Duke Ellington and George Gershwin – and in Grand Central Station we were delighted to be greeted by posters of those mythic movie stars, Humphrey Bogart and Marlene Dietrich. On returning to Edinburgh I arranged an exhibition in the New 57 Gallery as a tribute to Ronald on his 50th birthday.

"Without music, life would be a mistake" wrote Nietzsche in *The Twilight of the Idols*. What I can say is that my life would have been very different had I not known Ronald Stevenson. Throughout his seventy years as a composer and practising musician he has unflinchingly confronted the 'epic' reality of our times. As an artist he has placed great demands upon himself, but he has succeeded where others have failed. He remains a potent and very special figure for us all.

Stevenson's Soutar Settings in the Context of Some Personal Memories

Alastair Chisholm

When I was a student at Glasgow University in the 1960s I was lucky enough to hear Ronald Stevenson give a lecture to mark the centenary year of Busoni (1966). It was a wonderful talk, wide ranging in its references and captivating in its delivery. In the course of his lecture Stevenson alluded to the Anglo-Dutch composer Bernard van Dieren (1887-1936) whose music greatly interested me. After the talk, I introduced myself to Stevenson, and on the strength of our mutual interest in van Dieren an invitation to his home in West Linton soon followed.

Ere long I became familiar with Stevenson's own music, and the *Passacaglia on DSCH* made a lasting impression. Stevenson's generosity of spirit and his astonishing flow of ideas on a huge range of cultural matters had me enthralled. After a visit to West Linton, I would return home to Glasgow, my mind awhirl with ideas. I sometimes think that I learned as much from the Stevenson household as I did from my formal musical training.

Of course he introduced me to the poetry of Hugh MacDiarmid, and I too tried to set some of those astonishing lyrics to music. By way of response to this I took my mother's copy of William Soutar's *Seeds in the Wind* to Townfoot House on my next visit, and waxed eloquent on the Bairnrhymes and on 'Bawsy Broon' in particular. I am sure that Stevenson had encountered Soutar's poetry before, but with typical generosity he always claims that I introduced him to it. The reality was that perhaps my youthful enthusiasm for the Bairnrhymes sparked off his creativity. At any rate I was soon the owner of a tiny exquisite manuscript of his new song

– 'Bawsy Broon'. A series of other settings followed, and our friendship was further cemented by these tributes to my favourite Scots poet.

The majority of Stevenson's Soutar settings are for or about children, and in the same way as my mother had introduced *Seeds In the Wind* to me as a small boy, so Stevenson's own children were often the first performers of the Soutar songs. They remember the fun of his rhythmic setting of

> Wi' a chickie-chick-chickerie
> Dickie-dick-dickerie
> Tickie-tick-tickerie
> Jiggety-jig.

as they sang it at family parties and local concerts. Similarly, 'Day is Düne' was often sung at Christmas.

In the 1960s my own feelings about a Scottish identity were developing, and as I became more aware of the modern Scottish Renaissance through his enthusiasm, I realised that such enthusiasm was out of touch with the attitudes of Stevenson's composing contemporaries. Composers like Iain Hamilton, Thomas Wilson and Thea Musgrave demonstrated little interest in anything intrinsically Scottish. In them the wonderful flowering of Scottish poetry represented by MacDiarmid and his admirers apparently found no echo. To them Scots language seemed an embarrassment, and so was everything about Ronald Stevenson. Their compositions which reflected contemporary fashion in central Europe, together with their diffident performing styles, contrasted markedly with Stevenson's nationalist expression and his flamboyant pianism. I still remember the attitude of mockery which accompanied the reaction of some of the audiences to his performances at the McEwan Memorial Concerts in Glasgow.

The development of Stevenson's music at the time was therefore in complete contrast to that of his peers. He continued to work at a lyrical and intellectual musical response to MacDiarmid's poetry and ideas, by writing consciously nationalist settings of texts in Scots or Gaelic (e.g. his choral cycle *Anns an Airde, as an Doimhne* of 1968). All this when the musical establishment's attitude to him could be summed up thus:

> As long as the word Scottish in this context is understood as a geographically correct distinguishing term, it is perfectly appropriate. But it is not quite as simple as that. On the one hand it may give rise to a faintly patronising, if vestigial suspicion that the composer so described is a strange phenomenon, altogether different in kind from his English contemporaries ('does he write tartan music, ha ha?'). On the other hand it may inspire hope in some native breasts that the composer is a cultural standard-bearer who deliberately draws upon his country's folk heritage in his own idiom. Such views may sound exaggerated today . . . (Christopher Grier, 1966, quoted with permission).

Today it is worth remembering that thirty years ago Stevenson stood alone as a nationalist Scottish composer, scorned by the establishment. Scotland had its own musical mafia à la Glock. (Heavens, he was even known to write tunes!)

Stevenson's settings of Soutar show his awareness of the roots of Scottish folk music in their melodic outline and their consequent harmony. He deliberately roots his music in its Scottish context, but from that develops original ideas. The children's songs showed this well. In 'To The Future' the notes of the pentatonic-like tune also form the chords of the accompaniment – a favourite Stevenson device. In 'The Plum-Tree' the fleurs "flichterin doun in shoo'rs" are set in a chromatic pentatonic way. 'The Buckie Braes' has the real old-fashioned sound of children's chanted calls: –"our toun, our toun, our toun" and the later description of the happers "diddlin owre their tune" is a rhythmic delight, especially to child performers. At the climax of both verses in 'Bawsy Broon' he catches the child's fear of the dark with the *crescendo* on "I'm shair – it was Bawsy Broon" (lest bogles catch him unawares!). The utter simplicity of the accompaniment in 'Day is Düne' allows one of the great Scottish melodies of our time to speak to us directly.

Two of Stevenson's 'adult' settings are especially noteworthy – 'The Lea' and 'The Quiet Comes In'. The former has a melody which uses leaps of the seventh in characteristically Scottish way. The music matches the words with a high rising movement at "My spirit craves when it is free", and by a huge downward leap at "Only the largeness of this lea". In 'The Quiet Comes In' a slow wide-spaced melody contrasts with a rippling piano accompaniment which slows to a halt "When the quiet comes in". Stevenson's Soutar settings are a small but significant part of his large output of songs. His love for the poet's work is shown in the wide range of moods he captures within a group of about a dozen songs.

As a postscript to my earlier description of Stevenson's position in Scottish music of the 1960s I should mention a link with Benjamin Britten. By that time most of Soutar's poetry was out of print. When Britten expressed an interest in familiarising himself with more of Soutar's poetry, it was Stevenson who gave him a volume of the *Collected Poems*. Subsequently Britten set a number of them in his 1969 song cycle *Who are these children?*. It was curious to note that this thoroughly English composer, with an international standing, showed no embarrassment whatever in setting Scots poetry to music. Likewise Stevenson's pianism so impressed Britten that he was commissioned to write the *Peter Grimes Fantasy*, a concert paraphrase on themes from Britten's most famous opera. No scorn here!

So in the 1960s Stevenson, after his return from South Africa, tried to earn a living as a freelance musician in Scotland. Alone among his contemporaries he wrote music which showed a positive response to the artistic and nationalist ideas of MacDiarmid. The Scottish musical establishment, involved in their own serial square dance, rejected his work with disdain, and so he had to seek work elsewhere, both in London and abroad. A less tenacious man would have given up. Perhaps some did. Stevenson, following the example of MacDiarmid and Soutar, chose to gang his ain gate, and fortunately has lived long enough to witness his work being accepted and admired in this his adopted land.

Day is Düne

Poem by William Soutar

Music by Ronald Stevenson

To the Future

Poem by William Soutar

Music by Ronald Stevenson

13   *mf*

are   With - in   the   hand.   Such   a   sure

16

sim - ple - ness   As   strength   may   have;   Sun - -

18   *ff*   *mf*

- - - light   up - on   the   grass,____   The

20

curve_____   of   the   wave.

Busoni and Melody
(an extract from an unpublished biography)

Ronald Stevenson

Le style, c'est l'homme. The object of biography is to reconstruct the image of a man from the mosaic fragments of legend, data, fact and apocrypha. If, indeed, "the style is the man", and if we assess with a fair measure of accuracy what the style is at the same time we shall have reconstructed an image – however shadowy, however imperfect – of the man.

The style is the *stilus*: the man's mark. By definition, a man's handwriting is an inroad into his style. Busoni, though he wrote mainly in German from early maturity to his death, never wrote in the Gothic German calligraphy. His characters remained italic as his character remained Italian. The calligraphy of his early manhood is flamboyant and expansive as his music at that time was neo-baroque. Later, handwriting and music became more economical and controlled. In conversation he liked to use an occasional archaism: he who looked to the future did not disown the past. And in his handwriting he retained the generally obsolete 'f' for the lower case 's'. His writing sloped upwards, as if indicating the elevation of his thoughts and his optimism. It was a calligraphy of rare beauty with harmoniously formed letters. The artist's hand is shown in the variation of thick and thin strokes, though the general impression is of a fairly thin, wiry line. Every page was carefully composed with a generous margin. The tops of his characters were pointed which may have indicated a certain aggressiveness. The lower loops were gracefully garlanded to balance aggressiveness with agreeableness. The writing had much in common with that of Goethe: the sometimes separately formed and sometimes fluent characters indicating alternation of caution and confidence; the upward-curling terminals seeming to continue the thought beyond the sentence; and, above all, the clarity, revealing the logical thinker.

Busoni's calligraphy of music writing did not change as much as his handwriting did, because by his adolescence he had composed as much as many a middle-aged composer and had thereby gained facility. The note-heads in his musical juvenilia are smaller than in the later manuscripts. Later he gave himself more space, and in the last works often leaving the *verso* blank for the addition of any afterthoughts. The late manuscripts also give the impression of a freer hand – almost an impression of being drawn rather than written.

As a melodist Busoni's avoidance of vulgarity amounted to inhibition. The monopoly of Italian music throughout his lifetime by the *verismo* school of popular tune-mongers, in itself, was enough to inhibit such a mind as his every time he conceived a melody. The chief difference between his procedures and theirs was that whereas their practice of melodic construction was geared to a high powered climax, his interest in melody lay in subtleties of inflection. These subtleties were expressed chromatically, but whereas Busoni's contemporaries Delius, Strauss and the Schoenberg of the *Gurrelieder* employed chromaticism emotionally, without reference to formal structure or parenthetically within a form but not essential to it, Busoni employed melodic chromaticism with strict logic. Some of Richard Strauss's most lurid and inflamed music depends for its *raison d'être* on chromatic melody; with Delius the dying fall of a chromatic phrase sets like the sun, leaving the ache of remembered beauty; and the chromatic tendrils of Schoenberg's *Gurrelieder* climb and droop on the pages of his enormous score like hanging gardens of exotic melodic plants. *Au contraire*, Busoni's treatment of chromatic melody is related to his belief that music (of any sort) only suffers when the passions begin to dictate to the reason. This controlled chromaticism thus becomes a dialectic process.

Such subtle melodic inflexion is related to and is sometimes the result of Busoni's interest in exploring all possible chromatic permutations of the septatonic scale within the range of selection afforded by the twelve semitonal degrees of the octave. He already foreshadowed this possible extension of melodic language through new scales in his prose sketches *A New Æsthetic of Music* in 1906. These suggestions have borne fruit. In 1929 his friend the French composer Maurice Emmanuel, at Busoni's suggestion, composed a '*Hindu' Sonatine* for piano, based on Hindu ragas. Emmanuel was the teacher of Olivier Messiaen who continued and extended his master's interest in the fructification of occidental music by oriental techniques. Messiaen's pupils, Stockhausen and Boulez, have further extended the field of melodic possibility by venturing into the world of electronic music. This, too, Busoni forecast – not vaguely or mystically but on the firm basis of actual experience and experiments observed in his *New Æsthetic*. He also sought to graft system of thirds of tones on to the prevalent semitonal system, thereby also allowing the resultant refinement of sixths of tones.

To satisfy himself of the validity of theses expansionist ideas he had a harmonium in thirds of tones constructed to his specification and conducted certain experiments with the co-operation of musician friends, to address how the new sounds could be absorbed by musically intelligent people of the early 20th century. His conclusion was that similar extensions of music's vocabulary were inevitable, but that they could only be introduced gradually: could only be absorbed in an age of technology which would be the proper *milieu* in which such ideas could take root; and that finally, the new vocabulary should be embraced as an extension of, and not as a substitute for, the traditional one. Now in the second half of the twentieth century, with the technological age already upon us, Busoni's sagacious words are unfortunately forgotten by a generation of young composer-physicists, who, intoxicated by a glimpse of infinite possibilities rendered feasible through science, are only too prone to jettison the old for the new. There are hopeful signs, however, that exceptional figures among their ranks are beginning to realise the necessity of historical perspective which is synonymous with the realisation that man, and not machine, is the constant factor in progress; and that as long as man remains man, or better, becomes more fully man, the human medium will never disappear from the performance of music, though it may be implemented by the wonders of machines, which if man had not been a greater machine, would never have existed.

It is this acknowledgement of the human element in music which made Busoni utilise Italian popular songs in his piano *Concerto*, traditional Chinese melodies in his *Turandot*, and Native American folk-songs in no less than three works; the *Indian Diary* for piano, the *Indian Fantasy*, op 44 for piano and orchestra; and the *Song of the Ghost Dance*, op 47, for strings, six wind instruments and timpani. His use of these folk-songs is a frank admittance that the roots of all music lie in the soil of folk-song.

There is a mistaken current notion among the supposed intelligentsia of music that Busoni was one of the most abstract of composers. This idea is exploded instantaneously by the instance of his employment of folk-songs in no less than five of his major works. Unlike many later composers in the western world, Busoni never made formalism or abstract invention the basis for his composition, for he knew well that this could only be the most false of premises. He composed, not from the premise of abstraction, but from the ethos of experience. Even his *Fantasia Contrappuntistica*, which might be considered a Kantian "Musik an sich" was, nevertheless, composed directly from his accumulated experience of the music of Bach. This is not to deny that Busoni's greatest music, like all music written from supreme intellectual and spiritual striving, tends towards the abstract.

The order of precedence is important. While a composer may work from a base in real experience of people and places and ideas, to which myriads of impressions are bound to have contributed, and while, from such a premise, his work may tend towards abstraction, a composer whose work finds its *inception* in the formalism of technical tricks will never allow the enrichment of life's experience to contribute to what he creates. It is the scientist, not the artist, whose work begins in abstraction and ends in benefiting mankind. The composer, benefited by mankind in equal measure to his ability to put himself into perspective with society, allows his experience of everything affecting his musical sensibility to affect the conception of his work, so that the work ultimately gives back to mankind what the composer's experience gained from mankind. Such a composer writes out of experience of the speech inflexion of his native tongue and allows the characteristic deportment and physical movement of his nation to exercise a subtle influence on his sense of rhythm. All these things – and many others – contribute inevitably to a composer's work unless he consciously turns his back upon them by concerning himself with technical experiment for its own sake. Busoni's work as a composer was informed and instinctive. When he experimented, he did so in the spirit of an age of experiment, the age of the aeroplane which was rapidly becoming the atomic age and the age of the space rocket. This is experiment in the sense in which Leonardo understood the word: experiment which has its root, not only as a word, but as a reality, in experience.

An example of Busoni's creative process of inception in experience and fulfilment in experiment is the score of his *Song of the Ghost Dance*. The melodic material of this work draws upon the Native American motives published by Busoni's American pupil Natalie Curtis in her volume *The Indian's Book*. Busoni was strongly attracted to the Native American sense of values, which, during his lifetime more than now, placed poetic sensibility higher than business acumen and spiritual gifts higher than material possessions. This poetry and spirituality were conveyed musically in a melody almost as fragmentary as a birdsong. This economy of notes and the limpid, poetic image of wedded tune and poem persuaded Busoni to find a medium suited to the child-like transparency of expression. Here began the experimental process. He pondered the problem of how to instrument fragile material and finally chose to experiment with a very small orchestra. An experiment it was, for Strauss' *Grosses Orchester* was still fashionable during the 1914 war, when Busoni composed this work. Though Percy Grainger had written his *Hill Song 1* for twenty-two solo instruments as far back as 1901 (two years before he became a Busoni pupil), Shönberg, Hindemith, Berg, Webern and others did not begin to experiment with compositions for chamber orchestra until the Twenties. So, apart from the unique case of Grainger, Busoni was here breaking new ground.

He had a further problem with this particular work because its melodic material was motival and fragmentary, whereas, as Dr Paul Bekker observed, "new classicality leans on polyphonic art, as it particularly marks Busoni for a definite parting from the thematic idiom and a recapture of melody". What Busoni sought was not a mosaic of motives twisted and twined by every device of ingenuity, such as one finds in Shoenberg's dodecaphonic works, but what Busoni himself called "Auflösung", an interpenetration of all the elements of music till they fused in creative incandescence; a dissolving and melting and mingling of ideas till the music took on the aspect of a dream – not the atmosphere of impressionism but the vivid clarity yet immateriality of a dream. The Native American motifs he used in the *Song of the Ghost Dance* consisted of few notes and pithy phrases. Through refined harmonisation, resulting from the intersecting lines of freely flowing polyphony, Busoni transformed this rudimentary but elusive musical material into a work entirely characteristic of his mature style. But before he did that, he absorbed as much as he could of the Native American way of thought (much of which was familiar to him, for he had reached similar conclusions independently). Thus the finished work had grown from contact with people – in this case Native Americans – and, when performed would communicate with other people and so interpret to them something of their spirit as well as the equally mysterious Busonian spirit.

Busoni never interested himself in making collections of folk-songs by harmonising them for piano or setting them for chorus. Neither did he introduce them into his work to add a dash of local colour. When his friend, the conductor Artur Bodansky, asked him to write music for *Peer Gynt* in 1913, Busoni refused because he felt himself unequal to the task of writing Norwegian music, and his awareness of the play's suggestions of a Norwegian Wandering Jew, or even of a Norwegian Quixote or Faust, and his consequent high valuation of it, would not allow him to write pseudo-Nordic music for it, as so many lesser men would have done.

It is the capturing of the mood of awesome fear which marks Busoni as a true representative of his age, and particularly of the 20th century; this century in which for the first time in the history of man, since the Great Flood, there looms overhead the possibility of total annihilation. The fear which Busoni so palpably expresses is the fear of the destructive force of great knowledge wrongly used. It is this which makes Faust's heart pause to beat. It is this fear which has grown to such huge proportions today in the problems of mankind that no thinking person can possibly be unaware of its existence. We have all met this fear, between heartbeats, in moments of truth.

The 'fear' motive is never far from Busoni's music. His work is pervaded by it. So subtly is it woven into the warp and woof of his music, like a thread of destiny, that there can be no possibility of interpreting it in the sense of a Wagnerian *Leitmotif*: nothing could be further from a true realisation of how Busoni employs this 'fear' motive.

What we have termed the "semitone dichotomy" in Busoni's melody is related to his characteristic major/minor coalescence of harmony. In this he was foreshadowed by Schubert, in whose music, more than that of any other precursor (and particularly in his C major symphony, C major String Quintet and his last String Quartet in G minor), the tranquil but sudden transition from major to minor is the audible manifestation of a lifetime's mingled bliss and melancholy. This distillation of experience, this weeping joy and smiling sorrow, this Mona Lisa aspect, is yet another facet of the concept of Auflösung which was often on Busoni's lips towards the end of his life. It is this, more than anything, which links him with Schubert and Mozart: Mozart, whose most salient characteristic he felt to be *Heiterkeit* (merriment blended with serenity). It is no accident that Mozart and, to a lesser extent, Schubert, who wrote out of this ethos of tranquil joy were Austrians. As Austrians, their culture held in equipoise Teutonic discipline and Latin temperament.

Like Mozart, Busoni was a master not only of his own style but of many styles. Again like Mozart, Busoni was fascinated by quasi-oriental colour: only compare the *finale alla turca* from Busoni's *Turandot* with Mozart's *Rondo alla turca*. Unlike another 20th century Mozartian, Richard Strauss, Busoni never indulged his taste for oriental colour (or semi-oriental or, even europeanised oriental colour) in blatant poster-painting-in-sound, but in transparent pastel shades. It is not only Strauss's *Salomé* (as a semi-oriental semite) who casts off her veils in her notorious dance; the music also reveals the nudity of raw exhibitionism, an attribute foreign to Eastern expression in art. Nothing could be further from Busoni's musical portrait of the Princess Turandot in 'Turandot's March' in which his idea was to present four character sketches: cruelty, passion, the veiled beauty and the unveiled. The Strauss is "suggestive" in the most *risqué* manner; the Busoni has the elusive mystery of the lover's eyes glancing through the lattice in the 'Song of Songs'.

Apart from the exotic quasi-oriental colour and the Native American colour of certain works of Busoni, there is also the Italian colour in his other compositions, which is explicit in the piano *Concerto* and second *Elegy*, *All'Italia* and *Arlecchino*, but which is implicit in many of his works and particularly the later ones. The sound of an Italian tenor can be heard behind much more of the music – not only when Arlecchino sings his *lallalera* off stage; and the Italianate contours of Ferdinando Busoni's clarinet, which weaves the gently undulating lines of a southern landscape. But this Italian colour in Busoni's music is never impressionistic; it is always contained by the firm outline of the form. Anyone who has seen the sun-gilded Tuscan horizon and has inhaled a deep draught of the champagne-like air in that region will know that it is impossible for a Tuscan to be an Impressionist. He sees too clearly. In Busoni's one conscious foray into Impressionism, the piano piece *Nuit de Nöel* (which he even had published in France by Durand of Paris), the music's outline never becomes blurred as it intentionally does in the music of the French Impressionist school. The bell-like sounds are enhaloed in overtones, but they sound silvery-clear through the shimmer of sonority.

All the multifarious elements of Busoni's style melt into each other in what he called an Auflösung – an elusive word we have already tried to define, but which we shall attempt to describe further as a solution (in both sense of the word) of the musical idea and the notes by which the idea is expressed. Perhaps a dangerous analogy with the French Impressionist painters may clarify Busoni's concept of Auflösung (the analogy is 'dangerous' because, as already stated, Busoni was no Impressionist). Monet (in his *Débâcles des Glaces)*, Pissarro and Sisley repeatedly painted the subject of a flood. These artists considered this an ideal theme, because it necessitated the dissolution, not only of colour, but also of the elements themselves, in the merging sea and sky. Busoni's Auflösung began with a melodic idea which, as the music proceeded, dissolved into an aquatic flow of counterpoint which mysteriously dissolved into harmonies produced by the interweaving of parts.

Perhaps the best analogy is the enigmatic *sfondo sfumato* of the 'Mona Lisa'; that strange vaporous background of melting rocks and smouldering streams; that landscape lit by a smile which has been interpreted as variously a dream, but which continues to exercise its fascination because it is well-nigh intangible and immaterial as the music itself.

If the lines of Busoni's music could be translated into a picture (as Paul Klee has painted a transcription of Bach's *Chaconne*) it might well look like the background to Leonardo's masterpiece. That would be the hallmark of Busoni's *stilus*: not a signature engraved by steel on stone, but a name, like that of John Keats, "writ in water".

Alan Riach

Passacaglia

"The movement of a passacaglia is the movement of water flowing in a broad stream, underneath the ice upon a border river."

1

The miles of peat-bog, tufts of cotton and the rain pelting across
the flat expanse of moor, my friends and I, our jackets collared up,
marched over, with spring stepped stride and wide determination,
intentional, heading for the steeple edge and end of land
near Elgol, facing the sea. Soaked, our coats still warmed
us as we sclimmed and clambered down the cliff-cut
edges of rock, and through the fissured caverns to the open ledge
of stone that faced the sea front: the weight of the Atlantic breaking –
water smashes on the stone and ledge – drenched, clinging
to the wall of rock as the sea heaves monumental tides
of dreck-free ocean, threatening brutality and equal in its opposition
to rock, and in its natural indifference to creatures live beside it.

2

There is another place where broken ice-floes heave upon the weight
of the Atlantic under them, and the mass of waves is something else –
hard on the edge of the sea and land, the rock dropping down, our
puny human selves beside it, only fighting momentarily –

3

But these are coasts and cuts –
rock and ocean, massive oppositions.

Think of a river, in the borders, a
broad and curving stream, its
natural beauty covered with another,
closed over by ice, and the trees not bare
and skeletal, but crushed with the crystal salt
and diamond of winter's world.

And know our music
moves beneath, a movement going on, under
the pressure of that carapace,
running –
to all the trouble there is
to come when it reaches the sea.

The Stevenson Scandal

Philip Hutton

Or if you prefer, The Stevenson Case – it sounds like a roaring whodunnit or else some lingering jurisprudential enigma. Mention The Stevenson Case in a general way, in the context of artists careers and reputations and the dealings of just desserts, and people will think you are referring to "wheen sleazy tunes fur rascals tae spiel". It does raise the level of the conversation! That Ronald Stevenson has given us a music of astonishing beauty and absorbing interest, and that the lazy, indifferent and retrograde Scottish musical public has not, by and large, noticed, is the scandal.

In as far as RS has been written about and discussed in musical circles there has been acclaim, respect, affectionate reminiscence. There are many 'How I Met Ronald' stories, and perhaps something of their aura shines on these *Chapman* pages. But I miss the salt of controversy. There is no stimulating opposition. Those hostile critics are very reticent. Where are the 'Ronald Stood on My Corns' stories? Even the enthusiasts of The Stevenson Society, assailing the sluggards of the BBC and the directors of the Edinburgh International Festival could raise nothing better from them than an evasive smirk. We need a good battle in which those onlookers who are too lazy actually to listen to the music can take sides.

I am offering some tentative suggestions that might explain the lack of controversy.

An old gentleman feels that the pleasures of his youth have vanished away. (If you really want sherbet fountain, just go to the sweetie shop and buy one, though it'll cost you the equivalent of three shillings old money). "The line of impressive omni-competent musicians which was begun so boldly with Bach, so robustly continued with Beethoven, so colourfully overstated with Liszt and Busoni, disappears completely after Rachmaninov, Prokovief, Britten and Bartok."[1] This is precisely where Stevenson fits. The line has not disappeared after all. The paradox is that it is his omni-competence as composer/pianist/scholar that has occluded him from Said's view. Cultural identities are premised on division of labour. Artists are defined by their incompletenesses. Brendel is a celebrated pianist and a fine lecturer, but where are his concertos? Maxwell Davies is an accomplished composer, but when did he last perform an instrumental solo? Anthony Burgess boldly combined literature with musical composition and could illustrate his entertaining lectures at the keyboard. But as a celebrity of sorts, his music had more of a hearing than had been unknown, and found wanting. But Stevenson's musical roundedness made him, unfortunately, difficult to attack. That would have been like attacking Music itself.

The quality of hostile criticism in the arts has declined. Hans Keller had no real successor, and major assaults with his kind of flair and persuasive power are rare. Smarminess, faint praise, snide innuendo and libel-fearing

---

1. *Musical Elaborations*, Edward Said; Chatto and Windus (1991) p5.

caution are the norm. We see, particularly in the visual arts but in time extending to other areas, that celebrity upstages artistic repute and is upstaged in turn by mere notoriety. The loss of good bashing polemics trivialises the whole show.

Music audiences are tribal and sectarian, as every marketing manager knows. Although there is talk of global pluralism, cross-fertilisation and ecumenical what-have-you, this is about as unreal as Mr Major's classless society. Those who advocate breaking the barriers have no intention of relinquishing their own protective devices. Behind one set of barriers lies classical music. Having been in ill health for decades, it is now seriously dying. The insulation of cultures is such that this catastrophe barely makes news. Julian Lloyd-Webber admits that music can make it to the news media as long as it is hung on a scandal or a joke. Norman Lebrecht in *When the Music Stops* relates the collapse of CD sales, concert audiences and public funding to the vulgarity of the star system and the rapacity of the three tenors. These alarms make a picture of generational change. The musikants in their 60s and 70s die, retire or just can't be bothered any longer, the kids in their 40s and 50s loll around watching the soaps and sniffing glue, the tiny tots joyride through the wrecked underpasses. Paranoid stereotypes and a measured view of change are becoming uncomfortably close.

As the Beethoven who in his heydays, the 1790s, enjoyed the enthusiastic patronage of an enlightened Viennese nobility and a public who followed their lead, became the Beethoven of the dogdays, the 1810s, forgotten by the war-weary waltzing Viennese mob, so, a strong artist can find and be lost by his or her audience.

Meanwhile, the Edinburgh International Festival, stuffily resistant to the new in the 50s and 60s, nervously endorsing whimsies and fashions in the 70s, 80s and 90s, has not lifted a finger to support Stevenson's music. If cornered officials come up with evasions, confessions of ignorance or ignorant snap-judgements. At no point is the quality, seriousness or integrity of Stevenson's work challenged. One wonders if such apparatchiks ever make judgements of quality based on actual hearing.

Ronald on form is a charismatic performer, creating occasions which no amount of critical denigration could efface from the memory of his hearers. He is a master of imaginative programming and speaks the introductions, connections and associations of his pieces with grace and intimacy, never ingratiating, never cold or downbeat. Very few performers can bring off this equivalence of personal presence and inspired playing.

He concluded his 1989 recital at the Gallery of Modern Art with the great Bach-Busoni *Chaconne*. This is a piece on which Ronald spent a life time's craft, intensifying and aggrandising Busoni's 19th century piano writing as Busoni had intensified and aggrandised the 18th century violin piece. It was wrought up to a tremendous momentum and grandeur at the close, and a two-fisted rinforzando trill at the final cadence, a pneumatic drill that sent waves of horror through the squeamish. The loose sheets of music on top of the piano levitated at this point, spun (perhaps aided by the sweep of the hand) and cartwheeled out across the floor. A hard act to follow. Silence. Applause. Here was fierce concentration, high-voltage projection, overt muscularity. But some listeners do find it not nice, too much, over the top. They say so in private. Perhaps those who are attuned to the smoothness and polish of industrialised music, of recorded and marketed and market-researched music, do feel a too-muchness and a not-niceness when confronted with a totally committed performance. But no serious defence of industrialised music is forthcoming, other than its commercial viability. In the case of the "classical sector" now even that is in doubt.

Illustration by Philip Hutton

Ven Begamudré

The Lightness Which Is Our World, Seen From Afar

One

Ondu

She remembers how he railed
as a householder. His obsession
with rain, his need for it
to purge their previous life, promise
an end to rebirth. In the compound she stalks
are ninety-nine images he crafted of summer:
unglazed, even unfired,
pieces of some greater whole which holds
his longing for what summer could have been.
She dreams he will return in her lifetime
to finish them.

Eradu

There is a glimmer of dew; still every mouth is dry. He watches parakeets
circling without rest. Hopes if he must be reborn, he will return as a par-
tridge fed on moonbeams. Cobras stifle in the dust. If he had a child he
would not want it to hear parakeets without songs.

Muru

Vultures alight on the banyans.
They are heavy with flesh.

There is no rain
in a land where crocodiles weep.

This is what she hates. So much thirst
and how blue the sky.

Nalku

Even as a woman denying her loneliness
thinks of summer as a season for desertion,
thus couplets are composed of unlikely lines
and so much sadness emerges: the princess
hoping for a true prince who will not scorn her
for her flaws or learning or wit. He is merely
a dream, this long-lost mate, as if
the thought *We remember* is all she needs
to recapture their previous life. It is
never enough. She knows this.

Aidu

Shadows lengthen by a stroke, his need not hers. He thinks of the Adivasi, those original tribes. How the girls sleep together, unripe yet welcoming nightly visits of boys. The boy pretending to abduct the girl. The dowry to appease her clan. How simple their desires: shamans interpreting intentions of everyday gods; no need for clothing, coyness, shame; bands of cloth barely meeting in the back. He sighs, holding himself tight, a lone cloud refusing to weep.

Aru

Pausing near an evergreen banyan,
she eyes tourists at the temple
well after nightfall performing *pujas*
at the end of a picnic. All these prayers
for the boredom to end. She likes
to watch the Brahmins, their circling
disk of flame, the neon lights.
What she likes best is to hover
when worshippers leave the sanctum
for the muddle in the courtyard;
how they reclaim sandals
they know by feel, *ayahs*
shepherding children, parents
frowning at a hand-cranked carousel
creaking through the night. She listens
while novices close the inner gates
to guard the sleeping god. Inside
the Brahmins fatten on sugar and *ghee,*
making the best of this age
before the white horse comes,
Kalki with his sword blazing
like the comet of doom.

Elu

Hunger yet nothing will grow except doubt and envy. Where do all the songs go? What he craves is flight, an end to gravity, everyone becoming lighter. Hunger much as the Adivasi know scrabbling for roots while that other hunger dies, the hunger for flesh. All their doubts like *why?* and *how?* In this case, the phrase *much as* easing his pangs. Hunger and doubt and envy, the day growing hot.

Illustration by David Stephenson

94

Entu

She is chanting the end of *Ramayana*,
not the first end, not the one the children
are told: when Rama takes Sita back
home, the long road north lit by lamps.
It is the second end she likes: when Sita
stands accused of seducing her abductor.

It is a tale for autumn nights
told in the breeze: the endless
quest for that perfect love.

How comforting it would be,
she thinks, if there were only one end:
no question of Rama's faith
or questioning of Sita; no need for tears
from listeners or lovers. Yet the version
she prefers, her *Ut-Ramayana*,
is so much more like life.

Ombaththu

He reaches out and touches scales. Each night the cobra seems more
tame. He ponders the skin shrinking and splitting, shedding and drying
with such ease. Beneath the slackened hood, an emerald. He will harvest
it without killing his lone visitor, condemning himself to death from its
mates. First the bites, then his fleeting breath. Their justice too swift, his
execution slow. He could never do it, he thinks. He plucks a scale from
the hood, sucks at the root where it is moist, the blood green, and savours
it. Is this how she saw him, resenting her need? He urges the cobra toward
him. He thinks: *When it leaves to rejoin its kind, I will warn it of the sun.*

Haththu

Her *Ut-Ramayana* is ambiguous.
The first end led naturally to rain,
Not the warm rains of winter here;
the rain which plunges in relief
on summer afternoons,
a rain which leaves its mark.
The second end, as perverse as life,
leads instead to grief. She
recites the paradox to herself,
envying the poet his foresight:

*The presence of doubt
is the nature of love.*

Often she wishes Rama failed in his rescue;
let Sita save herself. Yet *Ramaraj*
could not have begun, the perfect reign
of an imperfect king, that once or ever.

Hannondu

Allow me to intrude. This is not some local diversion, didactic entertainment with an easy plot. We are what the Goddess dreams, able to direct her inventions as easily as we command the sun. Consider the footprints on a river bank after the Goddess crosses the river. We call it a sign but it is only she, walking in her sleep. Another way of being, which we envy. The question to be answered: *Yet why are we here?* The Goddess chuckling in her sleep when we seem so real.

Two

Hanneradu

The beggars have discovered her home.
A legless man propels himself at ease
on a wheeled board followed by a woman
cursing God for their lack of sons,
though she has no tongue. A girl without ears
dangles earrings on either side of her face;
swears she would never disfigure the child in her,
not above the neck. Every well is dry.
The icebox, as elsewhere, is locked.

Their hostess is in a dark room
clutching a statue: a goddess of erotic love.
She must emerge to greet the intruders
and feed them but for once she is not angry
with this image of summer, unfinished
like so much he began. She tells herself
he was not to blame and cups the breasts.
They are glazed and firm.

Hadimuru

He lies with his face to the old moon and tunes his ears to their whispering, the hooded hiss of the guardians. He will creep with them to the edge of their realm. He prays the night will not be too dark. He prays the many portals will be lit by the brilliance hoarded within. Inside he will discard his loincloth, shed his fears. Squirm his way down through their halls: here, in the labyrinth they rule. And yet he will not touch the stones. He will keep only the thrill of resisting temptation, prizing this above the emeralds, rubies and diamonds of night.

96

Hadinalku

All of us hunger alone. Beggars
wander, letting no one hold them back
with promises. No water to be had,
the sad water, and so much time for thirst.

*The goddesses of dawn and dusk
are sisters.* She mouths this and reaches
down in her shadows, aching to be full.
She feels nothing at her fingertips
but heat, resenting her need,
his restlessness, while beggars cackle
and a wheeled board creaks, the passing
shapes a reminder of life beyond the shades.

Hadinaidu

Cobras in these thick summer months shrivel within their loosening skins.
Shrivel and coil themselves on the hoard which galls them, drives them
from cool halls into a sun blinding them to their duty. The cobras, the
hooded ones.

Hadinaru

Dancing in her still dark room
she welcomes a four-armed god:
he so dazzling she closes her eyes
to his touch; she so ready she mounts him
before he warns her of the outcome:
ruining her for mere men.

Hadinelu

The man creeps again to their haunts. Trailing his loincloth, he enters to
squeeze himself through mazes to this: a ransom left for his taking, light
into light. He tells himself to relish his conquest. Soon. If there is any vestige approaching lust it is for these gems knotted in the cloth. He crawls
back to the hut, his skin rasping through dust like scales.

Hadinentu

Her cries fade, ebbing like the light
from her impossible lover's face.

If she lies perfectly still in his arms
she can hear a keening while the hooded ones writhe.

Haththombaththu

Let us be frank: for the man to creep at night in search of wealth is just another error in judgement, as a lion makes who leaves cover to be confronted by his trackers. To surrender to the surprise of life: now this is stoicism, the kind we Hindus are thought to have perfected. Even you cannot hope to resist it. *Satyagraha.* Soul force. No surprise the Mahatma lives. No surprise you still mistake what he did for the passiveness of a sea on calm days while under the surface waters churn: the peace of doves the one thing a sea cannot attain, as dust cannot know it is even in the eyes of a lion a cause for tears.

Three

Ippaththu

She lies with her god on a mat, starlight
piercing the shutters to dapple his arms,
two cradling her, two crossed upon his breast
rising and falling with his breath. The god dreams
creation, the cries of children in the sun,
food their only thought. And shade.
The image she tries to forget is of a man
moulding a child out of clay.

The arms release her when she rises
to open the shutters. She says, *Love
is for dreamers.* This is what the god read
in thoughts she could not speak:
children in a monsoon playing with toys,
the rain sweeping away the stars
and the rootless seeds.

Ippathondu

What the god finds on earth is what Manu forgot in the flood: the tracks he left filling into themselves, generations to come chafing at rebirth. The full load, the seeds rooted once more, *pujas* which are prayers of *Why?* The god cares nothing for this. He has come down in lust and learned sorrow. He is finding the footprints on the river bank are not even his. How touching his surprise, his arms thrashing in the heat. It is a wonderful irony, his consort waiting and he knowing he has been found out. If he were a man he could say: *She meant nothing to me.*

Ippaththeradu

Then there is the man who does not want to die rich. When it finally rains he will leave with nothing more than the clothes on his pilgrim back. This is how he wants to be remembered. This is the tale they will tell when the sun no longer raves. He is planning to head farther south. He will leave only if everything else survives this drought in which even the young have no will.

Ippaththamuru

Clouds appear with a rising sun,
lacy black in the dawn: the grieving clouds.

How many lives. How many ages.
Vultures wake to circle the compound.

Ippaththanalku

There is little strength to breathe left in the elephant plodding through the mud. It is as grey as the rain. If you could read the embroidered script on its cap you might see, *Come to the Circus,* an invitation the man fears. The chance to laugh without guilt. He longs for it the way he longs for all those old verses by Tagore, rivers teeming with tame golden fish, prayers for the ease of innocent days.

Ippaththaidu

She sees the elephant looming through rain
breaking figures in the compound. Lumbering
from bench to kiln and pondering the number
ninety-nine as though their maker must repent.
This is wishful thinking: an animal
hoping for completion with only memory
to goad it. No wonder she pictures vultures
rising from the banyans, laughing, expecting
only fragments to greet their return.

Ippaththaru

Darkness surrounds him in his hut. He lies with his limbs exposed to the hooded ones. They take back the gems he holds, slithering across his thighs, hissing at each other, then at the lone visitor who glides away and coils into itself well beyond their reach. This is how Manu must have felt on the mountain, he thinks, water everywhere beneath his boat, the bitterness of triumph, clutching the many seeds he saved, returning them to soil and silt and stones. These last the preserve of the guardians.

Ippaththelu

The flesh left on branches is a horror
she ignores while she gathers the fragments
and cradles them. Rain plucks the trees clean.
How she yearns for night, the four-armed god
returning with his emerald-coloured seed
and still it sprouts and withers and dies.
She is not ready, she thinks, to bear a child
for a god, one so dazzling she cannot face him
when he enters. Yet even riding him she thinks
of a man with two hands moulding a child
to which he gives his mouth, her eyes. This
is what poisoned their love: thirst because someone
has to light their pyre. Hunger because nothing will do
except their own flesh and blood.

Ippaththentu

It is a vestige of the rains he absently moulds: wet clay malleable as an
infant learning to sing. He could change it into anything he wants. He
could even make a child in his own image, bring it to life with fire. He cradles the form in the sun on his hands, hardening while the moisture
returns to the earth and air. He tells himself some things were never meant
to be. Not in this life, perhaps not ever.

Illustration by David Stephenson

The Sky Painters

Mark Tyler Edwards

We live in a house at the top of the world. It is a small, stone-clad house, with thick, interweaving tendrils of ivy creeping up to the thatched roof where a family of thrushes have fashioned a nest a few feet below the canvas of the sky. Sometimes, as I stand on my ladder and go about my work, the birds sing to me, which greatly inspires me as I sweep my brush across the canvas and daub it with the pastel colours of spring. I am a sky painter. We are all sky painters here, in this house, the four sky painters of the northern hemisphere: Isabel, Théodore, Leonardo and me, William.

Leonardo is the longest standing member of our profession, and Théodore is the baby of the bunch, as he only joined us in 1897. Isabel has been here since the end of the eighteenth century, a few decades before I was recruited. Leonardo has lived in this house since what might as well be the beginning of time. He won't speak of his origins. Whenever I try to enquire about what he did before he became a sky painter, he merely mutters something unintelligible in Latin and stalks off to his room. Leonardo is the only one of us who looks anywhere near his age, with his snow-white beard and dry-roasted complexion, the appearance of age heightened by the smock which he wears every day, which was originally white (I believe) but which has now been covered by so many different-coloured smatterings of paint that it now resembles one of Jackson Pollock's less revered efforts.

Isabel isn't much more forthcoming than Leonardo, but I know she was formerly the wife of a merchant in Andalusia. She is beautiful and serene and if I didn't think it would cause so many problems I would probably fall in love with her.

Théodore is the complete opposite to the other two: he never shuts up about his past. He grew up in Rouen, in Normandy, where he was, for a brief period, a student of Monet's, although the way he tells it, they were best buddies, drinking and whoring and partying together: Monet this, Monet that – I actually feel relieved when he starts talking about politics. Almost. Anyway, I know that everything he tells us about Monet is fabricated. One night, when he was drunk, he told me that all he ever did with Monet was sit with him and watch him paint Rouen Cathedral over and over again, until he was so sick of the sight of gothic spires that he fled the city, and that was when he was recruited as a sky painter. I don't know if Théodore remembers his drunken candour. I doubt if he cares.

So that just leaves me. I was born in Winchester in 1801, the son of a father who was a physician and a mother who fancied herself as a romantic poet. She was about as successful as Keats without the posthumous acclaim. I suppose I was influenced by her evocations of nature's beauty, but I preferred the paintbrush to the pen. When I was eighteen, I bade my parents farewell and set out on the road; I was going to find my fortune. Perhaps I would travel to Florence or Rome and study the fine arts in the shadow of those city's legends. But on my way to Portsmouth, from whence I planned to set sail, I was accosted by the woman I would later learn to call 'the Boss', and that's how I ended up here. I remember our initial encounter vividly: it was a rain-streaked April afternoon, and I was striding along the road towards the port when a horse-drawn carriage appeared on the horizon. As it drew closer, I admired the fine craftsmanship of the carriage and noted that the horses were draped in the finest purple velvet. Imagine my surprise when the carriage, which appeared to have no driver, halted beside me and the rouge-tinted face of an elderly lady peered out from behind the scarlet curtains.

"How do you do, madam?" I enquired, and the woman laughed and looked me up and down.

A minute later, she had invited me into her carriage and offered me a job. As I sat among the decadent finery that surrounded her, she grasped my hand tightly and told me all about sky painting and how an unfortunate incident (the exact detail of which I never discovered) had left a vacancy in the ranks. I ummed and aahed for a moment or two and asked her what my wage would be.

She laughed, stroked my hair lightly and said, "Your wage, my dear boy, shall be *immortality*."

How could I refuse?

So, a few days later, another carriage (a rather less elegant vehicle, I'm afraid) collected me from my temporary lodgings at a local inn and brought me to my new home, at the top of the mountain, at the top of the world. It was a long, rocky journey, particularly the final stretch, as we ascended the mountain, the altitude thinning as we reached the pinnacle where I would spend the rest of my days. Strangely, the moment I entered the driverless carriage, I found that the curtains would not open, so I passed the journey in darkness, unable to look out at the landscape. So don't ask me where the mountain is. Nobody's ever told me.

I often reminisce as I paint; today the instruction was to paint an overcast May sky, an undemanding task, just requiring three colours: cobalt blue, white and charcoal. When I came here, this was the first type of daytime sky I was allowed to attempt. My first few years were spent painting night skies. Isabel was my tutor in this task, with the occasional interference from Leonardo. They taught me how to apply the many shades of blue and black and then to splatter them with white dots for the stars, the precise constellations of which must never alter. The finishing touch is, of course, the moon, and we keep a chart inside the house to remind us of the exact pattern of the moon's cycle. You'd be surprised how difficult it is to paint a really impressive moon (it is much harder than painting the sun) and it requires a unique paint which one can only gaze upon, when it is in its pot, while wearing dark glasses.

Anyway, after several years, I had mastered the night sky, from dusk to dawn, and a message from the Boss advised that I should be allowed to try my hand in the daytime. My first task, then, was to create a skyscape of late spring. As I ascended the ladder to apply the first brushstrokes, I was trembling. Isabel murmured a few words of encouragement, I dipped my brush into the pale blue paint, and I was away. I think I did rather well, although some of my clouds looked a little two-dimensional. When I descended the ladder, later that day, Isabel greeted me with a round of applause and a kiss. Soon I was confident enough to move on to more challenging skies, and, although I do not like to blow my own trumpet, I think I have created some spectacular sights. My 1909 rainbow-chain, where I daringly linked three rainbows and let them arch across the hemisphere, was one of my greatest efforts. Another was my summer morning of 1942, where I used almost a whole pot of shepherd's delight to triumphant effect.

There is only one type of sky that I have not as yet been permitted to attempt: the autumn sunset, which is Leonardo's speciality. Whenever the instruction comes through to construct an autumn sunset, Leonardo gets terribly excited, pacing around before locking himself in the storage shed, mixing colours on his ancient palette. Then we all gather round to watch, Isabel, Théodore and me, because Leonardo's sunsets are probably the most beautiful images I have ever seen: a backdrop of the palest blue, onto which he layers scarlet and orange and tangerine and pink, the colours glowing, leaping from the canvas, glorious, dazzling, a blood-red sun fading into the bottom of the canvas. It is a transient spectacle: no sooner is it completed, Leonardo leaning back for a moment to admire his handiwork, the rest of us gazing up in awe, than it has to be covered and, effectively, destroyed. It always breaks my heart to watch Leonardo conceal his masterpiece behind gradually darkening shades of blue, from the lightest cobalt to the deepest midnight blue, which is when one of us, usually Théodore, as he is the relative novice, takes over, and Leonardo retreats to his room to consider his next sunset.

One day, perhaps, I will be permitted to attempt an autumn sunset of my own. I pray so. Until then, I will have to content myself with vermillion dawns and azure afternoons, amethyst storms and ultramarine evenings; I will have to amuse myself by painting the faces of movie stars in the clouds. I still have many aspects of my art to perfect. It is a never-ending challenge.

Let me tell you a little more about our existence here. Perhaps you are wondering where we receive our instructions from, which tell us what kind of sky is required each day and night? Well, the instructions come from the Ministry (of which the Boss is the boss); we are part of the Nature Department, of which there are many sub-departments. Nobody here knows where the Ministry is based, or even who works there. We know only what we are told by the Boss when she makes one of her rare appearances, once every three or four decades. She is a busy woman, so I would not expect her to be a more frequent visitor. Years ago, when I first came here, the business of garnishing us with our instructions was an arduous one: they were brought to us, daily, by a dwarf on goat-back. It wasn't always the same dwarf, and it wasn't always the same goat, but they may as well have been, as the dwarves were all mute and the goats did nothing but bleat (unsurprisingly). The instructions were etched in fancy calligraphy on parchment, explaining the exact type of sky required over which region of the hemisphere: 'Spain – rain on the plain', 'Siberia – snow again'. Earlier this century, the dwarves and goats were made redundant when we had a telephone installed, and the instructions were dictated to us each day by a bland, anonymous female voice. Now the telephone has been replaced by a fax machine (a marvellous invention!) and soon, we hear, this is to be replaced by something called 'e-mail'. I don't know – this century has moved too quick for me. Anyway, as long as we receive our instructions, it hardly matters by which method.

Each week, a carriage arrives with our supplies: food, drink and books and magazines, along with our painting equipment. We like to keep in touch with the rest of the world; I am particularly interested in keeping abreast of the latest developments in the art world, and in the shocking exploits of those glamorous people who live in Hollywood. Unfortunately, we do not have the facility to watch films here, although I have put in an official request for what I believe is called a VCR. Until then, I will have to continue to invent the movies in my head. Perhaps one day I may be allowed to take a holiday; I would love to visit Los Angeles and see the movies in the wonderful cinemas I believe they have there.

I have to go now: I have a spring evening to paint, and it is imperative that I am not late. That would be a sackable offence, and I would not wish to lose my immortality. I have paints to mix, brushes to clean and a ladder to climb. Once I have finished, Isabel is going to paint the sunset, and I shall be retiring to bed. I will dream, as always, of that glorious autumn sunset I will one day paint: the most breathtaking, spectacular sunset the planet has ever seen.

Goodnight then, from me, William, and from my companions. When you look at the sky tonight, or this morning or afternoon – whenever you are reading my letter from the top of the world – think of us, won't you? We are the people who frame your lives with beauty.

Gael Turnbull

A woman has

A woman has devoted her life to her family. One evening at the table as her husband talks of his day at work and the children of their friends at school, she picks up her half finished meal and turns it over on its face, carefully pressing it down onto the tablecloth.

The children stare open mouthed. Her husband finally gasps, "What are you doing?" She smiles at him sadly, shaking her head. "You understand nothing. It wasn't me who did that. The woman who did that, by doing it, no longer exists."

In my dream

In my dream, the real one that dreams of me, it's always the same house – I could tell you the town, street, number, you could go there yourself, I could go, though much rebuilt, even in my dream – and where I can't find the answer

to why I'm back or why I've been gone so long or why so careless as to leave, or to that implied "Was I not what you dreamed? Not all you desired?"

It was as if

It was as if she couldn't know herself. It was only other persons, who weren't like her, who could do that. When she searched her own image, there was always the reminder: one green eye, one brown. Her mother tried to reassure that it made her attractive, interesting, that it was an asset, not a defect,

which wasn't what troubled, or even the lack of symmetry, but that when she looked for herself in the mirror, tried to see into those eyes, she knew that she always saw herself reversed, with her green right eye on the left, her brown on the right. Only others saw her as she was. Only others could hear the affirmation, "I am". For her, it was always the reflection, "Am I?".

This other

They call me by the same name, the bank accepts my signature, even my wife and family keep up the charade, and what variation I can point out is no more than enough to make the deception convincing

but I know I have been replaced by this other that I didn't chose, that I don't recognise, that the mutation is now almost complete and I even begin to forget who I was.

Standing stones

Standing here in this pattern where they have been set by men and for
whatever purpose, they will stand here after we have gone, though some
have fallen, as we read in the guide book what little is known about them
and how much is not,
where we also stand, adding our pattern to theirs, and our words, for our
own purposes, then falling silent, silenced by their silence, and by our
need to understand and our understanding that we can't.

In the unfolding

Warned at the last moment they were coming for him, he pulled jacket,
trousers, over his pyjamas, then shoes over his bare feet but paused to tie
the laces and in his haste, knotted one, fumbled, struggled to re-tie,
succeeded, and in that
was too late, and was taken, tortured, shot. Only nineteen, and
supposing he had been eighty–nine or had gone barefoot? Even the
stars drift, the sun burns down, it is nothing, unremarkable in the
unfolding of whatever, and yet . . .

A man returns

Somewhere between the Danube and the Vistula, a man returns for the
first time to the town where he was born, of which he has only a few
confused memories. On the wall of what appears to be a synagogue, but
is only a replica, he finds the list of those deported who never returned.
He himself at the last moment had been sent to friends in the country who
were able to get him over the frontier and he had grown up with strangers.
He searches down the list for his parents and his grandparents.
Their names are there as expected but so is his own. Momentarily shocked
by the error, as he walks back to the railway station, he is overtaken by
a strange peace. That child he was has now rejoined them and the alien
he has become is free at last to live this other life that chance has given.

When I pointed out

When I pointed out that for her to bring her life to an end or ask me to
do it, whatever her suffering, was against one of the fundamentals of her
belief, she replied, after a pause, "Oh, God understands even if his priest
doesn't."

She said

She said, "My father never encouraged me, my mother never gave me any
affection. I was always alone against the world, and laughter, a luxury.
You had the fortune of a happy childhood."
but he replied, "Not at all. They taught you well. I was never prepared for
life and am still struggling to learn what you absorbed so naturally from
the cradle."

Airy Fairy's Son Aklim

Hamish M Brown

Once upon a time (which means nobody knows when) there was a fairy living below the hills of the fair county of Kerrouchen. She was known as the Airy Fairy for the good reason that she was lighter than air. This was a great inconvenience to conventional living. Her solution was to wear slippers with lead soles and the cover on her bed had little tassels fringing it, all with little lead beads she'd pinched from her husband's fishing tackle basket.

The husband had said, "To hell with her!" and run off with the pretty secretary of Birtam Tam, the fat Chief of State. The Honourable Tam was none too pleased as he was having it off with his secretary himself, hardly surprising if you'd met *his* wife. But it is really Airy Fairy's son Aklim this story is about. That his father left the land as an adulterer only has importance in his being no earthly influence on his son.

Aklim was a horror of a brat. When he was about twelve he'd begged Airy Fairy to use her magic and endow him with perpetual youth.

"I never want to grow up," he swore.

Eventually his mother gave in, as she usually did.

"Anything for a quiet life," she sighed.

Aklim, luckily for everyone else, didn't inherit his mother's genes as far as magic went. He hardly needed to for he was both imaginative and manipulative and his little fingers were made for twisting people round. He looked so bloody sweet too, the sort of child aunts loved to kiss and coo over. The last aunt who tried that he'd spat in her face.

Once in a blue moon Airy Fairy forgot her condition. Aklim once left the whistling kettle on the hob and went out to play forgetting all about it (knowing Aklim, of course he could have done it to annoy his mother) and when the shrieking noise blasted out Airy Fairy leapt from bed – and found herself spread-eagled against the ceiling. Not being a light princess but a right old nag her language was something deplorable. Kerrouchen houses have high ceilings and they had to get the painter in with his ladders to fetch her down.

Some fairy you might say, unable to sort herself out, but magic has its rules and regulations like anything else. Airy Fairy had seen the Fairy Shop Steward's rule book and it was a foot thick. There was nothing covering the removal of inherited personal characteristics. She was stuck with her condition. She stayed indoors and wore lead-weighted slippers.

Airy Fairy was a nasty bit of work herself so one can't altogether blame Aklim for disposing of her. One day he filled a bucket with boiling water and placed this outside the door of the house. He then pretended to be fearsomely hurt and writhed on the ground screaming and shouting. Airy Fairy naturally rushed out, checking nevertheless that her toes were well-lodged in her lead-soled slippers. Once she was beguiled out he wriggled free of her grasp, grabbed the boiling water and poured it over her feet.

Now, I defy anyone having boiling water poured over their feet not to immediately kick off their slippers. Airy Fairy did and went up, up, up and away, screaming blue murder. She drifted over the mountains and out of Kerrouchen, and also out of this story. Aklim was delighted. He nearly pissed himself laughing.

The resulting taste of freedom was to lead to all else. Aklim was determined no grown-up would ever control him again and when he saw the damnable captivity of other boys and girls he wished he had his mother's magic to free them all. The germ of an idea grew in the nasty abscess of his imagination. He'd have "Kerrouchen for Kids" and himself their king, just you wait and see. Oh yes he would.

As if on cue he gained two friends and allies who'd suddenly come to live in the hills above the town. I say town because capital city is altogether too presumptuous for a place of just 2000 people, ruled over by Birtam Tam, who was no more than an upstart lawyer who'd just yerred more of the law than most. Aklim hated his swank and swagger and painted "Philanderer" on his whitewashed wall – and then had to go home and look up the dictionary to see what that meant.

It was the shepherd boy Imlil who came racing into town with the news. He'd seen a giant and a dragon on the hill. They were devouring his sheep and he yelled at the Honourable Tam to do something about it or pay compensation on his losses.

The news went round like wildfire. That it was extravagantly, indecently shocking was the general opinion. Some places sometimes got lumbered with a giant and you had a bit of a pantomime before some hero came along and jacked it in. Or you were landed with a dragon and sent for St. George, or one of his understudies, and enjoyed a bloody good scrap, the sort of thing only seen centuries later in a so-called sport. To have a giant *and* a dragon was quite unconventional and probably unconstitutional. It just wasn't fair. But Birtam Tam couldn't think of anyone to sue.

"And what happens when they run out of sheep?" Aklim asked with a malicious gleam in his eye.

He'd been preparing his own *coup d'etat* for weeks and at once realised the potential of the pair up in the hills. He went off to visit them.

"Good evening, you two", he piped up as he neared their vantage point close by their cave.

"My name is Aklim, the future King of Kerrouchen. Who are you, pray?"

They were so astonished at this bold boy that they quite failed to gobble him up as he so richly deserved.

"Gallumph, at your service," boomed the giant and he held out a pinkie for Aklim to shake.

"Tounfite," roared the dragon and spat out a ball of fire over Aklim's head before giving him a warm lick with his tongue. It was a bit on the hot side of warm but Aklim bore it like a rascal.

"I hear you are eating Imlil's sheep," Aklim began.

"For lack of anything better," Gallumph interrupted.

"He – we would rather have humans," Tounfite explained.

"That was what I was hoping," Aklim grinned.

There's a marvellous innocence in the wicked. In all good fairy tales they would have snapped up Aklim with no more difficulty than a dish of *cuisses des grenouilles* (frog legs). Instead they sat talking for hours and parted with a treaty of friendship signed, sealed and bedevilled. Aklim needed a week or two yet; but till then Tounfite would make do with catching Imlil's now free-ranging sheep and sharing them with his mate Gallumph.

Kerrouchen was a prosperous place for the soil was good and the climate congenial. With all that grew there they not only ate well but had a fine range of things to drink like mead and cider and home-brew and the distillation of everything you could think of – and a few others. Thus, when the year's big festival came round, most of the adult population was blotto for days and the teenagers weren't much better so it was usually a time of trial and hunger for children. It was the perfect time in fact for the children to deal with the disgusting adults. This was to be a holy war, a purifying purge, a righteous crusade. Never was Aklim more persuasive and dominating. He both inspired and terrified the boys and girls of Kerrouchen. A rumour (quite untrue) went round that one boy who had hinted at something to his parents (a few boys actually *liked* their parents!) had had his throat cut by Aklim. They kept mum. There will always be a few doubters and fearful in any revolution but most were thoroughly behind Aklim. Parents were *numero uno* for extermination.

A few managed to sleep in and miss the hour of striking, which was 0300 on the third day of the festival, but 99.9% did their stuff, as the newspaper declared a few weeks later. It was the only issue they ever printed. Like much of the adult world it was something they could happily live without. Comics hadn't been invented, of course.

The action had to be swift but, within that remit, the boys and girls could act as they saw fit. Aklim had nothing against any of them cutting their parents' throats, except it was rather messy and they'd have to clear up afterwards as there wouldn't be any parents to do so. Most settled for simply tying up their parents and taking them along to the old Roman stadium where they were dumped, others relished putting a knife in a big brother's back and marching him to captivity.

As Aklim had no parents left to dispose of, he (and two henchboys) went along to the house of Birtam Tam. He broke a back window, they climbed in and sneaked up the stairs. There was no difficulty in locating their victim. He was noisily philandering. It was with relish (and a few encouraging jabs from a sword) that the Honourable Tam was delivered to the stadium. Even some of the bewildered captives already there were amused, for the Boss, as he liked to call himself, was no longer in his finery but in an extremely ill-fitting birthday suit.

By sunrise the old stadium was full and "Kerrouchen for Kids" was being chanted and scrawled on walls. Aklim's trusties made the prison secure and had also seized vital places like the dairy, bakers, butchers and so on. Aklim, while proclaiming glorious freedom (he was good at slogans) had every intention of being master of Kerrouchen. At a first rally held in the main square that morning a carefully-engineered spontaneous demand saw him proclaimed Honourable First Secretary. Three days later his council proclaimed him absolute monarch. Aklim was king.

The dragon, Tounfite, had a field day in the stadium, or rather, a whole week of playing the final solution. Starting with the fat and sagging Birtam Tam the dragon bore everyone off to, or over, the mountains, nobody really cared which. They just went. Gallumph actually came down into the town. As his was the voice moving that Aklim should be proclaimed king there wasn't much dissent. Any opposition would soon be eaten away. Gallumph then retreated to his cave above the town.

Strangely enough this boy kingdom worked. It was a boy kingdom because Aklim made it so. The council, his Protectors (a cross between secret police and arm), all the key administrative posts, went to boys. The girls were quite rightly expected to be home-makers. The system worked because Aklim was clever and, like most dictators, believed what he did was for the general good, and the generality accepted that it was.

Aklim, being bound to perpetual boyhood, rather overlooked the fact that everyone else wasn't. A few months after the successful *coup* not a few boys (and girls of course) were no longer as they once were. They began to be a bit bolshie too and Aklim panicked at the thought that these soon-to-be-adults in turn would stage a *coup*, and oust him.

So he made another proclamation, which caused both some complaint and some amusement to begin with but was soon so part of their life that nobody noticed at all. From that day onwards all clothes were banned. On cold days a blanket could be draped round one's shoulders but that was the only concession. Another was to be added later. Those working the land could wear sandals. (There was an awful lot of thistles in Kerrouchen!) For the rest, and at all times, everyone was to go naked. This at once showed up those who were pubescent and, strangely, they simply disappeared in quick order. Tounfite saw to that. He was quite a pet in the town but Gallumph preferred to live in the big cave up on the hill. The threat of being made Gallumph's supper was usually enough to bring the most dissident into order. Aklim kept very strict order.

Tounfite was a great favourite for, by climbing up onto his back, a kid could enjoy an exciting slide down his scaly slope, and once onto his tail, the dragon would give a flip and send the child back to the start. He kept it up, happily, for hours at a time. Everyone knew Tounfite, the friendly dragon, and Tounfite knew everyone. This eventually led to panic as one's body began to change, unmistakably heading for that never-allowed word "adulthood". Tounfite would always know. He found them out and would fly off with them over the mountains. "Over the mountains" was the euphemism all used for the end of being just a boy or girl.

Aklim thus saw all his trusties taken, whether literally "over the mountains" or on a shorter flight to Gallumph's cave (the giant had to be eating regular somebodies after the initial hoard of adults had gone) and he saw another problem arising. There was going to be a steady decline in population. In a dozen years even the babies who'd been left, to the great delight of the girls, who could play at being mummies for real, would be whipped away by Tounfite. He alone would be left. So he had a quiet word with Tounfite and came to a practical arrangement whereby every time he took someone "over the mountain" he would come back with another boy or girl from beyond Kerrouchen. Aklim was good at solving practical problems.

"Pragmatic", was Tounfite's comment at Gallumph as he dropped a trembling youth into the giant's hands. "Very", mumbled the giant, his mouth full with a newly bitten-off head. "Adolescents are far more succulent than those awful adults".

Aklim went as naked as the rest but it eventually struck him that this wasn't quite right. He was the king. He should be different. So he ordered some of the skilled girls to weave a beautiful checked and colourful length of soft cloth from the best sheep on the hill. Tounfite and Gallumph never needed to touch sheep now. (The shepherd lad Imlil had made a snack, though.) Aklim learned to belt himself into this new garment, which is reputedly the ancestor of the traditional Scot's kilt, and thus he could not be mistaken for anyone else in the kingdom. Kings have to be different.

There were certain murmurings later. "How do we know he isn't hiding his changing parts?" So once a month, at the elected council meeting (Aklim did the electing) he ceremoniously disrobed before them all to proclaim his pure boyhood. Later he showed himself more dramatically to the whole kingdom.

It then struck him that a king should have a queen so he chose the most beautiful girl he could find and made a grand ceremony before the whole population of enrobing her too. She became his private plaything. Playing was all he could enjoy and a year later the inevitable happened. Curiosity made Aklim keep her state secret but, even robed, it would show in the end. Another, far greater ceremony was called for. Every kingdom after all needed some sort of religion.

When he told his queen what he intended she burst into tears.

"But Tounfite will take you anyway", he comforted. "Far better become a loving sacrifice. Make going "over the mountains" seem a wonder to be desired, make all the girls long to be my queen?" Thus Aklim wrapped his first queen round his finger. Others followed.

He kept all his queens till they were beautifully rounded and marked by hair. They could sometimes drive him into a sort of turmoil which was usually calmed by his gracious sacrificing of their lives to the spirit of perpetual childhood. He wielded the knife himself.

On the day appointed everyone gathered in the square. He had a wide flight of polished granite steps built on one side, leading up to his "palace" (a rather ordinary house but full of the best furnishings in the land) and half way up the steps he had a platform which was visible to all the population when they gathered in the square.

The queen would come out in her gaudy robe, her hair tastefully dressed, her demeanour stately and calm, and slowly descend the steps to the platform. There she would unclasp her garment and let it fall to the

Illustration by Maura Bissett

ground. No matter how frequently it happened (and Aklim chose older and older girls to ensure it did), there would be a great gasp from everyone present. Queens were different. Amazing. And only queens ever looked like that. As Aklim foresaw they became desperate to be his queens. In the end he allowed himself three queens at any one time, which meant there could be several grand ceremonies a year. You have to keep the people happy.

After the queen had stood on the platform for a few minutes, Aklim would appear at the door. He would descend a few steps, then let his garment slip from him, to be revealed for what he was. There would be a great shout of approval. Their king was just a boy like the rest of them. Except he was for ever, for after some years, nobody could remember life pre-Aklim. They dated their calendar from the day he was proclaimed king.

King Aklim walked down the steps to stand behind his queen. He kicked her robe aside. He touched her shoulder. She knelt down. The young girl chosen as her successor then hurried from the side to hand him a beautiful jewelled knife. The queen leaned her head back and he quickly drew the knife across her throat. There was always another great shout as the blood ran down the little breasts. Aklim laid her kindly on the cold stone. The blood ran to the edge and formed a trickle down from step to step. Aklim's new queen then came forward and picked up the fallen robe. She knelt before Aklim, who marked her brow with a symbol from his bloody finger. After that she withdrew (till the robing ceremony) but everyone else, starting with his council in the front row, had the right to come and mark themselves with blood. It was all done with great decorum. It was all very wonderful. Later Aklim made it even more ceremoniously impressive by having a choir trained for the occasion.

We haven't anything else recorded about Aklim the King, Airy Fairy's boy. This little was written by someone obviously close to him but no doubt he went "over the mountains", like the rest. Certainly Kerrouchen does not exist today. Nobody lived happily ever after.

Kerrouchen eventually disappeared as a name on any map. When its dreadful history was discovered in an old manuscript the town on its site was given the name Douleur, now corrupted to Dollar. High above is King's Seat, the hill where Aklim always conferred with the giant and the dragon while the Burns of Care and Sorrow round down to the town and Gloom Hill is the hollow of Gallumph's cave, the roof long fallen in. Some try and say it is just a quarry but how do you then explain the tons of bones unearthed when indeed it was turned into a quarry during "the war to end all wars"?

Of course in our enlightened times giants and dragons are obsolete. The world is now a civilised place. You couldn't imagine an Aklim today. Yet he was made perpetual boy and every time one encounters a little horror (and there's plenty of them around) there is a twinge of questioning. Could this be Aklim, living unhappily ever after?

Derick Tulloch

Interference Pattern

Quick circles o rain on watter
A circle is a simple form
Geometry canna catch dat life
An wird is a mantation here

Dis is a mony-centred time
Quick circles growin fae aa places,
Meet, dan pass troo ane anidder
Fade away. Watter still remains.

Restit Fire

Me hate me love fur dee
Growes steedily
Lowin rid col aneath me hert

A gate is shut whaur we
Walkit free
Lowin rid col aneath me hert

A time fae syne whin we
Grew steedily
Lowin rid col aneath me hert

A flame slokkit fur me
Love is free
Lowin rid col aneath me hert

Timour mortis conturbat me
Timour mortis conturbat me

Flash!

He sees da bonnie lasses staund
Ilk ane is laek a lowin taand
In every toun troo-oot da laund
Wi hough high buits
He'd laek tae set a clammy haund
Abuin der cuits

He'd laekly get some dirty looks
Or markit bi defensive clooks
Wid be five tracks across his plooks
He'd thus retire

Tae da refuge o dirty books
Aside da fire

Dan – oot tae forder his career
Ahint a shrub he wid appear
Accost a maiden – an wid speir
(An cast a cloot)
"Hou does du laek dis ane me dear?"
An wave his troot

I winder whit wid be dafter
His pose or her helpless lauchter?
While his threatener'd get safter
Wi-oot a doot
Scho'll tell a teel fur ever eftir
FUR SIC A MOOT!

Educatin da Teacher

A'm joost six an thocht skule wis joost lovely
Whaur da bairns could play wis an fecht wis an laern
Til Mester Robertson telt wis at me, Jean an Ally
Coodna spaek right an widna laern tae write
At whit I laernt fae mammy an scho laernt fae granny
Wis aa bruck an a failure – weel lat me tell dee Mester
At whaups is NO curlews – an w're tirn bit no angry
So dee – du sood laern at tae pick on a bairn
Tae mak oot at du's clivver is sad an no funny
W'll tak dy brand new strap an w'll sneck him tae ribbeens
An bind dee tae dy desk wi bricht kokkiloories
Dan eftir dat plunkie w'll run oot tae play pickie
W'll skip an w'll skirl an sing up wir ain sangs
Fur it's owre fine a day fur tae smore i dy skuleroom
An wha's du tae tell wis da rights fae da wrangs?

Chapman Exhibition

A Literary Hinterland:

Over 25 years of Chapman history

Literary magazines don't get any better than this!

The exhibition shows Chapman's development from a slim eight page pamphlet to a substantial book-sized publication: from key issues, contributions from the greatest Scottish writers of the time and the up and coming writers of tomorrow.

It reveals the strange hinterland of the magazine and its impact on Scottish life and culture: those bizarre letters to the editor, how Chapman is produced, memorabilia of life in the office. And much more: newspapers cuttings, posters, flyers, illustrations, cartoons . . . and many oddities!

Information packs available.

An exhibition not just to see but to read and relish.

Sponsored by the Barony Bar, Broughton Street.

Runs 23 May until 26 July 1998.
Admission free, opening hours 10-5, Mon-Sat.

The Writers' Museum, Lady Stairs House, Lady Stairs Close, Lawnmarket, Edinburgh
0131 529 4901.

RLS Memorial Award

Initiated in 1994 by Franki Fewkes, a Scot and RLS enthusiast living in France, and administered by the National Library of Scotland with the financial assistance of the Scottish Arts Council the Robert Louis Stevenson Memorial Award is a continuing memorial to RLS and a way of perpetuating the tradition of which he was part. It awards a Scottish or Scottish resident writer two months residence at the Hotel Chevillon in Grez-sur-Loing near Fountainebleau, France. The hotel is an international centre for writers and artists from around the world, but especially the Scandinavian countries, with six self-catering apartments and specially adapted workshops. Stevenson himself spent several summers at the hotel and it was there that he met and fell in love with Fanny, his wife.

The award is intended to enable the winner to develop their creative work, to work on new literary ventures and to represent Scotland in the wider artist community. The award provides accommodation in a self-catering studio apartment and a grant towards living expenses. The Scottish Arts Council provides a travel grant, but the participant is responsible for all other costs.

Also, as part of the conditions for their awards writers can look forward to having work inspired by this award published in *Chapman* after their return. We are pleased to include in this issue, the 1996 and 1995 winners of the prize, two Scottish writers Angus Dunn and Dilys Rose who have each contributed two short stories preceded by a short essay describing each author's experiences during their time at the Hotel Chevillon.

For further information and an entry form for the award contact: The RLS Memorial Award, National Library of Scotland, George IV Bridge, Edinburgh EH1 1EW.

Putting Down the Words

Angus Dunn

My first month at Grez-sur-Loing was productive but cheerless. This part of France is nearly a thousand miles south of Dingwall: I hadn't expected sleet and frost in March. The Hotel Chevillon has been converted into self-contained flats for writers and artists. The rooms were comfortable, but the sense of chill remained, even though the radiators kept the rooms warm.

The surrounding countryside was bleak: empty fields, lots of bare trees. There was no height in the landscape at all. A dreary fuzz of far-off oak branches lined the horizon. I walked around the village, but it was not attractive: the houses had no gardens, abutting straight onto the street, and they were all tight shuttered. A derelict house had the word *Poignee*, painted on its door. This meant that the place was booby-trapped against intruders and 'YOU HAVE BEEN WARNED!'

I stayed in my flat and worked. Four hours writing in the morning. Editing in the afternoon. There was a bistro nearby. I spent one long evening in there, in the company of a gloomy Swedish artist. It was not appealing. In the evenings, I made notes towards a novel.

I wrote a lot, in March. In April, though, the pollarded willows by the river woke up, producing masses of catkins. There was a small rowing boat at the Hotel Chevillon and I took it up the river, finding that the village houses had fine long gardens that stretched down to the river, most of them with small jetties in a variety of wonderful styles from raw-timber-and-six-inch-nails to fifty-year old oak planking slowly subsiding into the water. As the weather warmed up, the place grew better every day. Dozens of geese arrived and quarrelled over nesting places along the river banks. Plane, ash and chestnut leaves grew thickly. The willows were cascades of greenery. The hotel lawn was covered in violets, then primroses.

Suddenly one day it was pleasant to eat on the hotel terrace at mid-day, and even more pleasant to sit there after dark, drinking wine with the Finnish writer and listening to sad Estonian music.

I continued to write at my desk in the mornings, but the afternoons were spent on the river. I rowed upstream until I reached the weir. I sat in the bows and wrote in a notebook, letting the boat drift in the slow current. Every half hour or so the boat would bump into the bank and I would scull out to the middle again.

The village had come alive, too. There were people on the streets, the shutters were opened. I tried the bistro again and found that it had improved enormously. The Swedish artists seemed to have cheered up too. They smiled a lot. Sometimes, they laughed. We all drank Calvados and spoke French confidently.

Poetry had begun to appeal more than fiction. Short poems, especially. As April passed, the poems grew more concise. If I'd had another fortnight, they would have disappeared entirely.

I wrote fewer words in April, but they were better words.

Relicts

Angus Dunn

Harry returned from the Middle East like the conquering hero. I'd not seen him so excited since he visited the Pentecostal Church and discovered that he could talk in tongues.

He came round to my house at that time to demonstrate his new-found talent. "Listen!" he said, then he produced a distinctly liquid babble, not unlike birdsong. I listened politely, then pointed out to him that it wasn't much use if he couldn't understand what he was saying. Harry took the huff, and relations between us were strained for a couple of days, until he forgave me – at which point I felt bound to apologise. I expected the novelty to wear off after a while.

But it didn't. He spent more and more of his time with strange folk from strange churches and his conversation grew increasingly bizarre. Quite stimulating, in its way, but increasingly impenetrable to the uninitiated.

That was just the beginning of the change. Next he came across Hugh Miller's work with the fossil fish in Eathie Gorge. Harry thought that if God had hidden fishes in the sandstone, then He must surely have hidden proofs of Christianity where men of faith and diligence could find them.

Harry saved up for two years and managed to get some kind of grant from a religious foundation to go to the Middle East. He was away for six months, starting in Turkey, then Lebanon, Jordan and other dangerous places of a Biblical sort. Then it was Egypt, and finally, Israel. When he got back he had a dozen packing cases with him and he was all lit up from inside with enthusiasm.

But Turkey was where he realised that he'd found his life's work – so he said, – as a Biblical antiquary. He was taken into the wilds by a guide who led him up on a mountain and showed him ancient relics which no westerner had ever seen. After a great deal of persuasion the guide sold him one of these, which Harry brought back.

He told us the story in his front room, after showing us his slides of Holy and Interesting places of the Near and Middle East. The rest of his audience were churchmen and Pentecosts of one degree or another. They all oohed and aahed, while I suggested that he should have brought a camel home to work the croft.

He looked hurt and disappointed and awesome all at once. "Sorry," I muttered, "Silly of me. Where would you get a harness to fit a camel?"

He was certainly an impressive figure. He had developed a splendid white beard on his travels, and he looked for all the world like Moses himself as he sat there expounding, the lights shining on him. He spread his arms in a most prophetical way as he spoke. I wondered who had arranged the lighting.

"And tonight," he said "I will show to you, my chosen friends, the very first relic which I was led to find."

He lifted a small wooden chest to his lap. We sat there agog as he opened up the chest and reached inside. He held up a shirt.

"Here it is!"

An old shirt, certainly, but not very remarkable. Quite long, made of sheep's wool or something similar.

"That's very nice, Harry, but just what is it?"

Harry nodded sagely. "Mrs Donnely in the Nairn church has holy water from Lourdes and a crucifix blessed by the Pope. She even claims to have a fragment of the One True Cross. But this is even holier than that, and certainly more ancient. Preserved by the miracle of high-altitude desiccation, saved down the centuries for our wonder and worship."

I leaned closer. It just looked like a shirt. "It's a woollen sark, Harry. It looks fine and warm, but what's so special about it?"

"It's older than Christianity . . ."

"No! A pagan artefact? That's very broad-minded of you."

"Pagan? No indeed. This is a relic from the true Judaeo-Christian heritage. Older than the Law and the Prophets." He paused and looked around at us portentously. He held up the shirt for us all to see.

His voice was hushed when he spoke again. "This is Noah's sark."

There was a moment of silence. I looked around, surreptitiously. Surely some of the better educated were considering explaining the basic facts of Bible hagiography to Harry. But no, most of them seemed ready to accept its authenticity.

I began to wonder if this was an inspired piece of anarchy devised by a mind no longer wholly normal. He continued.

"And that is not all. That was only the beginning of a pilgrimage which brought me in touch with the living lands of the Bible, a pilgrimage in which it seemed that my steps were guided to the most precious evidences of the faith, lain unnoticed for hundreds, sometimes for thousands of years."

I broke in. "One moment, Harry. I have some doubts about the authenticity of the – relic. You see, the word 'sark' is a Scots word. That such a word was in use in early Biblical times is very improbable."

"But that also is revealed in the scriptures. Not only is the Bible a true story of the Jewish peoples, it is also an allegory, a symbolic representation of the history of God's chosen people. The British race."

I was staggered. "That's why the Bible is written in English?"

He nodded approvingly. "Just so. All the major incidents, even the individual words, are coded references to the real nature of the Book. It is a guide and an instrument to lead us."

"I suppose you all know about numerology," he continued, "and how it is used in the Bible?" I mumbled something amidst the general murmur of assent. "The wonderful description in Revelations, fulfilling the words of Jesus, when He said, there is not a sparrow that falls from the sky but my father knows of it. He watches over us and numbers our days, and even the beasts of the field. And Saint John tells us in Revelations – 666 is the number of the beasts. That's precise. And Biblical."

The scholar in me could not be silent in the face of such factual error.

"I'm sorry, Harry but that's just not right. Henderson Glaickbea has over two hundred head of cattle himself, and Glaikbea's not a big farm. There must be more than a thousand beasts on the north side of the Black Isle alone."

Harry leaned forward to look me in the eye. "I was just about to say, that it is precise and Biblical – and symbolic." He nodded his head forcefully and settled back in his seat as if the matter was settled.

Then he sat up again. "And after all, our language is divinely structured. What language do they speak in North Africa?" He answered himself. "Arabic. And what language do we speak here? English. Now look at a Spanish phrasebook sometime – you'll be surprised at how many words we share."

"For instance, mañana," I said. He nodded to me.

"When the Moors overran Spain, they brought their language with them and it seeped into the local language so that there was a kind of mixture. A language that spans the gulf between the two languages. It spans two cultures. So of course that language is called Span-ish."

He smiled at us, inviting us to enjoy the inevitability of the name.

I could see that Harry needed no encouragement. Evidently he was a master in the anarchic style – if that's what it was. I stood up to make my excuses.

"Just a minute, Jimmy," he said. "There's another holy relic that you really must see before you go."

"What is it this time? Aaron's rod? Jesse's thorn?"

"Ach, someone's been telling you about my collection, I can see that. But I think we'll save those for another time. No, what I want to show you now is a greater wonder than that. You'll need to come through the house."

He raised himself from the chair. His white beard seemed even more venerable than before. He shuffled through the room to a doorway, beckoning us to follow.

The room beyond was dim, with niches in the walls. Each one was lit from above, and each had something in it, with a label on the wall below. There was a model of a head on a shiny plate, a basket full of dusty seeds and so on. As I passed by, I thought I could make out the name Onan on the label below the basket.

Harry beckoned me to the far end of the room. The crowd had followed, and they were quietly marvelling at the room and the relics.

At the end, in a rectangular niche, was an aquarium. There were corals in it, and brownish seaweeds that waved as the bubbles from the aerator drifted past.

"This is one of my greatest finds. In Jordan I managed to get a guide who was deeply versed in Bible history. I persuaded him to take me south, down the sparsely populated shore of the Red Sea, to where the Israelites crossed from Egypt."

He bowed his head.

"That holy place. I will treasure the memory of that day for the rest of my life."

Someone murmured. "Hallelujah." I peered into the tank.

"So you brought back some souvenirs then?"

His lips pursed. "I do not collect souvenirs. I am a serious antiquarian. This collection is in many ways superior to the corresponding section of the British Museum."

I could feel the hostility of the crowd, at having thus offended the old man. "I'm sorry. The word was not well-chosen. But what relic did you bring back from Jordan?"

He pointed. "Look close."

I leant down and peered into the tank. There was a little sand, some rocks, the weeds. A bit of algae on the glass. Nothing living at all.

"There's nothing there."

He chuckled. "None so blind, eh? Look close, now, at that greenish rock there, and tell me what you see."

It was just a smooth green rock. I was about to say so when it moved. There was a puff of fine sand, and I saw its claws.

"It's a partan. A crab."

"Aye. What do you say to that?"

"Well, well," I muttered, being a bitty baffled. He waited. "It's a crab. A fine crab. But what of it?"

"Losh man, d'ye not know a religious relict when ye see one?"

My patience had stretched to its limit.

"I am as well versed in Archaeology and Church History as the next man," I snapped, "but my studies of invertebrate animals of the Red Sea was sadly neglected. Perhaps you could tell me what that is, so that I do not have to guess."

"Well, well," he sympathised smugly. "They didn't teach you everything at college, did they?"

"Obviously not. Perhaps you could enlighten me."

"Stand back a wee, then, so that the rest can see."

We all moved back and stood in a semi-circle around the tank.

Harry pointed at the crab.

"That wee darling," he said, "is the partan of the Red Sea."

There were sighs of awe. As the rest crowded closer for a better look, I slipped quietly through the house. There was a set of keys hanging in the hall. The label told me they were the Keys of the Kingdom. There was a picture of a washerwoman on her knees in a field, scrubbing. It was entitled 'Rebecca Cleaning in the Fields'. Was Harry an inspired agent provocateur in the house of God? Or was he just demented?

As I opened the front door, Harry called to me.

"Jimmy, wait. I brought you back something specially." He pressed something into my hand. I thanked him, but he just smiled and turned to go back to his guests.

As I walked down the road, I stripped off the paper wrapping. There in my hand I held a small white pill box. Undoubtedly it contained the Tablets of Moses.

Parts

Angus Dunn

From my corner of the classroom I could see my cousin Enrico's seat by the door. He was showing something, a photograph, to the boys on either side of him. His black eyebrows waggled suggestively. One of the boys peered at the picture curiously, then looked shocked. He handed back the photo and faced the teacher as if paying attention, but his eyes were blank.

The teacher turned from the blackboard. "The skin is an organ." He said the words firmly, then his mouth clicked shut.

"The basic unit of biology is the cell." That's what he'd said the very first day in class. He'd articulated the words carefully, letting the short dry sentence emerge from his mouth. Then he waited until we began to write the words down. "So we will study the cell," he continued. His face was old and dried out, his mouth could have belonged to a tortoise.

"The basic unit of chemistry is the molecule. We will occasionally refer to it." It seemed as if the saliva in his mouth had dried out, so that when he spoke he had to pull his lips apart against the tacky residue. He paused again and looked around.

"Classical physics deals with the atom, so we will not." From the tortoise mouth sentences emerged. He'd used them so often they were lifeless: they sat in the air, waiting until we'd all taken note. Then the next one emerged. Once a week we had a double period – nearly two solid hours of biology. Week after week I watched his mouth in horror, unable to ignore it.

"People are cells," he said. The words meant nothing to me, but he emphasised them as though we should note them.

"Meat is muscle." I wrote the words down, week after week.

"The kidney is an organ." Every Tuesday afternoon more raw images of bodily parts emerged from the desiccated mouth.

At dinner time, Enrico was at my table. He was showing the photo again, flushed with excitement, but nervous of getting caught.

Plates rattled at the other end of the canteen. The supervisor turned towards the noise. "Quiet now!"

While Enrico was watching the supervisor, I reached across and took the photo. It was a Polaroid, bent and creased. All I could see was an ambiguous jumble of black and white. Then I made out a recognisable shape – the pale blob was a girl's face. She had one arm across her eyes. Her other hand was holding something dark. It was her dress. She was holding it right up to her neck. Below, there were white shapes that might be her breasts – so that must be her belly, and there was one of her thighs – most of the picture was still an abstract pattern when Enrico snatched the photo away.

All through the afternoon I held the black and white shapes in my mind, trying to make out what they were.

One of the annoying things about Enrico staying with us was the way my mother behaved as if he was an adult. She practically simpered at him. As soon as his visit was arranged she did a big blitz on the house, touching up the paintwork, replacing the old tablecloth. She even bought a plant for the living room – a Swiss Cheese plant. It had big glossy leaves with holes in them. It looked as if a cat had clawed it while it was growing, so that when the leaves unfolded there were tears in them. I don't know why she bought it. Maybe it's fashionable to have ugly plants in the house.

Enrico was standing in front of the hall mirror again. He'd greased his hair with Brylcreem, and now he was combing it into shiny black waves and hollows. It looked like sculpted lard.

"They say that Michaelangelo once made a lion from butter," I told him, "for the centrepiece of a feast."

"Heh?" He didn't understand, but he saw me grimacing at his hair.

"What wrong with your mouth, little cousin? It look like a hen's arse. You gonna lay an egg, maybe?"

"It looks horrible, Enrico."

"Hey, when you big enough to chase the girls, you old enough to yap about my hair. Jesus, I bet you ain't even seen a girl's tits. eh?"

I turned away so that he couldn't see me blushing. He laughed and turned back to the mirror.

Later I was reading in my room. I heard Enrico walking down the hall. He opened the door and threw a magazine at me. "Look at that, little boy. See what you're missing." He laughed and shut the door.

The magazine was called *Parade* and there were pictures of women in it. Most of them had hardly any clothes on at all, and there were some pictures in full colour. One of these was in the middle pages, a completely naked woman lying on a bed. One of her legs was crossed over the other and her hand was on her hip. She was twisted round so that both of her breasts were visible. Her nipples were huge, much bigger than mine. "James! You haven't done the dishes yet! And have you finished your homework?"

I grabbed the magazine against my chest with the picture hidden, as if she could see through the walls from the downstairs hall. "I'll come right down, mum." I looked frantically round, then stuffed it under the mattress.

Of course she couldn't have known about the magazine. In fact, most of the time she didn't seem to know much about anything at all except keeping the house and cooking. In fact, that was the best way to know what she was thinking.

She still thought I was a child, so she could just walk into my room and tell me to get it tidied up. But she never looked in Enrico's room, and it was much worse than mine. She gave him more food at the table too, like she did for Dad and Grandad. But not for me.

I remember once, when I had discovered what it was to feel unrequited love. She made a jam steam pudding because she thought I was looking miserable.

"You must be sickening for something," she said.

I was furious at her. I could hardly eat the pudding.

Compared to biology, physics was a relief. Nothing oozed. Nothing had unpleasant juices. No glistening organs or dissected portions of animals. Instead there were subatomic particles, inelastic collisions, interference patterns and complex lens equations.

Also, the teacher was young and friendly. He explained. He wanted you to understand. He ran a physics club: we built our own radios, and later on, a simple cloud chamber.

We needed a radioactive source for the chamber. He borrowed my watch. "The luminous hands have got radium in them," he said. "Watch."

He put the watch inside and evacuated the glass chamber. We leaned over it, waiting.

"There!" A tiny white streak of cloud had appeared in the chamber.

"Is that a Radium atom, sir?"

"No, no. Much smaller than that. Even an atom is made of smaller bits. It's mostly empty space with a collection of tiny particles whirling around in it. That was one of them, an electron, leaving its mark as it shot through the chamber."

So that was it. One of the basic bits that make up everything else. I was silent, thinking about it.

"Of course, even that is probably made of smaller bits," he said.

Grandad was long-sighted. He had to use a big magnifying glass to read the newspaper, but he could still see well enough to drive.

Every Sunday he'd clean his car and we'd go for a ride, usually out in the country. It was an old car with leather seats. I enjoyed the feeling of being taken somewhere, but I didn't like being out in the country, which is where he always went. It was full of scrappy bushes and old fences that were falling to bits. Most of the houses looked as if they were empty, or no-one looked after them. Mostly I looked at the sky while Grandad told me he was brought up in a place just like this. Wherever we went he'd tell me that. I suppose that was the sort of place he went.

Enrico came with us once, then never again. "I got better things to do," he told me, and laughed. After that I was embarrassed to go out with Grandad. He still went, by himself.

The day Enrico left, he gave me his collection of magazines. Most of them were like *Parade*, black and white pictures of women with naked breasts, printed on cheap paper, with just one or two of colour photographs on glossy paper.

One of them, though, was different. He must of sent off for it. There was a set of photos of a woman wearing only stockings and a suspender belt. She was standing with her legs apart, staring out at me.

After everyone had gone to bed, I sneaked into the sitting room and took Grandad's big reading glass. I scuttled up to my bedroom, closed the door and turned off the light. Under the blankets, I turned on the torch and opened the magazine. There she was, smiling grimly at the camera, hands on her hips, her pelvis thrust forward. I lifted the heavy magnifying glass and held it to the picture, first over her face, then her breasts and then, closer, over the dark place where her legs joined her body.

The illusion of skin and hair broke up into tiny dots. I snorted a laugh. Of course that was the way printed pictures were made. I moved the lens further away, then closer again. Now you almost see it, now you don't. After a while it stopped being amusing. I put the reading glass aside, feeling uneasy. Something moved in the room. I turned off the torch and looked out from under the blankets. The door was still shut, but something unpleasant was moving in the dark. I turned on the torch. The room was empty but the unpleasantness was still there. I could feel it. It was getting worse.

I jumped out of bed and turned on the light. It didn't go away.

I felt the sudden chilly presence of the biology teacher.

"People are cells."

A cold air moved through me. I felt it pass between the cells of my body.

The magazines did not burn well. I crouched over the living-room fire for an hour, stirring the ashes.

At last there was no recognisable piece left. All the lights were on. I was huddled close to the fire.

It hadn't helped. It was still in the house, somewhere near, waiting. I tried not to think about anything. The wrong thought would bring it close again. I stared straight ahead. There were tiles around the fireplace, cheap bright ones with pictures. From close up, the coloured dots that made up the pictures were clearly visible. I turned away. In the corner of the room, the plant drooped its mutilated leaves. The chill in the room grew worse.

I jumped up and put out the lights, then put coal on the glowing fire and pulled the damper out. In the dimness, the pattern on the tiles was barely visible. I stared at the flames, letting the light drive out thoughts, letting the heat soak in.

Slowly, I warmed up, and fell asleep on the rug.

One Sunday in Spring I went out with Grandad again. Just like before. We came onto some country roads that had been freshly tarred. The road looked like a smooth black ribbon. I sat up and watched it. Among the dreary scraps of hedge and rusted fences it made such a clean line.

We had a puncture but Grandad didn't mind. He had all the right tools in the boot. He left me to get the spare wheel out while he jacked up the car.

When he got the damaged wheel off, I rolled the spare over to him. He had put a pair of overalls on over his Sunday clothes and he was kneeling on the black road. Scraps of tarry grit had stuck to his knee.

I dropped the damaged tyre on the grass verge and sat on it. From inside the car, the edge of the road had seemed to be an exact line. Black tar on one side of the dividing line, grass verge on the other.

Out here, I could see where that tarmac edge was already breaking down, from cars driving close to the edge. Even where there were no car tracks, the road-edge was rough and uneven, if you looked close. There never had been that knife-sharp edge. I'd only imagined it.

In the car on the way home, an unpleasant dizziness twisted inside my head whenever we went round a corner or over a bump. I had to ask Grandad to stop and I was sick. I'd never been car-sick before.

For the rest of the journey Grandad drove slowly with the windows open. It didn't help much. Acid was burning deep in my throat. The sour taste lined my mouth and I couldn't stop thinking about it as Grandad drove home. All that stuff had been inside me. It had been part of me.

When it came up, at what point did the sick stop being me? The thought made me feel worse, but the question wouldn't go away. It roiled with the sick giddiness in my head. It wasn't just car-sickness. For a week I lay in bed listening to my breath wheezing in and out. In and out.

Mum made jam steam pudding for me and brought the plant into my room. "You need something green in here," she said. "Something growing."

I was too weak to argue. The plant sat near the window with its sad leaves hanging. I had nothing to do. I couldn't concentrate on a book long enough to read. Most of the time I lay with my eyes shut, but when I opened them, the plant was there.

And one day, when the sun shone in the window, I saw the plant, really saw it, for the first time. Saw why my mother liked it. Each irregular piece of leaf was helping to make a shape. All the bits were working together. I could see the leaf they were trying to make.

That summer my mother let me go down to London to stay with relatives. I'd never been away by myself before.

I think she wanted to warn me about city ways, but she just said good-bye at the station, and told me to take care.

I was taking the overnight train and managed to get a window seat. I watched the countryside falling away behind us until it was too dark to see out. The train was crowded and hot, but eventually I managed to doze in my seat. When I woke, it was daylight and we were in the outskirts of town. I reached down my luggage and waited for the station. The rest of the passengers stayed slumped in their seats, dozing. I looked out at the sea of houses and small gardens. The train showed no signs of stopping and after a while I fell asleep.

When I woke again, the compartment was empty, but the platform outside the window was crowded. I clambered out and stood amongst the bewildering rush of people, looking for the exit. I spotted the barrier, with Aunt Iza standing by it.

From far down the platform I heard a voice raised, and then I saw him coming. A crazy man. People made room for him, and he used all the space they gave. Striding confidently down the platform, dirty grey coat flapping and grey hair waving behind him, he looked as if he didn't care about anyone or anything. I tried to avoid his gaze as I made for the exit.

He stopped and pointed at me. "You!"

I stopped. I couldn't help it. He strode over and stood in front of me. "In the heart of the atom lives Jesus the Christ!"

Past his shoulder I could see Aunt Iza waving. I tried to step past the man, but I couldn't break from his intense gaze.

"No," I heard myself saying. "No, I don't think so."

His eyes lost their fire and he looked puzzled. Then he walked away muttering to himself.

I walked through the barrier and waited for Aunt Iza to kiss me.

She stretched up and pecked my cheek. "My," she said, "haven't you grown!" Then she took my arm and we walked out of the station.

A Hundred Shades of Green

Dilys Rose

What I did in Grez: I walked, I rowed, I wrote. The village was a sleepy place, its shutters closed and lace curtains drawn by ten at night. Sunday afternoon was the busiest time; families in their Sunday best would stroll over the old stone bridge, stopping to throw bits of baguette to the river birds and young bikers from nearby towns played pinball in the café across the street. I didn't spend much time in the café: apart from Sundays: the same half-dozen (male) drinkers lined the bar.

Spring's first shoots coincided with my arrival. By the time I left, the countryside was in full bloom, the woods a hundred shades of green. The sun shone almost every day and much of the time it was warm enough to go out without a jacket. Good weather – for a Scot – is all too seductive when you're supposed to be sat at a desk. There was the garden, where last year's chestnuts sprouted in their hundreds, blankets of violets unfolded heart-shaped petals and colonies of chic French ladybirds dotted the tree trunks, mating on the move. There were the woods, dappled, untidy, busy with birdsong. Overhead, huge boles of mistletoe hung like dark planets and at night Hale-Bopp added sparkle to the sky for a week or so. The lake was occupied by swans, the canal side by men pretending to fish. Best of all was the wide, lazy river Loing on which to row, to watch the sunlight on the water, to wonder who could afford the riverside mansions and be grateful that their equally massive guard dogs weren't fond of swimming.

Looking after myself was so simple and quick compared to life at home that the most mundane chores became almost enjoyable diversions from the screen. Towards the end of my stay, I was even hand washing most of my clothes. As I'd taken a couple of unfinished stories with me, it took only a day or two to begin writing. Two months may sound like a long stretch but time has a nasty habit of disappearing fast when it's on limited offer. During the first half of the fellowship, I worked on stories. The family visited for Easter and no work was done. The second half was spent on a draft of a stage play. At home, it would have probably taken me six months or more, to cover the same ground. Though quantity isn't really what counts, I was pleased with my output. Not only that; a couple of stories came into being as a direct result of my surroundings.

Socially, life at the Hotel Chevillon was quiet, verging on non-existent at first. Days went by when I saw no-one and the ghosts of Stevenson, Larrson, Strindberg and the rest were at times a more palpable presence than the living artists from Sweden and Finland. We did eventually organise a few meals together, which turned out to be jolly, boozy occasions, and provided welcome punctuation in what was otherwise a fairly solitary though hugely useful time.

Electricity
Dilys Rose

There's something I'd like to experience before I die. In some parts of the world, the American mid-west maybe, or Canada – wide open places where thunderclouds roll across the sky and dust balls roll across the ground – it happens. But maybe the place doesn't really matter, maybe it could happen anywhere and it would prove the thing scientifically, it would make sense of the invisible workings of body and mind. At some time or other we've all experienced this jolt and maybe we spend the rest of our lives trying to experience it again because it felt so shocking and vital, so impossible to resist. You will know what I mean. We will understand each other. Perhaps we have different ways of describing the sensation but both of us believe it can be rediscovered, if the conditions are met.

One condition, one essential condition is not to try too hard, so I haven't gone to too much trouble, just a little trouble, in case you might think I hadn't made any effort at all. I'm wearing something nice but not too nice, not my favourite clothes; that would be taking too much of a risk. It's odd, going through my wardrobe trying to imagine how you might react to the colour of a dress, the texture of a skirt, the cut of a pair of jeans. I realise that I don't have many items of clothing that I like – even though I did buy for myself everything I own – so in the end the choice is fairly limited; but I must at least like what I'm wearing. To meet you in clothes I hated – the whole thing would be doomed before it started.

I hope too that you'll wear something I like a little, but not too much. I don't want to feel intimidated by your clothes. Or your appearance. Your appearance does matter, your voice too and your smell, everything about you matters and it's better you look quite nice but not perfect. Though I'm not remotely perfect you might like some things about me. My teeth are reasonable and as they are I smile quite a lot which makes me appear to be a cheerier person than I really am. I had my hair trimmed a couple of weeks ago so it's tidier than usual and I've found a rinse which replaces the grey with gold. Instead of dreary wintry tones, I now have summery glints through my otherwise unexceptional brown hair. With the help of some little inexpensive tubes of ammonia-free colour, I intend to go slowly blonde.

The flat I've cleaned and tidied more than usual and tarted up just a bit, but that's because I prefer it that way for myself; a clean house feels happier than a dirty one. I've watered the plants and sprayed their leaves so they glisten like wet skin. Would you prefer the fleshy succulents or feathery scented geraniums? Do you know that geraniums are named after crane bills? Will you find this fact as strange as I do? I considered buying cut flowers but buying flowers for myself always feels dismal or extravagant and neither mood is appropriate. Of course I changed the sheets and aired the bedroom so no stale odours or memories cling to the dusted walls. Lightness and space are required.

Of course you may not see my home. You may see nothing of my hand-sewn curtains, my scrubbed skirting boards, my pressed linen and polished woodwork, or the tidy pile of ongoing projects which keep me busy and hopeful most of the time. You may not see any of it, but if you do, I'd like it to be in reasonable order, I'd like to create a positive reinforcement of myself; if you are in my home you should be able to look around it and discover something – but not too much – of me.

My home; it has rather a lot of me in it, possibly too much. Too much of me has been put into paintwork and curtains and carefully chosen linen but you have to put yourself somewhere, don't you? I wonder if you ever feel you have put too much of yourself into objects which could manage quite well without your efforts. Have you, too, come to the conclusion that all these things around you will go on existing perfectly well without you taking any notice whatsoever? In colder moods I feel this is also true of people.

There is food, too, in case it's required, though sometimes food is just an added complication; accompanied consumption isn't always a pleasure. Too much attention can be paid to the wrong details, the handling of cutlery for example, all that clattering and clinking, the scraping chairs, all these hard inanimate objects to deal with when they are not the point at all. And the eating itself, the chomping and chewing and swallowing, the forkfuls of food to be negotiated from plate to mouth; perhaps eating with you is too intimate a beginning. Just in case, however, I set the table, checking the cutlery for streaks.

The food itself; if you didn't like my cooking, would it be something we could ignore or would it lessen the voltage ever so slightly, loosen the connections? Would we find ourselves shifting in our seats and turning our eyes to something other than each other? If there is food, perhaps it should be a meal which has nothing whatsoever to do with me or you, food which someone somewhere else has made, food which has been bought from some pretty boy or girl in a smart shop though that too can be dampening, the lack of effort, of care. Even if the food is too wonderful and exotic for me to have attempted to make, offering you precooked food seems a bit like a trick, like cheating and cheating is not attractive unless it is clever and dramatic, the way it's portrayed in films and plays. In life it's small, mean and grubby. As for the ridiculous image of me whizzing down the aisles of a supermarket, tossing precooked treats into my trolley, forget it.

The weather is good and it might be better to be outdoors although – as you'll have noticed – as soon as the sun shines, the world is crammed with courting couples and families milling around whatever green space they can find. All these other attached people might be a bit distracting. And the public setting might feel a bit contrived, a bit obvious; strolling amongst all these composite blocks of humanity, strolling a suitable single distance apart . . . perhaps not.

Thinking just gets in the way too, doesn't it, so once I've sorted myself out as much as I feel is enough but not too much, I try to slip you to the back of my mind, that little mental glory-hole. If you could look inside it, you'd see my most cherished moments all piled in together, squirrelled away like nuts for the winter, for dark days when the sky is a frozen blanket of boredom. Don't worry, I'm very greedy when it comes to cherished moments; I'll share them with nobody, not even you unless the unimaginable happens and we can also share unflattering clothes, bad haircuts, tummy upsets and toothache, bills and Christmas cards, cleaning the toilet – maybe then.

To think that such an amazing thing can happen in what can't, by the sounds of it, be a very interesting place. So much of nothing. The desert. A landscape of absence. But maybe these are the ideal conditions, maybe it takes a certain level of lack to reach the point where something really spectacular has to happen. Not that I'd want to share that kind of absence with you, I prefer to have all that out of the way first. I think you'd prefer that too so I've spent more time than usual dealing with dull things – with a reasonable amount of success. Dull things don't demand every nerve in your body to be alert; they require practice but not enthusiasm, or any other emotional response.

Friends have not been informed of this possible rendezvous. Already friends are too familiar with a number of those not-so-cherished moments in my life. You won't hear about those; there will be no sob stories, no confessions, above all not even the slightest hint of desperation because that would set up a different kind of circuit; one of sympathy, need. Friends have not been informed; I have managed to avoid any mention of you; I don't want to encourage their opinions and questions at this stage.

Is this a good thing for you at the moment?

Have you thought it through?

Have you thought how you will feel if it doesn't . . . ?

And friends would want all the details of you that I could provide; your looks, personality, politics, bank balance and, of course, marital status. Married or divorced are the only options. And there would be the inevitable if tacit speculation on the other intimate possibilities. Friends would knit all the facts together and build up their own identikit images of you, which I'm sure would be nothing at all like mine. They'd pass judgement. I don't mean to be hard on my friends but this is not the moment for listening to advice. I can go into a day feeling briefly, recklessly *engaged* in it and then I'm given some good advice and inside me a little crystal of hope is chipped away by doubts.

So I have been keeping you a secret. There have been times when I've been tempted to slip a *By the way* into interminable conversations about other people's husbands, wives, lovers, children, parents, when I've had the desire to mention ever so casually that even in the emotional desert which my industrious, single life has become, between you and me – given the right conditions – a spark, a literal visible electric charge just might – as can happen in other, similarly monotonous landscapes – leap across the void.

Handholds

Dilys Rose

Summer dusk. Three leggy, teenage girls, in silhouette, tilt backwards, bracing themselves against the steep slope of the hill. Laughing, they link arms, sway and stagger from side to side, kicking up their legs in a ragged chorus line. Above them, a flicker of late birds or early bats, a spatter of stars. Below, a single pale wave licks the shore. In the hills, the distant waterfall appears to flow upward, to grasp at the cliff like a huge silver hand. The evening smells of sun-dried seaweed, heather.

Where they are is barely a village; a spill of cottages clings to the curving bay, at the bend in the road a red, unvandalised telephone box is waist-deep in thistles and the shoreside campsite contains a solitary, unoccupied caravan. The single-track road whips around the fretted coastline, a wild reel of hairpin bends, rockfalls and sheer, deadly drops. In the distance, the headlights of a car wink and vanish, wink and vanish.

– It's nice here, says Sarah, but . . .
– But borin, says Dianne.

Dianne sighs loudly and chews a strand of her long, straight hair.

– Ah wish Glen wis drivin that car. Ah wish Glen wis beltin roon they bends tae meet me, says Dianne.
– Has Glen got a car?
– Nuh.
– Still. At least you can wish aboot somebody real, says Sarah.
– Ah miss him, says Dianne.
– It's only been four days.
– Ken. Feels like forever.
– Fuck off, says Sarah. Ye're makin me jealous. Ah've naebody tae miss. God, mibbe ah'll never huv naebody tae miss.

Above their heads the sky is inky. At the horizon, it's pink with thin mint-green lozenges of cloud.

– See they clouds, says Sarah. Ah fancy jeans that colour.
– God, says Dianne. Make yer arse look massive, a colour like that.
– Ken, says Sarah. But ah'd get noticed.

The third girl, Ciara, breaks the line, waves her arms above her head and jiggles her hips until she stumbles and falls face down on the hill, laughing helplessly. A harsh, strangled cry pierces the sun-scented evening.

– Nae m!ir Hooch for her, says Dianne. You hear me, Ciara, NAE MAIR HOOCH! Ye're pissed awready.
– OOOOHH!
–Ye can hear that all right, can ye no?

Ciara rubs her bluish, moonlit cheeks against the hillside, trying out the feel of grass, moss and heather. Her head feels hot, bubbly and everything is funny, everything. Lying on the grass is funny; it's like being on a boat, rocking. Dianne and Sarah shaking their heads at her is funny. The sea is funny. The car bobbing along the coast road is funny.

– Are we goin doon the beach, then? says Dianne.

– We could try the Pizza Hut first or the chippie. Or one of aw they discos doon the road, says Sarah. Or we could just eye up the talent on the streets.

– Fuck off, says Dianne.

– CAAAA, says Ciara.

– Aye, says Sarah. Car. Dianne wishes Glen wis in it.

– GEHHH?

– Get up ye deef bugger and come oan.

Like a traffic policeman, Sarah beckons to Ciara who stumbles obediently to her feet. The three girls walk, skip and stagger down the hill until they reach the short stretch of road which leads through the caravan site to the beach. A couple of munching sheep scutter in front of the girls, unable to decide what to do next.

– Stupit things, says Dianne.

– Pea brains, says Sarah.

– Shhhh EEEE, says Ciara.

She stretches out a hand to stroke one of their silly, bony noses but the sheep back off nervously; one of them slips into the ditch. Ciara laughs but she's sorry that the sheep don't trust her. She'd never hurt an animal. She loves animals, their warm, comforting smells, their uncomplicated eyes.

As they pass the empty caravan, Ciara stops, presses her face against the window. There's not much to see but the glass is cool against her skin and when she steps back, her mouth leaves a kiss mark. With a finger, she draws two mismatched eyes above the smudged impression of her mouth.

Dianne and Sarah race each other to the shore, trainers thudding softly and throwing up arcs of fine sand. Clownlike, Ciara follows, arms and legs flying out in all directions. When she reaches the water's edge, she birls round and round.

– Get back, says Sarah. Ye'll fa doon daein that. Ye'll get soaked and us two'll get the blame for it.

– Ye're wastin yer breath, says Dianne. She hastae see yer mooth. And ye huvtae say everythin dead slow.

– Ken, says Sarah. Ken. Ah've kent her as long as you, Dianne. But she willny look at ma mooth, will she? She willny fuckin stand still.

Dizzy, Ciara veers into the water; Sarah grabs her and pulls her back. Ciara's head jerks backwards and a thin harsh sound, like the cry of a gull flies from her mouth as she twists free from Sarah's grasp and hits out, a frenzy of elbows, fists, knees. Sarah gasps and groans, doubles up and clutches at her stomach.

– Fucksake, Ciara!

– Ye ken us, Ciara! Sarah roars. Ye've kent us since ye were wee. It's deep, the water. And ye cannae swim.

Sarah slowly straightens up, wipes the sand from her jeans.

– Ah'm sair all over.

The small waves make a secretive, whispering sound. Ciara clomps off along the shore, hugging herself. Nothing's funny anymore, nothing's a laugh, it's all gone dark and cold. Dianne and Sarah watch as, at the far end of the beach, Ciara disappears behind a jagged stack of rock.

– The rocks here are really really old, says Dianne. Millions and millions of years old. Folk say they're the oldest rocks in the world.

– Huv ye finished yir geography project, then? says Sarah.

– No yet, but there's tons of leaflets in the cottage. Ye widnae think there'd be much tae write aboot a wee place like this but there's stacksa stuff. Aboot rocks and deid folk, ken.

– But nae much need for an entertainments guide. *For visitors to the area, there are nice walks and nice walks. And if ye dinnae go in for walkin, fuck off.*

– That car cannae be far away now. Ah can hear it.

– So can ah.

Dianne and Sarah look up at the road expectantly.

Ciara begins to clamber up the smooth black rocks, still warm from the day's sun, warm as a body. Her hands feel for holds. In the hairline crevices, crisp, salty weed and striped cockles crackle beneath her fingers. She pulls a cockle loose and lets it roll onto her palm. In her ear, her inner ear, as the doctor explained, pointing to the chart – there's a clever wee cockley thing, the cochlea; inside the cochlea fluid swishes about like the sea in a shell, and the hearing hairs – all twenty thousand of them – send messages to the brain. Since she was wee and had the fever which made her eyes burn and zapped so many of those hearing hairs, she's seen the ear chart so many times she could draw it with her eyes closed.

With one ear flat against the rock, she can hear her fingernails scraping against it. The sound is very faint, as far away as the stars but she can hear it all the same. She's out of sight of her friends, alone with sea, rock and sky; safe, though she must be careful, her trainers are wet, her legs long and thin, too thin. Her mum's been worrying about her and since they've been here, she's been baking cakes; every day's been like a birthday. Before the holiday, they went shopping three days in a row and her mum bought her piles of new stuff, just like Dianne and Sarah's, exactly the same.

– Must be dead cosy in a caravan, says Dianne. Wouldnae like it on ma ain, ken, but if Glen wis here . . . if he had a phone ah could phone him.

– But he doesny huv a phone. Or a car. Or a job.

– Ken.

– Ye'll just huvtae enjoy missin him. Lie doon in yer bed at night and pretend he's yer pillow or somethin. That's whit ah dae, says Sarah.

– Eh?

– Pretend.

Ciara pulls herself on to a ledge where she can dangle her legs over the edge and look down. A clear patch of violet water swarms with flashing green strands like seaweed but too fast, too muscular; not seaweed but baby eels, pretty now, like little neon ribbons but she imagines all those babies stretching and swelling, filling up the water. Her mouth is dry. It doesn't make sense that drinking loads of Hooch makes you thirsty. Sliding back from the ledge, Ciara looks up at the sky, at the stars. She likes stars, the way they breathe out light and throw their shining rays across millions of miles of nothing. Sometimes they don't seem so far away . . .

She has climbed higher than she intended to. It's as far back down to the shore as it is up to the road, where the approaching car dazzles her with its headlights. Ciara blinks and shrinks back on to the ledge, out of sight. The car slows down, turns in through a gap in the dyke and draws up outside the caravan. A man and a woman get out, stretch their dark, bulky bodies and stride around aimlessly, like people who've been driving all day, then they wander to the edge of the grass, stop and stare at the sea, the way people do, just stand with their feet apart, bodies slack, gaze fixed on the sea, they stand and stare and do nothing for ages before making their way back to the caravan. The woman waves an arm in front of her face; midges. When the sun goes down midges blow about the campsite in clouds but out on the rocks where Ciara is crouching invisibly, it's mostly bloated flies and creepy crawlies.

The man moves from the shoulders; Ciara sees her dad in his thrusting shoulders, his jutting, angry chin. Her dad and Horse. Horse walks just like her dad, though she's never thought about it before. She doesn't ever want to see Horse again but she'd like to see her dad, if only he didn't get so cross with her. But when school starts, Horse will be there day after day, his jutting angry chin, his yellow teeth and sore looking skin . . . and her dad will tell her off for her table manners. She makes a noise when she eats, he says, she's like a pig at the trough, it makes him sick, the noise she makes, the noise that she can't hear.

On the beach, Dianne and Sarah are pretending to talk but they're not really concentrating on what they're saying; they're watching the couple in the caravan. Ciara can tell by the way their heads flick back and forth. Sometimes they look over at the rocks but they can't hear her; they're looking at the wrong places, at a route she might have taken, but didn't.

A yellow brick of light glows in the window of the caravan. The man bends into the boot of the car, pulls out bags and boxes and dumps them on the caravan step; the woman takes them inside. They move quickly and smoothly, without looking at each other, as if this fetching and carrying is a natural routine. And when the door of the caravan is closed, the curtain drawn, the man and woman pass back and forth, flat grey shadows, sometimes one at a time, sometimes sliding across each other, darkening at the overlap like layers of tissue.

Her mum is in the cottage on the far side of the bay, drinking wine with her best friends' mum, enjoying the peace and quiet and not wanting to think about what might happen when school starts again. Ciara doesn't want to think about school either. What's here now is enough, plenty. Dianne and Sarah are somewhere below her on the dark sand, maybe squinting into even darker crannies and wondering where she is hiding. The sea is swallowing the dregs of sunlight. Ciara is on a narrow ledge half-way up a stack, searching for handholds; in her head she can hear a deep, deep booming.

George Vafopoulos

The Mirror

I have never heard the footsteps
of my neighbour,
he who lives beyond the wall.
I have never received any signals of sound,
any message from his voice.
Yet he exists, I think,
as I exist.

A wall separates our two rooms.
Yet a small window exists
though hazy and crystalline as ice.

I pace up and down,
trying through the restless movement
of my own existence
to fathom the meaning of our situation.
Discretely I project my gaze,
to the next room
I seek to explore through the blur
the barrier
that room of my neighbour.

The rooms are much alike,
so much so
they could be duplicates of the same image.
The same portraits are on the walls,
the same sculpture
is placed on the table,
just as on mine.

I stand astonished
as I confront the eyes of my neighbour.
Stunned, astonished, he too faces me.

He is wearing my mask.
He has surrounded his shape
with my body.

Maybe he too is saying to himself:
"this man
has stolen my veneer".

And can it be possible, that my clothes
are really those of my neighbour?
Can I possibly be my own neighbour
encased within my own veneer?

So, who now can show me,
when the moment is crucial,
my real, my authentic self?
Who is there who in grim conviction
will confirm my existence,
debate or deny this apparent split?

Desolately I turn my face,
seeking an answer in vain.
On my table,
and I am no longer sure
if it is my own table,
the cheap sculpture
rears up before me,
a Sphinx of many meanings.

I pounce and grab at it
and hurl the sculpture
through the crystalline barrier
and search for an answer
in the shattering of the glass.

And now I confront the form of my neighbour,
darkened now, black and blank,
as if he has been blotted out.
And I touch to the delineations of my own, intact, face
to be sure of my self,
my own unbreakable unity.

The Well

As I reach over the mouth
of the dark well,
I recognise in horror
the dichotomy of my being.

As I turn away my face in fear,
edging away from the crucial chasm,
with one hand alone I search
and find one half of myself, only, intact.

I return once more and send my half-voice
echoing down the well,
becoming as one
with my other half-voice
achieving a composite phrase.

But,
below the inescapable chasm,
still water awaits
holding to the one disjointed image
of my divided face.

For how long must I curve
my severed body
over the well's dark edge?
how long must I delve so deeply
to recapture my other hand?

Will I have to stretch down to
the watery lips of this deep well,
to be capable, with one jump
to re-assemble
my inherent secret sense of unity?

But, can I
dare undertake such a venture?

Here is the jump.
Here is the unity.

The City

The city submerged in night.
A crammed cemetery with cumulative
high-stacked tombs of the dead,
who snort and snore.

How many here are aware,
of this deep and heavy snoring,
the leaden steps of the guards?

Seven soldiers pass.
The steps of seven soldiers echo
through to the hearts of the dead,
who, really, have yet to die.

I myself am the first.
The second too, it is I.
One and the same, I am the third and fourth.
I am the fifth, the sixth and the seventh.

I walk with fourteen feet,
I hold to the seven rifles
with fourteen hands,
rifles which could shatter
the uneasy eardrums of the sleepers.

I am one within seven souls.
I am bound by seven bands.
I prowl this night,
a sinister-polypod-insect,
I prowl the slick and clammy face
of this city as it snorts and snores.
touching gently beneath its many gaping nostrils,
unsettling its drowsy sentience.

The City Walls

"Carelessly with neither sorrow nor shame
they built the city walls, huge and broad around me
And now, here I sit, lost in despair".

So, the worthy Alexandrian
he sits and he despairs.
Maybe, among the decadent poets
this offers "some kind of solution".

But, "between the joy and myrrh of my life
and with deep reflection, with wisdom and sagacity,
I raised these walls around me by myself.

It may be that those who know so much more will say
that my wisdom amounted to no more than stupidity
We are all human after all and can all
be mistaken in our presumption of deep knowledge.

But, from the currency born of such intense study,
who among such learned men,
could barter with me for these simple joys:
to strongly stride and dance in my garden,
to scatter seed among the birds,
to take myself aside from myself,
and so to double my joy before my own eyes,
when, from upon high, from the apex of the blue-light dome,
the eye of God will see only me?

It may be that my own knowledge is too meagre to grasp
the implications of the Poet's despair
as his thoughts gnaw away at his mind,
that "he had so much to do on the outside".

But what is there to do on the outside
when so much awaits within you?

With the permission, always of the learned of course,
it is a sensible, wise action
to raise your own walls around you.

But, to allow others to construct your walls without your own due care,
and so "slowly, to be excluded from the outer world",
that is the jurisdiction of the gods, and this is the Fate,
I suspect, the cunning Alexandrian,
adopted in pretence, as if in despair
so that he did not feel that hand on his brow.

For he knew in himself, very well, what the sense was
in the saying "as much as you can: don't debase it
with too much congress with that outside world,
in too many preoccupations and aimless debate".

The River

This vast river
is no longer
the river of Babylon we knew.
It no longer carries the current,
where in days long gone we came
to swell its rolling waters
with the tear-fall of our bitterness.

This vast river
no longer admits
our tears to its depths.
They remain estranged, unassimilated
as unwanted droplets of oil
gathering only on the unwelcoming surface.

Now, as is appropriate,
I sit alone by the shore
shrouded in the unfeeling mask of serenity.
I sit alone,
observing,
contemplating
the funeral procession
of silent masts
passing down, down along the river.

Drifting vessels,
their faces irretrievably lost,
bearing the tolls of death,
carrying
the last immutable
forms of man.

In this malleable mirror
the immobile facsimile
of myself is poised.
If floats yet remains still
while every moment is changing,
my fellow traveller time,
yet, solely, to a finite juncture.

On the wet kerbside of the pathway
I sit, ready and waiting.
I am waiting for the barque
which will shatter
this unmoving facsimile of myself.
I am waiting for the barque
with its deficient chronometer
which will carry away
my final immutable form.

Translated from the Greek by Thom Nairn and D Zervanou

A Wee Fuckin Send Up

Ian Shearer

Ye hud tae watch his fists. Ah mean ye *hud* tae watch his fuckin fists. If ma faither wisnae holding his pint at 120 degrees the radge cunt wis liable tae lash oot. Ah had the scratches tae prove it. And there wisnae ony point greetin aboot it either. Ah'd go home minus ma teeth, a few pints o blood or wi a fuckin major internal organ missing and ma Ma wid literally pish hersel. Whit kin ye say?

Ye hud tae learn the hard way and if yers dinnae agree ah'll kick the shite ootae ye ya wee cunt, ma faither telt us. It paid amends in the long run. Ah mean, ye couldnae afford tae put a foot wrang when ye wir this far north – no unless ye didnae mind a startled grouse catapultin itsel ootae the heather an intae yer baws. Ah ken whit ah'm talkin aboot mind; ah've goat the bruisin tae prove it.

Anywey, ah'm in the pub wi ma faither an he's tellin us aboot this religious revival that's takin place in Scotland at the minute. Some o ma Pa's mates an fellow worshippers are wi us talkin aboot Scotland's spiritual thirst an how other great world religions didnae take their communion seriously enough, and ah'm gettin intae aw this, kindae gettin imbued with the spirit ken? So ah ask ma faither aboot holy orders.

Away tae fuck, ma Pa sais. You jist worry aboot the last orders. Drinkin's the religion up here, son, an ah'm the high priest if ye ken whit ah'm sayin.

Ma faither then telt us aboot his wee flock and how many hud given up everythin for their beliefs. Hud given up comfort, their families an friends tae wander in the wilderness o hostile cities, the subjects o violence an scorn. Many were imprisoned, an there were documented cases o demonic children settin fire tae them as they slept. Through unrestrained hunger an the blisterin caul they didnae relinquish their faith. In squalor they offered their libations. Ah'm almost greetin at this stage. Ah'm proud of ye Pa, ah telt um.

Ma faither goes for a pish an ah'm jist watchin ower his flock: Auld Jimmy MacArthur whae turned tae the religion fur comfort when his wife hud left um; Mickey Docherty whae turned tae the religion fur comfort when his wife hud married um; and wee Jimmy Cranky – whae hud eyes like bruised erseholes - whae wis sortae born intae a religious family. Ye hud tae admire them right enough. I couldnae help noticin their generosity either. It far ootstripped that o ither religious fanatics. Freely they parted wi their money. Clearly too generous, fur their bairns wir hungry an needed clothin.

The bell ringin heralded the end o the service. But ma faither's returned wi a tray – Ah love ma faither, ah really do. Ah ken we mightnae be the fuckin Walton family but this wis Scotland: ye could afford tae dispense wi the social niceties. Furthermore, ah cannae help feelin that ma Pa's gaunnae be proud o me yin day. Whae kens? Perhaps ah'll receive the callin masel. Ah really enjoyed the service the night an meetin the congregation. Mibbe ah'll tak ower ma faither's parish yin day, 'cause ah have a feelin ah could get intae this. Mibbe even die a martyr fur the cause, an then ma Pa couldnae help but be proud o us – end ae fuckin story.

The Minutes of the Meeting

Menzies McKillop

Whilst channel-hopping in the wee small hours with my house party of nymphettes, dollymops and hurdy gurdy men, in search of the Open University programme which would provide complete enlightenment, I chanced upon one of the Channel Four's excursions upon the wilder shores of love which depicted red wine running down a nude, young woman and being slurped near her nether parts by her male partner.

There were some sniggers from my house guests which I swiftly silenced by slapping my thigh-length rubber boots with the riding crop I carry with me at all times.

My guests said the only thing missing from the Channel Four tableau was a voice-over from the female oenologist in "The Good Food Programme" rabbiting on about the vintage.

Three pornographers renounced their calling after saying that the participants in the vignette looked like utter prats.

One feminist objected to the scene as exploitative and, when we poo-poohed her political correctness, said that the girls were often threatened, beaten and drugged, and, if we thought that was OK, then she didn't.

We said of course we didn't, but, in our lifetime, respectable patriots had killed tens of thousands of foreigners with less compunction than we strangle a rooster at Walpurgisnacht.

"Furthermore," added a defrocked bank clerk, "financial speculators and those with their darbies in pension funds cause infinitely more harm than bonking enthusiasts."

An elderly, male lecher misheard "bonking" as "banking" and asked if there were any money in writing spicy romances. He offered his services as a consultant if anyone wished to pen a lubricious novel.

A clapped-out, middle-aged seducer, hovering on the brink of renouncing his way of life and heading for a monastery, said that, when the fires of lust burned low, one should rejoice and not lash oneself into a sexual frenzy by reading erotic literature.

The matter was put to a vote (elsewhere recorded) and I brought in the absinthe and sandwiches cut into improper shapes.

There was a vote of thanks to the chairman's Mum for her help with the catering.

The Road to Wembley

Pete Fortune

– Here's your coffee.

– Thanks, Jim.

– Was that your boyfriend?

– My boyfriend?

– Yes. The big guy I saw coming out of your office earlier on. The boyfriend, was it?

– Donald? Good God, no, he's not my boyfriend.

– I kind of wondered . . . I mean . . .

– Actually, he was here to . . .

– Political nutter, isn't he?

– Not that I'm aware of.

– Yes. I remember him from years back. He used to sell one of those socialist rags on Saturday mornings. Down by the market. He used to stand there bawling and shouting like some kind of maniac.

– Did he indeed?

– He landed beside me on the bus to Wembley one year as well. Christ! From here to Carlisle I got nothing but socialism, socialism, socialism.

– Really?

– Yes. But I told him straight. Listen pal, I said, I'm not interested, right? I just want to go to Wembley, see Scotland give England a good hiding, and then get steaming drunk. So take your socialism pal, I said, and stuff it up your arse.

– That wasn't very subtle, Jim.

– No wonder. I couldn't have listened to that rubbish all the road to Wembley.

– Oh Jim!

– What?

– You've put sugar in my coffee again.

– Have I? Sorry. The new boy slips up again. Here, I'll make you another one.

– No need.

– Bloody hell. All the road to Wembley, eh? Up the revolution. Imagine it.

– I'd rather not.

– But he's not your boyfriend, eh?

– No.

– Glad to hear it. Suppose you've a boyfriend hidden away somewhere though, eh?

– Jim . . . eh . . .

– Yes?

– Be a good boy and fuck off home. You're fired. It's Donald who pays your wages actually. And mine. As for the socialist revolution – well – seems he took your advice, eh?

Joanna Ramsey

In Memory of George Mackay Brown

Evening Visit

In your room dark and heavy with books
firelight moves upon the walls.

Your lamp inverts its triangle of light
and pictures hang in the mysterious shadows.

There are always flowers on the table
from a Deerness garden,
a blue bowl of fruit, a cup, a plate.

You go to make the tea and I hear you
singing 'Bread of heaven' as the kettle boils.

We talk of everything except your work,
exchanging the small details of our lives.

Later I walk home beside the cold black sea,
the sky's rim shivering with Northern Lights.

The Guest

Christmas Eve tomorrow.
Inside the house a smell of candles
and cinnamon; outside
the moon-glazed sea
and clouds snow-laden,
a light in every window
but yours –

At supper, at our table,
shall I set you a place?
Will you sit amongst us,
a benign Banquo's ghost?

After George

How is it possible
that dwindling light
falling on broken stones
should so wring the heart?

The harbour water ebbs
unflawed by any trace
of breeze.

Gleam and reflected gleam
merge indistinguishable
in the stillness.

Your death distils
all things, all beauty
to this one pure ache.

Images

After you died I searched for you
in the newsprint words.
You were distant, changed; a stranger
staring out in monochrome, jaw jutted
against a skyline carefully composed.
Once a smile flashed from the page
but still you evaded capture.
You used to sing to my daughter.

I visited your house
but it was stripped;
nothing but dust and an old coat.
I pressed my face against it,
seeing your smile in the doorway.

I looked for you at Warebeth:
lapwings cried into the silence;
the stones said nothing, gave no name.
An empty jar stood beside the place.
We walked there once, the sun
slipping behind invisible hills.

I hunted for you everywhere,
opening a drawer to find your letters,
neatly put away against this day.
I held them in my hands a while,
still folded: they will keep.

I woke each day, forgetting –
only to taste again the souring fruit.
I want you back; I want to keep
one moment, to possess you.

I dip again into the pool of images,
and catch you: holding my hand
in a taxi, rain on the window –
you lie gleaming for a second
in the net.

Arseny Tarkovsky

Photography

To O M Grudtsova

A subtle wind will buffet your heart,
And headlong away you'll fly,
But love that's been captured on film
Seizes the soul by the sleeve,

And, bird-like, steals from oblivion
A single grain at a time,
Not letting itself be scattered,
Even if, living, you've killed it –

Not whole, but in some little part,
In silence and sleep, you relive your love –
As though in an otherworld meadow
You wander.

If the camera's angel unfurls his wings
To embrace your world,
Then everything visible, breathing and dear
Repeats once more its trajectory.

The Ring at the Door at Night

Why have you put up your chain
For the night, like a prisoner,
Ivan Ivanych? I'm standing outside
Your door while you sleep.

Killer-night, in black rubber shoes,
Is on its way to get me.
I'm ringing your bell to beg for shelter –
I can tell you don't want to help.

You've blocked up your ears with cotton wool
And hear the muffled ringing through your sleep.
Damn him, you say, let him scrabble about,
You think it's a sign of the times!

You don't believe in hell or look for paradise –
And if they don't exist, then what's the point?
Whatever will you say if I stain
Your threshold with my blood?

How can you leave for work at half-past-eight
To earn your healthy salary
When you've betrayed your brother and your friend?
How can you just go walking down the street?

That street is turning black with blood,
The cross is daubed on every house.
"What are you going on about?" I hear you say,
"I didn't get this sleep for free – I've earned it."

Invitation to a Voyage

Let's go, get ready, let's pack the cases,
I've stood you plenty of tickets from fate,
At last we'll visit my faraway countries,
Towns like Blessed Childhood and Family Graves.

If you like, we can visit the town of Loving Terror,
Centifolia City and Open Grand Piano,
A lovely ash-butterfly flits above each district.
And we mustn't forget old Insult-Town:

There stands the armoured train tarpaulinned at the station,
My brother gives me lessons on firing a revolver.
Then in Music-Town children play sonatas by Clementi,
But the streets are deserted, alien to the soul.

Moist salt will assist you in divining all the distances,
And from the grass you'll read that at earth's edge –
Beyond the steppe – the sea exhales in freedom
And ships are anchored in the bay.

If something can be salvaged from my promises,
I'll recompense you with the towns
Of Smoke at Sea from Steamships,
And Daybreak on the Ocean.

"But in your towns," you'll say, "I'm bored to death.
How can I live in Music, where there's nobody to love?
As for dawn on a sea which curves at the horizon, –
I had a blue sea of my own – I don't need yours."

Untitled

A battery stood below this hill;
We heard nothing, but here the thunder rumbled.
Corpses are lying everywhere beneath the snow,
Waving their hands in the frosty air.
The signs of death freeze us to the spot.
Today as other days the freshly slain arise
And soon the birds will sing.

Untitled

My stupid dream, foolish drowsiness,
Forever bowing and scraping by the house,
Peeping at me when I least expect it,
Always needing questions and encouragement,
A clear conscience and a flattering caress . . .
In no hurry to step into the light.

What have my early years left me? –
Those early years of radiant waters,
White sand and grass of the steppe –
Bitter, ringing, malevolent and arid,
Beneath the blueness, misty at the edge?
Only these empty words.

Where is my power over earth and sky?
I tried to be fastidious with my daily bread,
Letting the wolf drink from my cupped hands in the heat,
Feeding the cuckoo a grain of corn in his hunger;
And still I don't rest my head on the pillow
As if I hadn't spent all my strength,

As if your speeches gave me comfort,
My shoulders not bowed down with grief,
As if I hadn't learned my lesson
And didn't know how deaf you are,
My stupid dream, foolish drowsiness,
My stupid dream, oh stupid – my dream.

Translated from the Russian by Virginia Rounding.

The Packaging of Gaelic Poetry

Wilson McLeod

The role of translation is fundamental to contemporary Gaelic poetry, for matters have reached the stage where hardly any volume of Gaelic poetry is published without an accompanying *en face* English translation. This phenomenon has intensified in recent years, seemingly unnoticed, with the English words steadily increasing in visibility and prominence. The Gaelic aspect of this "Gaelic" poetry is becoming ever more marginal and the English ever more dominant, an overshadowing that comes close to blotting out Gaelic poetry entirely.

Consider the three new collections of Gaelic poetry published by Polygon over the course of the last eighteen months: Meg Bateman's *Aotromachd agus dàin eile* (Lightness and other poems), aonghas macneacail's *Oideachadh Ceart* (A Proper Schooling) and Rody Gorman's *Fax and other poems*, which ironically but tellingly does not even have a Gaelic title. The spines of these books bear their English titles only, and the back covers give descriptions of the book and short biographies of the authors in English only. All the poems in all three volumes are given in Gaelic and in English, with the English on the eye-catching right, with both languages printed in the same typeface. The English texts are not described as translations of the Gaelic – their presence is not explained at all – and no translator is identified: one may assume that the poets themselves provided the English texts as well as the Gaelic.

Presenting this poetry in such a fashion has serious consequences. The two texts can be understood as two functionally equivalent versions of the same thing, the same ideal 'original' – the difference being essentially one of format, like the difference between the compact disc or vinyl version of 'the same' record. Or the two texts can be seen as two distinct and different compositions, two 'originals' of essentially identical legitimacy and importance, each the fruit of the author's labour, and not necessarily dependent on each other. What no longer seems a realistic interpretation is the most obvious one – that the Gaelic texts are the originals, and their English translations are ancillary and mediated compositions in whose production "something has been lost." aonghas macneacail, recently honoured as Scottish Writer of the Year by a panel of judges unable to read Gaelic, gave a simple but incisive illustration of the process at work: "They took the translations at face value and read them as workable poetry".

Given that there are a hundred readers of English in Scotland for every reader of Gaelic, the consequences of this shift are grave. Once the English version is accepted as free-standing and fully valid in its own right, the Gaelic version/counterpart/original, once visible at the margin, is arguably pushed beyond the horizon altogether. A short newspaper review of Meg Bateman's collection, for example, gave almost no indication that the book contained Gaelic poems: the word Gaelic was nowhere used and the quoted lines, the cited poem titles, and the title of the book itself were

150

given in English only. The sole hint was to describe the collection in brackets as "bilingual," but the language in question was not identified, and the uninformed reader would not know it from Bateman's name (as one might, for example, from macneacail's).

A similar understanding was apparent in the recent plagiarism scandal in which a 'poem' of Bateman's and several of Derick Thomson's were allegedly appropriated by the Cornish teacher Alan Kent. The poems that appeared under Kent's name were in English, and the controversy arose because the wording of these English texts were substantially identical to that of certain English text that appeared in the 1991 group anthology *An Aghaidh na Sìorraidheachd: Ochdnar Bhàrd Gàidhlig* (In the Face of Eternity: Eight Gaelic Poets) and Thomson's 1994 *Smeur an Dòchais* (Bramble of Hope). Though Kent's conduct certainly cannot be justified, the charge of plagiarism is evidently premised on a view of Bateman's and Thomson's English words as primary compositions with an integrity in their own right, distinct pieces of the authors' property. Would the crime have been worse if the Gaelic versions – it no longer seems safe to say "the originals" – had been stolen? Would it have been different at all?

If not entirely new, problems of this kind have now reached an unprecedented stage of seriousness for in recent decades there has been a distinct shift in the way bilingual editions of Gaelic poetry have been prepared. It was once the prevailing practice to translate only some of the poems in a collection, and to place these in the back of the book rather than *en face*. Domhnall MacAmhlaigh's important 1967 volume *Seòbhrach às a' Chlaich* contains 78 poems, of which only 27 are translated in the back; Ruaraidh MacThòmais' *An Dealbh Briste* (1951) and *Saorsa agus an Iolaire* (1977) gave translations of 20 of 50 and 20 of 42 poems respectively, again clustered at the end. Significantly, there were no English titles for these volumes and the poets did not provide translated forms of their own names.

During the 1970s, a more thorough bilingualism was taking root, though the Gaelic remained clearly privileged over the English. The 1972 anthology of the work of Somhairle MacGill-Eain/Sorley MacLean, *Reothairt is Contraigh* (Spring Tide and Neap Tide), and the landmark 1976 anthology *Nua-Bhàrdachd Ghàidhlig* (Modern Scottish Gaelic Poems) gave translations for every one of the poems, but printed them in italics, on the less prominent left side. The introduction to *Nua-Bhàrdachd Ghàidhlig* (Modern Scottish Gaelic Poems) appeared in Gaelic and English, Gaelic first in roman type, English second and in italics, and the book jacket was bilingual. Yet by 1991, which saw the appearance of the next major group anthology, *An Aghaidh na Sìorraidheachd*, this careful, Gaelic-privileging bilingualism had been superseded, so that the English text rated roman type and the right side of the page, but there was no Gaelic on the back cover, no Gaelic introduction, no Gaelic biographies of the poets.

This trend towards increasing and privileging the English content of these bilingual collections has been accompanied by a noticeable reduction in the number of Gaelic-only collections published and in the proportion of monolingual to bilingual volumes. Until the 1980s, such collections appeared with some regularity, but this flow, trickling though it was, seems to have stopped almost entirely, with the consequence that there is now practically no contemporary Gaelic poetry (outside *Gairm*, the one Gaelic magazine) that appears independently and stands on its own without an English *doppelgänger*. At the same time, of course, there is almost no literary criticism in Gaelic, and the sole general work on the subject of Gaelic poetry, Derick Thomson's *An Introduction to Gaelic Poetry* (1974), is remarkable for not containing a single word of Gaelic poetry, relying exclusively on English translations. There is thus no space in which Gaelic poetry exists on its own, to be considered and assessed on its own terms: from the first moment of exposure to the world it is over-shadowed and usurped. Things have long been bad; but it is nevertheless important to notice when bad things get worse.

In this respect, the Scottish situation can be distinguished from the position in Ireland, where the politics and symbolism of translating Irish poetry have not only been noticed but debated. Although bilingual, English-privileging editions of the Scottish style are becoming increasingly visible in Ireland, the bulk of collections appear in Irish-only format, with translated versions coming only after a reasonable breathing period, and a poet like Biddy Jenkinson can choose not to have her poetry translated at all. (A noteworthy phenomenon, too, is Coiscéim's practice of issuing collections of Scottish Gaelic poetry – by Meg Bateman, Maoilios Caimbeul, and most recently Màiri NicGumaraid – with accompanying Irish translation).

Of course, the number of readers of Irish exceeds those of Gaelic by a factor of three if not ten, and among the folk who buy poetry books the disparity is probably greater still. The condition of Gaelic poetry in Scotland can be understood as a reflection of and metaphor for the decline of the language itself. The Gaelic speech community has shrunk by three quarters over the last century, from a population substantially monoglot to a bilingual population dominant in Gaelic, to a bilingual population ever more obviously dominant in English. With English being universal, Gaelic is no longer needed for communication, indeed no longer *needed* at all. In a sense, then, packaging Gaelic poetry in such a way as to push it into a kind of existential limbo is only appropriate. The utilitarian logic seems impeccable: why bother with the expense of printing Gaelic introductions when everyone can read English? Why bother with printing Gaelic versions of the poems? And the inevitable last question: why bother with Gaelic at all?

If one believes that the language is not destined to suffer an imminent and justified death, that it deserves to exist and survive, and, most specifically, that it deserves to be studied, learned and used, then it is unacceptable to have Gaelic poetry presented as an irrelevant decoration to an English text of equal validity and greater importance. The publishing practices of even recent decades show a range of options – printing translations in less privileged typeface in less privileged places, translating some poems in a collection but not all, publishing some collections without translation. The problem is fundamentally a political one: today's Gaelic-denying approach needs to be recognised and named for what it is and what it says.

Being Gaelic, and otherwise

Aonghas MacNeacail

I was born into a particular language community and brought up as a natural – i.e. monoglot – child of that community. Neither my parents nor I had any reason to modify my circumstances. Does a peaty stream have any reason to turn alkaline or vice versa? At the age of five, I went to school where it was the task (and bounden duty) of my teachers, who came from the same language community as myself, to introduce me to another linguistic mode which would become, effectively, the monoglot means by which I would recognise and communicate with the wider world including their pedagogic selves, my classmates, our reading material and every other contact then possible.

I'm talking about a time when there were perhaps five private telephones in our village including the merchant's, the doctor's and the telephone exchange equipment which occupied our local postmaster's front room. With no mains electricity supply we listened to the radio only to receive what was considered essential – news, weather forecasts, Scottish Dance Music Programmes, religious services, all in English, and the very occasional programme of formal, piano-accompanied Gaelic song (as approved by Marjory Kennedy Fraser and sung by tried and tested National Mod Gold Medal Winners, introduced, of course, in English). There wasn't much access to the indigenous demotic outside the home. Even the Gaelic church services to which I, like most of my peers, was dragged with some reluctance, were conducted in an 'elevated' register based on a fusion of Argyll and Perthshire dialects which had been evolved and ossified two or three centuries ago.

We may have been taught the occasional Gaelic song by peripatetic music teachers who visited our school on an occasional basis. I know the one who taught us in the upper primary was a Gaelic speaker, interested in participating in the local Mod and therefore prepared to introduce us to songs suitable for that event. Our primary school headmaster, being an elder in the Free Church, recommended the Gospel according to John, chapter 1, in the parallel text Gaelic/English New Testament with its incantatory repetitions as a good introduction to the reading of Gaelic.

Otherwise, I have no recollection of any educational access to Gaelic until secondary school where I was able to choose between my own native tongue and a modern European language. Given such a background it should hardly be surprising that my class of native-speaking Gaels was taught the rudiments of the grammar and introduced to the literature, of our own language, by a fellow native speaking teacher through the medium of English.

My first attempts at writing poetry were, inevitably, in English. As far as school was concerned Gaelic poetry died out around the beginning of the 19th century. It would, indeed, be true to say that I found my voice as a poet, in English, just around the time I was being introduced to the Gaelic poetry of the 20th century and the realisation that we had, in the works of Sorley MacLean, Iain Crichton Smith, Derick Thomson and others, a continuing tradition that was not only alive but vibrantly trailblazing in tune with its past while responsive to all the intellectual currents and cross-currents of the wider world. If I then began to write in Gaelic, as well as in English, it was not because I thought I had anything important to say in my own language. There was an element of curiosity combined with a sense of obligation about my early attempts, but, essentially, I considered them a channel for expressing my more *personal* prosodic thoughts. English remained the language for more 'seriously' addressing the wider world.

Thus matters might have continued had I not been invited to accept a Writing Fellowship at Sabhal Mor Ostaig, the Gaelic College, in 1977, before it had become a fully functional educational establishment. At that stage I had no collection published – only a scattering of English poems in a few magazines, a share in a new Gollancz anthology of emergent writing, *Poetry Quintet* (in English, of course), and a small but steady stream of poems – some, on reflection, very rough indeed – in the Gaelic quarterly, *Gairm*.

Although there were, as yet, no full-time students at Sabhal Mor, it was nevertheless a place conducive to study, which was just as well for me as I found myself, immediately, in the anomalous position of holding a community-orientated post with no community to address. I also found myself quite unable to write in either language for several months. What rescued me was the existence in a building undergoing restoration (and, as it had formerly been a traditional Scottish farm square, reinvention) of a small library of books devoted to Gaelic culture and Celtic culture in general.

For the first time in my life, with no one looking over my shoulder – other than to answer my questions – I was able to immerse myself in the entire question of who I was and where I came from right back to the mythical Scythians and, to a point of dizziness, beyond. So many questions presented themselves, although, often the answers came first in the form of information gleaned from my reading. The questions tended to focus on the generally low status afforded to Celtic cultures in our society (Teuchters, Taffs and Paddies, perjoratively expressed, were inevitable parts of the vocabulary I had lived with). The material I discovered presented a people rich in art and industry who learned how to process iron, to extract salt from the variety of sources (e.g. Hallstadt), to use wheeled vehicles as weapons of war (and, I'd like to hope, as carriers in peace), who'd traded as equals with the great empires of Greece and Rome. The list goes on and includes Nora Chadwick's chapter on literature in her Penguin book on the Celts which begins, "Celtic literature is the oldest literature North of the Alps".

Much of that earlier literature may be subsumed into the oral tradition, but it's still with us, and the practitioners of today represent a continuum that stretches back at least 2000 years. Having been brought up with the implicit attitude and assumption that all our remoter and some of our more recent forebears were illiterate, uncultured and unregenerate savages, it was and remains salutary to consider that I belong to a culture at least as old and distinguished as the so-called "Classics" of Greece and Rome.

The Gaelic I now use is the product of an act of reclamation. The appointment to Sabhal Mor Ostaig brought me back to my native community after more than half a life spent in non-Gaelic city environments. My fluency in my native language had become decidedly rusty. And there wasn't much point in being there if I couldn't tap into the experience of my fluent colleagues, to improve my own ability to communicate with other Gaels. Once I'd begun the process of using the language as a means of 'serious' communication, (in the sense of formal broadcasting, journalistic and literary, as distinct from everyday, colloquial, expression), while seeking to accommodate both constituencies, I knew that the process of renewal and experiment can never end – whatever language, or dialect, you choose. Those who see Gaelic as immune to, beyond, or protected from, such exposures are engaged in an act of denial which can only ultimately destroy what they would most dearly wish to conserve.

If I have dealt at some length with my own personal history, which may also be familiar territory to others who have had similar experiences in relation to Gaelic, Scots or any number of marginal languages, I hope it will, at least, make clear that my native language is a matter I could never be indifferent to or blasé about. It must also be obvious that my generation lives in a fully bilingual and bicultural world. The fact that we are fluent in English doesn't make us any less rooted in our Gaelic psyche. We can laugh and weep with equal facility in either language.

It should also be remembered that, as good little Christians, we were introduced at an early age to Biblical stories that had their origins in languages and geographies far removed from our own. Nobody questioned their validity as literature or as presumed truth. Nobody warned us that we wouldn't be able to taste the full nuanced richness of Hans Christian Andersen or the Brothers Grimm because we were not able to have access to them in their original forms. The translations are themselves readily accepted as accurate representations of great literature.

The same criteria stand for adult literature. I have never heard anyone declare that we cannot assess the greatness of Tolstoy because we can't read *War and Peace* in the original, or Stendhal, or Gunther Grass, or Juvenal. How do we know Chekhov or Ibsen are great dramatists? What about Baudelaire, Dante, Neruda, Holub, etc? We buy their works in translation only – or in parallel text, which allows us at least to play guessing games with sound or meaning. But we know the meaning, don't we, because we trust the translator to have conveyed it as accurately and sensitively as humanly possible. And what are we to make of Samuel Beckett who wrote most of his original texts in French, a language not his own, *then* translated them into English? Why should anyone be surprised if the Gaelic goose demand the same privileged sauce as such illustrious ganders – that we also be judged without prejudice?

It may, however, be useful, from time to time, as a Gaelic writer to trace one's own individual relationship with the choice of languages made, in terms of essential creativity, commercial necessity, or simple emphatic need to say "I am thus, and this is how I say it". When I start a poem in Gaelic, it stays Gaelic. Afterwards I'll set about translating it into English. If the triggering thought drives me toward an English word or phrase, the poem will be written in English, and not translated. Because I have worked creatively in English even before I did in Gaelic, I see no problem in constructing the translation as an entity which ought to work as an independent poem in English, different in a variety of ways, but every bit as realised and, I'd hope, as effective as the original. Nor do I see this reworking as a dilution of the strength or integrity of the original.

Why a poem should manifest itself in one language or the other, I cannot really say. I do know that, having itself apparently decided on which side of the linguistic blanket to be born, the poem demands to be articulated in that particular language. If it takes shape in Gaelic, that's because what it has to say can, for me, only be said (in the sense that a thought shapes itself into words) in Gaelic. So, if you want to have access to all the nuances and resonances of sound and sense, you'll have to come to terms with the original. I will, however, do my damnedest to weave as much into the translation as is possible of that original: and I do so because I believe it is, at present, not only possible but imperative for Gaelic poets to communicate with a wider audience than our own language community can provide.

That very question of numbers is a crucial factor. At the basic economic level, it makes our books more viable and we, surely, are as entitled as any other serious writers to seek viability. By doing so, we also offer yet another door, however narrow, for those who are curious about Gaelic to peer in, and perhaps eventually to step into our world. It should also be remembered that a high proportion of Gaels, particularly older Gaels, cannot comfortably read their own language. In such circumstances it has to be said that the mere act of writing in Gaelic, no matter how instinctive or involuntary, is a political act, a gesture of defiance against a history that has conspired relentlessly against the language. And why shouldn't we argue that translation is also, and overtly, a political act, in that it offers a reminder to the outside world that "We are still here"?

There are still those around us who, by their willing declarations of ignorance concerning Gaelic culture, would confine it to a ghetto beyond whose walls they need not look. There are those among us who would keep it behind equally high walls, pristine pure and insulated from the outside world. I believe that if it didn't trumpet its vitality against both the wall constructed from without and the one built from within, Gaelic would wither inexorably, and inevitably, into extinction. But we know there is a great deal of goodwill toward Gaelic in the wider community already. We have to reach out toward it with the richness and diversity we still have to offer, and beguile it in, not snub it.

I am happy to let my poems speak for themselves as poems, but should the translations come alive in the readers' imagination, I think I'm entitled to entertain the possibility that some of those readers will be prompted by sheer curiosity to enquire more deeply into the language. I know that's the effect that Ordnance Survey maps of the Scottish Highlands have had on many climbers, that Runrig have had on many of their non-Gaelic legions of fans in Scotland and abroad, and that Sorley MacLean has had on a great many lovers of literature who have felt it was imperative that they learn Gaelic in order to read his work in the original.

Gaelic literature is currently in an astonishingly healthy state. New young poets are appearing from the native Gaelic communities and there are those from 'outside' committing themselves to the language as a creative (and/or polemic) medium with the same rigorous urgency as Meg Bateman and others have done before them.

It's perhaps just a little curious that Wilson McLeod takes Gaelic writers to task for representing their works in an accessible form to English readers, as his own essay is, essentially, a reworking of an article he wrote in Gaelic (for the Gaelic page which now features regularly in *The Scotsman*). He raises a number of interesting questions, some of which I hope I have answered adequately, and some which must, of necessity, be responded to in detail.

At a technical level, I am genuinely puzzled by his reference to the "eye-catching right [-hand page]" – I'd have assumed that conditioning would have drawn the eye to the left-hand side of the left-hand page. I am also not sure how to read the statement "Aonghas MacNeacail, recently honoured . . . by a panel of judges unable to read Gaelic, *gave a simple but incisive illustration of the process at work* (my italics): 'They took the translations at face value and read them as workable poetry.'"

If the italicised passage is to be read as an inference that my words support the argument that presenting Gaelic originals in parallel with English versions is detrimental to those same originals, then I must protest that what I said has been taken out of its context, to suggest the opposite of what I intended. Yes, the judges clearly took the translations at face value, as I would wish them to have done, but Donny O'Rourke, convener of judges, also clearly expressed the view that the originals, being the originals, were presumed by them to be even better. Whether that is the case or not, I am content in the knowledge that they are different.

I know that Wilson McLeod, though not a native speaker, has been engaged in reclaiming the language of his ancestors, and more power to his elbow, fist and shoulder! We need many more like him, for Gaelic, despite many signs of apparent revival, still hangs on the edge of extinction unless it can generate new speakers at adult as well as infant levels. We have lived for far too long with *Mì-rùn Mór na Gall* (The Great Ill-will of the Lowlander) which still lurks in some dark corners. It seems a pity, however, when a Gael, as Gael, has been honoured due to the generous-spirited open-mindedness of a panel of "Lowlanders" that the occasion should be seen as an opportunity for nit-picking disputation. Rather it should be an uncluttered celebration that a Gaelic literature survives at all, let alone one vigorous enough to win national awards. There are, after all, many other questions that can be raised concerning the status of Gaelic culture, and of Gaelic generally, in the world it inhabits.

Why not, for example, criticise those magazine editors, mostly furth of Scotland, who, if they accept Gaelic work at all will *only* publish the translation, leaving their readers with no sense of the originals? Why not indict the editors of so-called "National", i.e. British, magazines and anthologies which by exclusion deny the very existence of the older British cultures, and, for that matter, many of the newer?

Why target writers and their publications when we live in an environment where, for all the excellence of programmes produced, there is no truly adequate Gaelic broadcasting service on radio *or* television? Where Gaelic medium education, though it has done much good, remains in the perception of public, politicians and educational professionals, essentially peripheral to "mainstream" schooling, subject to the vagaries of capping limits, ethnic selection. Where there is a shortage of resources the wider community can take for granted such as audio and video material, comprehensive modern dictionaries, thesauruses, etc. (which would also be to the benefit of Gaelic writers) and where the language still has no legal status in its own homeland. Deal with those issues first; then we can enjoy the luxury of debating how Gaelic writers should present their works to the wider world.

Bilingual Poetry

Peter France

The Edinburgh Festival is full of plays in foreign languages with sur-titles or simultaneous translation for those (often the great majority of the audience) who need them. In the same way, it is common practice now for foreign poets to be published in bilingual editions, irrespective of whether prospective readers know both languages. Given the famed insularity of British culture, such awareness of the Other seems something to be welcomed, a step towards the wished-for state in which we find our identity not only by being rooted in a monolingual culture, but also by our ability to exist between cultures, between languages. But what does it mean in practice?

Different types of bilingual edition serve different purposes. One variant is the volume where a functional prose version sits modestly at the bottom of the page or at the back of the book, a crutch for readers who know some of the foreign language or are trying to learn it. (At the same time, these plain versions can be impressive in their own right, just as the 'literals' provided by linguists for poets to work on are sometimes sharper and more interesting than what they later become.)

At the opposite extreme, it is the translation which relegates the original to the back of the book. In such cases the original seems to serve partly as a guarantee of authenticity. It is also a reminder that we are reading a translation – and after all, it's likely that all translations of poetry, even in monolingual editions, are read in a rather different way from non-translated poetry, with a greater awareness that there is something else is lurking behind the text we read. Even so, in such cases the translation has to take its place in the host culture as a poetic text in its own right. It may be worse than the original, it may be better, but it will certainly be different. And it won't harm the original which remains available for those who can read it, whether they are many or few, and for further translation.

Then we have the edition with two texts on facing pages, probably the norm today. This may serve a similar function to the previous two variants, but it is also, at best, an invitation to readers who understand the original language to read both at once, stereoscopically as it were, to compare, perhaps to admire or regret, but above all, to reflect on the difference between languages and cultures. One of the most translated modern poets, Baudelaire, is characteristically presented in this way – and of course an even better way of doing it is to offer not just one but several translations of the same poem.

This way, translation, far from being just a pale copy, becomes a source of new insight. In his famous essay, 'The Task of the Translator', the German critic Walter Benjamin writes of the way in which the translation ideally points not to an 'original' but to something that exists beyond either the original or the translation, a primal language. Less mystically, the contemporary French poet Yves Bonnefoy writes, as Pasternak had written before him, that while the poem cannot be translated, poetry can. In other words, the translator can give voice in the new language to an impulse which is never fully realised.

The problem raised here, as it is in the case of Gaelic-English bilingual collections, is "what is an original"? It might seem obvious: a poet writes a poem in his own tongue, and someone comes along afterwards and turns it into another, more or less faithfully, more or less successfully. In such a common-sense view, the original is the real thing, the translation something secondary and almost always inferior, the handmaiden (often, as Montaigne's translator Florio put it, the translation, being necessarily "defective", is "reputed female"). But modernists and post-modernists have muddied the waters. Jacques Derrida and his followers cast doubt on the very notion of an authentic original presence in speech or writing, and the provocative Jorge-Luis Borges argues that translation, because it comes after, is more knowledgeable and hence better than the original.

Whatever one thinks of these paradoxes, there is one practice which does cast doubt on the normal original-translation hierarchy: self-translation. This seems to be the norm for Gaelic poets (less so for Irish ones), but there are plenty more examples, some of them famous: Brodsky working by himself or with English-speakers to make his Russian poems English, the South African novelist André Brink rewriting his Afrikaans novels in English, Samuel Beckett turning French texts into English and vice versa.

In the case of Brodsky, even if the English texts have an oddity and originality which make them more than shadows of an original, the Russian remains in charge, and the translation provides an entry to the culture that Brodsky was trying to adopt. Brink, who chose to write in Afrikaans for political reasons, as part of the liberation struggle, enters the much wider world of English-speaking culture through his translations; in doing so, he apparently works on both texts interchangeably, rethinking and 'refeeling' them in the framework of different languages. As for Beckett, his English and French versions of *Waiting for Godot* or *All that Fall* are equally marvellous pieces of writing, and it seems irrelevant that the first was originally in French, the second in English. In all these cases, ideally, we should be reading both versions, neither should destroy the other. One hopes that this is how the collections of Sorley MacLean or aonghas macneacail are read by those who have both Gaelic and English.

But if the publishing of Gaelic in bilingual translations is a tricky issue, it is no doubt because it raises questions of the relation not so much between texts as between cultures. This links up with the growing discussion in recent years about the political significance of translation. There is by now a well-established school of thought that sees in translation a kind of aggression or colonisation. Far from being a handmaiden here, the translator is a raider, bringing home booty which is then made available like tea or sugar to consumers in the dominant cultures. Titles such as Eric Cheyfitz's *Imperialism: Translation and Colonization from 'The Tempest' to 'Tarzan'* (1991) tell their own story – the argument being that Western discourse colonises by imposing its own preconceived patterns on the Other. On the other hand, there is a school of thought, based in South America, which praises translation as 'cannibalism', giving new life to the dead by assimilating and remaking it.

It's a tricky question, especially for an English-speaker who is born into the role of coloniser. I have translated, via Russian, an anthology of poetry much of it ancient popular poetry, produced in Chuvashia, a small, Turkic-speaking country in the east of the Russian Federation, and in doing so I have no doubt assimilated it to certain English-language traditions while trying to keep it strange. The Chuvash themselves have recently enriched their own tradition by poetic translation: MacDiarmid's "ae weet forenicht i' the yow trummle" or the city poetry of Edwin Morgan offer them the shock of the unfamiliar as did the poems of Rimbaud or Eluard. At the same time, they welcomed the translation of their own poetry into English, French, Italian, German and Swedish – the anthology is their 'visiting card' to the wider world, seen as essential to their survival. It is perhaps significant that the anthology has not been translated into the language of their powerful neighbour, Russia. Even if it were issued in a bilingual Russian-Chuvash edition, however, the Chuvash language seems well enough rooted to survive as a language of poetry, and the volume rather than stifling Chuvash poetry might well encourage the Russian-speakers of Chuvashia to learn the language of the country they live in.

It isn't necessarily so much the fact of translation which critics see as harmful, as the manner. The norm for most literary translators has been for a long time to make a text that seems to belong naturally to its new culture – as a child I read Jules Verne without thinking it originated somewhere else. Against this, much current thinking about translation argues for 'foreignisation', rubbing the reader's nose into the strangeness of what he or she is reading. It's not always clear whether the agenda here is the defence of the Other against colonisation or the desire to stir up the complacency of domestic habit. Whatever it is, though, this may be what is hardest for the bilingual self-translator who will naturally, like Brink or Beckett, adapt the material to its new environment. I'm not in a position to judge how far the translations in Gaelic-English poetry collections go along the road to domestication, but maybe Brodsky with his strange-seeming style would be a good model if the aim is to resist the colonising effect of English translation.

Louis Aragon
Moscow Night

Here I have walked and dreamed so much of the future
That sometimes I seemed to remember him
And in my fever took his bare hand in my hands
He sang with me the same extravagant songs
I felt his breath and already our words
Easily expressed unknown things

Here I have loved so much the night and the silence
So often lost my way like a second childhood
So often for fun taken the wrong road
So often found again my ghosts in rags
Shadows of my past in a side-street[1]
Whose name slipped my mind like water in the hand

That I have finally at the back of my eye
Confused what is to come with what I imagine
Without knowing that every dream is to-day's sorrow
That man sees the flame and cannot doubt it
And though he is no longer lost where our eyes were lost
Later by other fires his eyes will be attracted

History spins at such speed between our fingers
That to-morrow will ask of to-day What was that
Forgetting the songs which pleased our hearts
How shall we get used to what overtakes us
We have called space our cage
But already its bars no longer hold us

To restrict life to our evidence
We mark in vain the limits of our graves
The grass overgrows the stone
And our shining mirrors will have to discern
Not the dying torches but those about to burn
And not our dream and not our law

In this century zenith of war
The deeper and darker the injustice
Men turned their eyes to the star in amazement
And I was one of them sharing their anger
Believing the dawn near each clearer shadow
At every step in the night believing in the outcome

---

1. Pereoulok (Russian) Translator's Note. I had the benefit of correspondence
with the late Dr. Max Adreth in the translation of these verses.

Star we forgot the hardship and the fear
The minotaur at this winding of the labyrinth
Star like water in our drought
You we could touch climbing the hill
Star so far star so near
Star on earth star in my reach

I put its opposite in place of everything
I imagined life and its changes
As an immense planned fairyland
It was a blue garden sparkling like a crystal
Where fabulous feet walked on the petals
And yet the flowers had never faded

I expected a happiness as wide as the ocean
From dawn to sunset colour of the chimera
Love torn from its profane fetters
But reality hears with another ear
And works wonders in her own way
Too bad for the dreamers too bad for utopia

If spring flowers if man finally changes
Is this the work of elves or angels
Or lines of the hand for palmistry
They will smile at us as false prophets
Who took the horizon for an immense festival
And did not see the nails in the hands of the Lord

They will smile at us for the best of our souls
They will smile at us for worshipping the flame
So far as to feed it with our own flesh
And as it is easy after the event
To reject the burnt hand on seeing its burn
They will smile at us for our self-sacrifice

What if I took the wrong road a hundred thousand times
You harp on the negative virtues of doubt
You crack up the roads of caution
Well then I've wasted my life and worn out my shoes
I am in the ditch I count my cuts
I'll not arrive at the end of the night

What does it matter so long as the night tears at the end
And the dawn rises to see it turn white
In the darkest hour I hear the cock crow
I carry victory in the heart of my disaster
Had you put out the eyes of all the stars
I carry the sun within my darkness

Stanzas in Memory

Poem written for the naming of a Paris street, 'Groupe Manouchian'. The Armenian poet Manouchian, a hero of our Resistance, leader of the group called 'Strangers' or 'Red Mark' was shot by the Nazis in February 1944.

You neither claimed glory nor tears
Nor the organ nor the prayer for the dying
Eleven years already how quickly eleven years pass
You had simply used your arms
Death does not dazzle the eyes of the Partisans

You had your portraits on the walls of our towns
Black of beard and of night hirsute menacing
The poster which looked like a blood stain
Because your names are difficult to pronounce
Looked for an effect of fear on the passers-by

No one seemed to see you Frenchmen by adoption
People went without eyes for you during the day
But under the curfew straying fingers
Had written under your photos DEAD FOR FRANCE
And the bleak mornings were different for it

Everything had the uniform white frost colour
At the end of February for your last moments
And then one of you said calmly
'Good luck to everyone Good luck to those who will live on
I die without hatred in me for the German people

Farewell pain and pleasure Farewell roses
Farewell life Farewell light and wind
Marry be happy and think of me often
You who will live in the loveliness of things
When it will all be over later in Erivan[1]

A bright winter sun lights up the hill
How beautiful nature is and how it breaks my heart
Justice will follow in our triumphant footsteps
My Mélinée my love my orphan
And I tell you to live and have a child'

They were twenty-three when the rifles flowered
Twenty-three who gave their hearts before their time
Twenty-three strangers and yet our brothers
Twenty-three in love with life so much as to die for it
Twenty-three who called out 'France' in falling

[1] Armenian capital

From *Le Roman Inachevé (The Unfinished Romance)*, 1956.

Translated from the French by John Manson

With Friends like us, What do Enemies Matter?

Martin Bennett

Bright Gold sat on a ragged armchair and wondered what quirk of fate possessed his parents to give him such a name. Stephen, Ignatius or any number of martyrs might have fitted. But why Bright Gold? And he had not been paid his salary for three months running . . .

But his thoughts were interrupted by his wife Gladys's discontented muttering from the corrugated-iron kitchen nextdoor.

"It's not me who's to blame for the state of the economy," he felt like screaming, his empty stomach tightening with anger. But he did not want to start another argument.

"If only I'd married Ebeneezer," his mind echoed with Gladys's latest reference to his ex-rival, now a big government contractor and commander of kick-backs. "Now there's a man who knows what's what." Next, like salt into a wound, she had added a proverb. "If you do not buy your wife enough cloth, her buttocks may become a public spectacle." Half an hour later had come, "Absence of powder turns a gun into a stick."

A few months ago such discord had been unknown. Yet now his marriage was in the doldrums at best. Austerity was setting apart what God had joined. Meanwhile Gladys had appeared in the doorway. " . . . And we don't have sugar, we don't have eggs, we don't have milk," she recited, presenting him with a shopping list of blames.

Bright Gold's stomach tightened another notch.

To prevent her inevitable "If only I had married Ebeneezer", Bright Gold rose from his chair and said, "Alright, my dear, alright. I will go and do some shopping then."

A minute later he was across the open gutter and in the potholed street. The diagonal green and red stripes of his T-shirt flashed in the morning sunlight. The sky was a peaceful blue, and from a record kiosk flowed the sounds of highlife. For a hundred yards or so he felt an uneconomic surge of well-being. Only several streets later did this turn back to anger as he recalled the purpose of his mission. He was not a beggar but a qualified teacher. Inside his head that highlife was replaced by a quote from one of this year's set texts: "Neither a borrower nor a lender be". But then Polonius had not had to suffer the austerities of a Government Reconstruction Programme. Why, he had even been a minister of sorts. No salary problems for him or perhaps the old fellow might have advised otherwise.

Bright Gold's jaunty gait had become a hesitant plod. No, indeed, borrowing was not good, he knew as well as anyone. But what choice had he? And he began rehearsing what he would say to Festus, his creditor, this time. As an inroad into Festus' pocket which would work better: A falsely nonchalant, "Well, Austerity has caught me again, my brother", or should it be a frankly shame-faced "I'm sorry to trouble you yet again but . . ."

As Bright Gold balanced these bleak earthbound alternatives, somewhere at the sky's blue edge Miles Wheeler smiled sweetly at the air-stewardess unloading two miniature champagne bottles from his table. A minute later he was lighting a postprandial cigarette. Making the most of his company-paid Horizon Class ticket, he stretched his legs. "We shall shortly be making our approach to . . . The weather clear . . . Our height . . . " So the in-flight speaker crackled and swallowed information. Down below, the capital's outskirts wheeled into view like a massive switchboard. He could make out corrugated roofs small as microchips, ant-sized vehicles and pedestrians going about their business. Miles Wheeler put out his cigarette, clutched his briefcase tighter as the plane touched down and was soon making his way across the sweltering tarmac. Few would have imagined his well-manicured hands held the inventories of enough weaponry to lay waste to half the city and turn thousands of its bustling citizens to corpses.

This was something Miles found difficult to imagine himself, he had his euphemisms so well-polished and stamped with government approvals. Why talk of war – especially of civil war – when there was a ready translation in 'projected threat development'? 'Combat efficiency', 'damage limitation', 'readjustments in inoperative personnel': these were the elements of his sales pitch. He was here in Dhira to market a product, not put prospective buyers off with needless candour. Particularly as the profits came not in tens of thousands and even millions. This was real money, unlike the trickling amounts he had once made selling hospital equipment.

It was a good sign then when General Ali, Deputy Minister of the Interior, boomed across the airport concourse in his best Sandhurst English: "Hey, Mister Miles, my good friend, absolutely marvellous to see you!"

And true to rank and title, the General was soon brushing aside immigration officials like bluebottles, and clearing a way with his swaggerstick to the limousine outside. Beggars, hawkers, drivers gawped fleetingly at the sleek-haired and suited European VIP. The car-doors thudded shut. No spare parts problem there, the limousine purred though the morning go-slow while out in front rode two burly and jack-booted military policemen on fat new motorbikes.

Behind the tinted glass Miles unlocks his briefcase. Inside, amidst glossy brochures of armoured cars, weapon suites, stenguns and other hardware, nestles a fresh bottle of White Horse whisky. "Just a small token," mouths Miles as he hands it over. Later there will be other larger tokens. Much larger and almost as secret. But who is Miles, a foreigner, to question local customs? It was their country after all.

"Ah, these people!" General Ali scowls a commentary at the line of over-optimistic shoppers spilling into the road outside Safeways Supermarket.

"Hmm, money miss road!" scowls back a man in a diagonally red and green striped T-shirt. If that limousine were to stop and its passengers to exchange tinted glass for a so-called 'walk-about', the man might have explained to them how he had just borrowed some money. But now there was nothing to spend it on. Even after two hours queuing. Unless one counted wooden ducks from Bulgaria, a shelf full of ladies' gloves for when this tropical country hit another ice-age, dozens of jars of Rumanian

166

greengage jam with which, if the worst came the worst, he might have to
make do instead of the sardines, sugar, meat listed by his wife back home.
All this the man in the T-shirt might have mentioned, one educated somebody to another, along with that problem of unpaid salary. "Neither a
borrower nor a lender be." That might be alright for old Polonius, except . . .
Except the limousine and its outriders have moved on. What are greengage jam, grumbling wives and so on set beside the nation's security?
Another official thud of doors and Miles Wheeler is being hush-hushed
through corridors to the plush heart of state, General Ali marches alongside with his swagger-stick now tucked beneath his arm. Secretaries and
clerks drop away behind. European visitor and Deputy Interior Minister
are ushered to fresh leather seats. The door of thickest mahogany closes,
a guard in place to ensure it stays that way.
"When one's guns are few, one's words are few", the main Minister
winds up his introduction with a proverb. Around the big polished table
echo five star chuckles, top-level murmurs. "And now Mr Wheeler, it's
over to you."
The gathered faces grow suddenly grave. Again Miles Wheeler unlocks
his briefcase, flicks on an overhead projector set up for his use. " . . . Oper-
ational flexibility . . . penetration-optimised warhead . . . " Miles' voice
matches the images beamed onto the wall. " . . . Superior accuracy . . .
user-friendly . . . tailor-made to meet customer needs . . . " The faces
around the table look suitably impressed. The talk moves on to flow
charts, cost benefit ratios, post-sales back-up, matters of commission. So
in the teeth of who knows how tough competition from elsewhere, the
deal is sealed, the order secured. On behalf of his company, Miles hands
over a model of an armoured car. Toasts in bottled water, Johnny Walker,
bottled beer are drunk to "unity of purpose", "this special friendship", et
cetera, et cetera.
Later Miles gazes from his suite at a mountain of rubbish inhabited by
several families of lizards and counts the hours till his arrival back in his
London suburb. The other side of the settee General Ali clinks down his
seventh whisky. Now that peace has been successfully underpinned,
Miles starts to find his escort rather less-entertaining company. Or maybe
it's just jetlag, the tropical climate, the stress of having so much money
hanging on each word and gesture. Already the jokes are repeating themselves. The silences between the two men get longer. Then, to Miles'
relief, the limousine arrives.
As the outriders set about instilling the necessary deference into a
sprawling cyclist, a watching market-woman screams, "These soldiers,
may God deal with them!" Miles glimpses through the tinted glass only a
mouth going open and shut while General Ali laughs whiskily into his ear,
"So you see, my friend, how important you are!"
A protest rises in Miles' mind. But then, overriding the unfortunate
cyclist and other facts on the ground, he recalls that 'special friendship'.
An air-conditioned silence prevails until the limousine reaches the airport
and Miles, half-asleep, is stirred by an urgent tapping at the window.

Coup! He impulsively translates the noise into clicks of released safety-catches. He freezes in his seat. Only by the ensuing wail of "Allahu ar-rahman ar-raheem" does he register the taps as coming from a beggar too blind to recognise the limousine's special number-plates, the status of its passengers.

"A good trip, darling?", Helen Wheeler, Miles' wife, enquires a safe ten hours and however many thousand kilometres later.

"Excellent, as these things go", Miles smiles back.

A fortnight passes, summery and peaceful, roses and chestnut trees in the garden outside come into bloom.

Then, one evening, five minutes into the nine o'clock news, Miles hears, "Government troops in Dhira, the capital of Suridan, opened fire yesterday on crowds protesting against the latest price rises. Unofficial sources put the number killed as high as twenty with many more people injured . . . Last night gales off the coast of Florida . . . "

"Anything on the news?" goes Helen, arriving downstairs from her evening bath.

"Just a spot of trouble in Dhira", says Miles. "After what I saw there, I can't say it's a surprise. But let me fix you a drink, dear. What will it be? The usual?"

As Miles crosses from sofa to cocktail cabinet, Bright Gold feels the piece of metal in his thigh expand. A cold upward pressure threatens to take over the whole body, barging his sense of self aside.

No, no, no . . . Against loss of consciousness he deploys memories in a a counter-offensive: his mother and father back in the village; the affectionate before-austerity Gladys, his wife; brothers, sisters, cousins; Festus, his friend and creditor. Even those shopping lists are converted into a sign of life and therefore hope. In priceless quantities he feels the air enter, leave, enter his lungs. He concentrates upon it lest it suddenly slip away: breath, then the sounds going on around him, nurses' whispers, clink of surgical instruments, somewhere beyond the window-blinds the ground-to-air cries of black-marketeers and beggars, harmlessly lowtech, dozens to the pound.

Robin Hamilton

Stanzas

Winter's weather capers in my bones
Like an old familiar ghost come home.
After the long dry furlough
I'll pick up a stock-taking pen,
Craft out some words against futurity:
The pains of a second life are new
Lessons to be re-learned, old ones
Forgotten. A sere autumn of the heart.

Coming to terms with it, as men
At a certain age must do. Less time
Ahead than there is behind, the weight
Of choices which made up our life:
Now turning into a new country
With a child in each hand, my best
Guests who save me from despair –
And drive me crazy, sometimes, with their love.

Where have they gone, the high ones, my heroes?
In the arms of what malicious god are they embraced?
Generation after generation that crafted wise words
That did for themselves no good whatsoever.
That hectic verse that drew no girls to their bed,
Those consoling words that stilled no fear of death,
Those poems only to mark out their tomb – an epitaph
Cut with a pen of bone, coloured with our heart's blood.

Crossed by some buskined fancy-man, the hard god
Who plays out tricks within our dreaming time.
Cries no mercy to the risk taken, turns us
Insides out to show the whole loving world
What we have become – raw meat that cries inside,
A heart pulsing out words, words, words,
While we, invert, inhale our grief;
And the maenads waiting, with their flensing knives.

No guilt, friends, not none. When God sent me out
Breech foremost onto this crying ground, She left out
A conscience, stoppered the gap with irony instead.
Only to take it all quite seriously! But as it is,
Each flush moment of grief or passion or despair
Is undershot: "What does it matter?" some cold voice
Whispers, "The best are dead. You've spoiled their world,
And only words remain." But still the words remain.

I know I'm talking to myself
When the words go fuzzy. Those abstract
Counters that mean much to me –
Love, joy, desire, despair –
But none of them are shareable, until
They're kitted out in images:
Drawn on that token I call Love,
Your face, and on your face, Despair.

Three Poems for John Berryman: That Worthy Man
(for Brian Jarvis)

1: Remembering Him Today

Datum, the insignificant: at a cold time,
Thinking on Henry's bones, how he rhymed
His Lise, left the hot sonnets on ice for
Fifteen years till
the blood cooled, husband gone,
Harpsichord silent, Henry well gone into his
Long walk to the river, to the Mississippi.

White bearded sage, old risk-taker, clown
In blackface, reeling drunk off a stool
At your readings, squirreling away at rhymes
While you squired your daughter, endured
Sudden lust on an aeroplane, coughed words
And watched your friends die, still wondering
Why you were still here, until it became
Too much.

I salute you, mi compañero,
Man of the high bulls. I'd fight in your ring
If my spirit had a partner for that game.

2: Yet Another Dream Song

Hey, man, don't put yourself down so. Sure
You is overage, underweight, and got that
Slight problem with the juice. So what?
You can still pull the girls. You flash out
Like some crazy neon in the dark. What you want,
To live forever?

No, Mister Bones, but I want
To live for now. Somewhere there's an allowed world
With like trees and food I want to eat
And people listening careful to my every word.
Let's hear it for that old, nostalgic paradise!
I build it up and put it down in verse.
But there you stand, with your damn
Sword, by the gate.

That's how it goes; you can't
Have everything. You chose the words, you live
By your choices. Be grateful you got that.

3: Henry's Whimper

Life is a griefy dream, friends.
I go round today like a tooth-sick bear:
Save me an individual shoulder to dump on –
I need someone to hear my weeps, mostly one who's
Female, intelligent, and soft-hearted. Surely you is out there
Somewhere? Call Henry collect in his heartbox.

Allen Wright 1932-1997
Raymond Ross

"Gentleman of the Press" would be a difficult phrase to use to describe a career journalist in the 1990s; and yet it could be applied without hesitation whatsoever to Allen Wright, the former arts Editor of *The Scotsman* who died in November of last year.

In his role as that paper's first ever Arts Editor, a post he held for nearly 30 years, Allen created the Fringe First awards, a lasting testament to his endeavours to widen the appreciation of theatre in Scotland.

A quiet man of ironic temperament and with a wry sense of humour, he was as self-effacing as he was fair-minded. In his own reviewing he was sharply aware that theatre itself should never be, nor ever be seen to be, under attack.

Not that he didn't dish out his fair share of bad notices but, characteristically judicious, it was the theatre that mattered to him first and foremost and he had little regard for the kind of opinionated criticism that was willing to blooter a show in order to gain the reviewer (or maintain the reviewer) an inflated reputation. That is to say, he was a true professional and he had both quality and style but was devoid of self-serving cynicism.

Generous and open-minded he was willing to listen to others and to take new ideas on board, always remaining his own man. His work-load during the Edinburgh Festival was gargantuan, yet he always seemed to take it in his stride. He was typically generous to younger journalists, reviewers and writers. People mattered to him as did words. But people mattered more. He was therefore acutely aware of the power of words.

On Being The Scotsman Arts Editor
Robert Dawson Scott

I did have to think hard about taking on the job of arts editor at *The Scotsman*. There were all sorts of negatives; the daily commuting to Edinburgh from Glasgow, the loss of flexibility in moving from a freelance life to that of a dependent employee, the grind of a daily as opposed to a Sunday paper, the rumours emanating from North Bridge about the tyrannical regime of Martin Clarke, the new editor (which subsequently turned out to be largely exaggerated). It must have taken me all of 30 seconds to make my mind up. For any journalist concerned with arts and culture, it is simply the best and probably the most important job in Scotland.

As it happened, when I was first approached, at the beginning of June last year, I was reaching the climax of a one year masters degree at Strathclyde University which I wasn't going to interrupt for anyone. I had intended to take a sabbatical from covering the Edinburgh Festival – every arts journalist's dream and nightmare all rolled into one – while I wrote the dissertation and I certainly did not want to start the new job having to mastermind *The Scotsman*'s exhaustive and exhausting coverage of the event. It's an undertaking which takes its toll on mind and body, the sort of thing, as one seasoned arts commentator put it to me, for which you need a long backswing. Happily, I was able to negotiate a September 1 start and I looked forward to easing my way in gently.

My smug plans were utterly confounded by the death of Diana, Princess of Wales. Far from starting on a quiet note, I was pitched into the biggest media frenzy, whatever your view of it, of the century. It was quickly followed by the most important story for Scotland of the last three centuries, the devolution referendum. Newspaper people are often said to be at their best when a big story breaks; they slip into a routine of familiar skills, they are too busy for the usual bickering and squabbling and the level of adrenaline is almost visible. For a newcomer, one who entered journalism by the side door as a theatre reviewer rather than through any kind of news training, it was, I must admit, heady stuff.

Not much to do with the arts, do I hear? Well, in the first place, largely due to my long-standing inability to keep my nose out of other people's business – I quickly became involved in all the features coverage in the paper. Even had I not been, those two epoch-making events were fraught with profound cultural implications.

Readers of *Chapman* do not require lessons from me about what art means but perhaps I should start by saying that whatever my job title says it is the whole culture of Scotland – and indeed further afield – which I consider to be my domain. My view of the task in hand is an inclusive one; I occasionally think, when time permits, that I really also ought to oversee the pages on food, drink, gardening, fashion, design, everything to do with the way we live now. In that light, it is a short step to seeing that the result of the referendum was an event of profound cultural consequence for Scotland – not least since many of the most articulate and vocal supporters of devolution have come from Scotland's creative community.

When I first arrived in Scotland from London in 1984, to take up a post at the Royal Lyceum in Edinburgh, I was, I liked to think, alive to the distinct nature of Scottish nationhood, to the idea that this was a proper country with its own history and its own culture. I soon discovered how little I really knew about that history and culture and also how quickly any discussion of the potential of Scotland – economically, politically but especially culturally – ran up against the rock of the then political status quo. History one can read; I devoured everything from Christopher Smout to Nigel Tranter (whose vivid storytelling I unashamedly commend to anyone who, like me, tends to founder in the detail of more conventional histories). The politico/cultural thing took longer; it takes a while to get to grips with the famous Caledonian antisyzygy, the swagger of 'wha's like us' side by side with the craven forelock tugging which allowed, for example, Scottish music and dance to be so perversely undervalued by the Scots themselves, especially their leaders, for so long. Devolution will not solve all that. I hope that it will help, but the growing assertiveness of other small nations (and before you ask, yes, I am aware of MacDiarmid's rousing rant at anyone who dares describe Scotland as small) was already showing the way towards greater self-confidence in a number of areas before the vote came along.

The death of Princess Diana was every bit as culturally instructive. To take one example; a popular song was placed at the heart of a great state cere-monial occasion. And nobody laughed or thought it absurd or improper. Could this have happened fifty years ago? Could it have happened even at Diana's wedding to the Prince of Wales in 1981? There the central musical moment came from the heart of the western classical repertoire – Handel's *Let the Bright Seraphim* – and was sung by a representative of the art form which above all, rightly or wrongly, still symbolises proper art, Kiri te Kanawa, an opera singer. Yet Elton John's performance of his sad little song was for many millions of people the emotional heart of that funeral service. His obvious sincerity was important; but so was the fact that a simple 3 minute pop song could sustain the weight and depth of emotion that people had brought to that occasion. Sentimental? A cheap trick? No, rather this was an eloquent demonstration of why the products of popular culture have to be considered alongside the older art forms which are subsidised by the taxpayer, taught in academies and sacralised in the temples of high culture, the gallery, the concert hall, the theatre and so on.

Culture is there to be described as much as prescribed. I do not believe that one form is inherently superior to another or that excellence can only be found in a limited number of forms which have survived largely unal-tered since the last century. Art and entertainment are not separate entities but broad overlapping areas strung along the same continuum. There is a small group in Scotland, as elsewhere, who would rather maintain the old hierarchy, for whom the symphony concert or the classical ballet rep-resent the zenith of man's cultural achievement. I am fascinated by the way that a certain class of international businessman, for example, from Sin-gapore to San Francisco, gravitate towards classical music for their spon-sorships, their corporate hospitality, their official entertainment despite the fact that they clearly don't understand it, are bored by it and usually choose not to visit it on their own time and money. My feeling is that this class is shrinking; the debate over how much public money should be spent on its 'entertainment' will intensify. Incidentally, this does not mean that there is anything wrong with classical music or any of the other so-called high cultural forms. A Beethoven symphony is obviously a far more sophisti-cated organism than a 3 minute pop song and potentially can reveal more, can stir more complex and satisfying responses, just as a novel by Muriel Spark can, in time, tell us more about ourselves than an advertising hoard-ing. My point is that it is unwise to ignore the impact of the pop song or the advert or the creative process behind them. Regardless of whether people like them or not, the sheer distributive power behind them means they impact on almost all of us far more of us than Spark or Beethoven. My instinct is not to condemn a song like the infernally catchy 'Barbie Girl' or the weirdly popular *Symphony of Sorrowful Songs* by Gorecki but, hav-ing realised that they do, to ask why they get to the top of the charts.

If you think this all sounds rather theoretical by comparison with the daily struggle to get the paper out, you'd be right. The daily fire-fight is ferociously demanding. Even if it wasn't, *The Scotsman* is a newspaper which must satisfy its readers, many of whom would certainly not endorse much of the above. It's a complex relationship, part leading, part follow-ing. The choices of what to feature and review and what not to are similarly complex. It is not easy to describe how those choices are made; many of the factors are banally functional such as how much advertising has been sold. So perhaps it is better to look back at what has actually happened over the last six months and see if any conclusions can be drawn.

I was fortunate to inherit some excellent principal critics; Duncan Mac-Millan on the visual arts, Mary Miller, Alistair Clark, Barry Didcock on music of all sorts, Christopher Bowen on dance. Catherine Lockerbie, the literary editor, ploughs her own furrow and is not beholden to me. However, her long experience of the paper as well as of the Scottish arts scene makes her a much valued colleague and friend. I am pleased to have brought in some new writers. Simon Frith, formerly my professor for my master's degree, is now a regular columnist (fortnightly on Thursdays) taking pop music seriously. Ninian Dunnett and Bob Flynn are both contributing to a broadening of the base of the music coverage. Elizabeth Mahoney interprets some of the more abstruse areas of contemporary culture with a lucid prose whose simplicity belies the sophistication of her argument. Of the others I inherited, Colin Donald, who had been covering Scottish drama for some years, has left to work in Japan, the country his wife comes from.

I was delighted to be able to lure Joyce McMillan away from *The Herald* and back to front-line reviewing, perhaps the single most gratifying event since I started and something everyone at the paper and in the theatre world, albeit slightly nervously in the latter's case, have warmly welcomed. Angus Wolfe Murray, whose commitment to and knowledge of film is beyond doubt, had developed a personal style which no longer suited the paper which has gone through massive changes. The editor decided and I agreed, that it would be best for everyone if we made a fresh start. He was replaced by Trevor Johnston, a dry-witted Ulsterman now based in London where he is better able to access the high profile interviews which have become an essential part of cinema coverage. I genuinely feel, though you would no doubt expect me to say this, that we have the strongest reviewing team in Scotland, quite as formidable in terms of knowledge and judgement as anything the London papers can throw up.

The departure of Angus was, nevertheless, a difficult moment, the lowest point in a series of early teething troubles most of which can be traced back to the fact that there was no real arts editor for a number of years. Individual critics had been left largely to their own devices within a fixed framework of the 'if it's Tuesday it must be drama' variety and there was an inevitable bout of everyone getting used to each other. Much good work had been done but there was obviously a lack of overall direction or agenda and there was not enough specialist attention to the news of the arts, the politics and the economics of it. Since I took over I have been able to influence and inform, if not actually write myself, the stories of Scottish Ballet's fresh start, Wildcat's funding cut, the SAC's appearance before the Scottish select committee, the National Gallery of Scottish Art saga, the rehang at GOMA, the Burrell hearing, the major events of Fotofeis, Celtic Connections and New Moves and many others in ways which would not have been possible before.

In many ways, the man I succeeded was not Douglas Fraser who nominally had the title but the late Allen Wright who had been forced to retire by ill health over four years ago. When Allen died last autumn after a long illness, I felt eerily conscious of a sense of the baton being finally handed on. I knew him well enough to be pretty confident that, given the choice, he would not have picked me for we had very different views on some of the issues I have touched on above. I hope however that I learned something from his generosity to those who did disagree with him. He did a great deal for the arts in Scotland in his own quiet way. I think he would have approved of my first executive act which was to increase the rates of pay to contributors and reviewers from the previous derisory rates. I also made reviews longer; 200 words is really not enough and although 300 is often not enough either, especially for new work, it's a step in the right direction. It means we review less but I don't think getting reviewed in *The Scotsman* should be an assumed right.

This has already provoked outraged reaction from more established organisations. The door remains open for them to argue that the umpteenth tour of some tired old musical comedy should be covered but at present I see no compelling reason to alter my basic approach. In choosing what to cover, I try to favour the new and the untried over the hack and the workaday, the excellent over the merely apprentice (which generally excludes student work). That said, big events whether it's an Oasis concert or a new production by Scottish Opera have to be covered simply for their news value. I have reservations about the value of short overnight reviews in terms of responses to the artwork although their long-standing function of providing the news of the arts means they will be with this particular newspaper for some time yet. Indeed discussions are ongoing over finding a regular slot within the news pages at the front of the paper. In general I prefer the more considered, longer and more contextualised essay type piece which you find in some weekly publications and Sunday newspapers and I may be able to introduce more of that in time.

I have dispensed with the themed days because it was too much of a straitjacket. Film coverage still appears on a Thursday because each week's film releases appear in cinemas the following day. Coverage of popular music is also on a fixed day though that is not to ensure that I include it. The editor feels that a large enough constituency of the paper's readership needs to be reassured that pop is not completely taking over. Coverage of new CDs has been rationalised and brought together in its own slot on a Friday. Far more people buy records than ever go to a concert and similarly, watching movies at home on video is something now widely practised in all social groups. Gareth MacLean's hilarious Flat Screen column, with its cast of characters on the video watching couch, attempts to reflect that difference. I have also reintroduced some architecture coverage. As this is, quite simply, the art form that none of us can ever avoid, we might as well try to have a sensible debate about it. The proposed Parliament building and Glasgow's Year of Architecture provide two obvious foci. I would like to do more on design and applied arts but am still looking for writers and commentators in this area and, of course, I am desperately short of space. Right now, that long Festival backswing has already started. *The Scotsman* has certainly changed and its arts coverage has changed too. For the better? That is for you to judge.

Strange Fish Are Moving

Tom Bryan

"Beneath the tides of sleep and time, strange fish are moving."
Thomas Wolfe (1900-1938)

I was released – on strong medication – back "into the community": another way of saying they were finally rid of me. I had a problem: hearing voices in my head. No, not loud voices telling me I was Napoleon or Jesus, but just faint whispers like scrambled radio reception late at night; voices sometimes jumbled together, relentless, persistent. I never knew what the voices were saying. They were confusing me, but the medicine stopped most of it. Finding a job became my problem because people asked what I'd been doing for the last three years; what could I tell them? I needed a job in order to buy some sunshine because all my life I have been cold and wet; but when I paint (I learned to paint "inside") I paint sunshine, golden sands and Italian villages where men sit under ancient chestnut trees, spearing watermelon with sharp curved knives. The men's teeth glisten. The women in my paintings are brown. and have great red lips. There are ripe fruits growing. In my paintings, people can just reach out and pick the fruit any time they wish because it is so plentiful. There are vines and huge pink flowers growing up the houses. The windows are always open; the sky is always dazzling. Not like the sky the day I got the job; a November drizzle, the Highland sky an angry blotch of spilled ink. The rain was horizontal in the wind as water dribbled down my socks. Voices were beginning to churn in my skull.

The interviewer was Irish. "I'm John Blackaby," he said. We shook hands. He was pleasant but got right to the point. "Mr. Brown, you've been unemployed for over three years?"

"Ye . . . yes, I was away for three years, in Craig Insh. I was troubled by voices in my head. I don't hear them much now. Doctors say I am as cured as I need to be. I'm harmless though, and dependable. I could use the job."

Blackaby went into a kind of trance. Took off his glasses. Rubbed the red spot on the bridge of his nose.

He cleared his throat, "Three years is a long time. Do you like being on your own, being your own boss. Do you like animals?"

I told him I would like very much to be on my own. 'Inside', you are never on your own. Patients talk, shout and follow you around. Staff wake you up to feed you. They hover, but the worst part is the fear and contempt in their eyes. So, I told Blackaby I liked animals. (I do because I sometimes felt like a caged animal myself). I didn't tell him that though. Just the part about liking animals.

He finally spoke. "You can start Monday."

That was that. My ordeal was over. I shook hands and walked down the long flight of stairs. The sky was whipping up. Voices were growling inside my brain. But I had a job – a real job.

On that November Monday, we drove slowly out of town. We went up the Strath, onto the single track roads. I saw all the colours of the land;

brackens turning to rust; the leaves of the rowans and birches curling into brown. Mr. Blackaby told me more about the job.

"We grow salmon from when they hatch until when they are ready to go to sea. Salmon remain as parr in fresh water but nature prepares them by giving them silvery scales to protect them against salt water. We raise the salmon to this 'smolt' stage. They need fed and protected from predators like heron and weasels. Their tanks need to be kept clean and free of disease. We rear salmon up here because the water is so pure and the site is isolated against vandalism. We fatten the fish up over the winter and keep them healthy. In May, we transport them by helicopter to the sea. We sell them as smolts. We give you a place to live and a basic allowance. When the fish go to sea in May, you get a bonus of £5,000, in addition to your basic weekly salary. We'll give you a sub of a few hundred pounds for some food and we pay for your fuel – mainly wood and coal."

Five thousand pounds! That was meant to be my ticket to Greece, Italy, or northern Spain. I could buy sunshine, buy my way out of the wind, cold and rain! I would do it! Meanwhile, the sun had come out over the Strath and I watched a lone buzzard drop slowly in the sky.

I can't forget first seeing the site. It was up a long track between two cliffs. The track curved down again. The sea glistened far in the distance. Ben Ruachan towering to the left; a frothy, fast-flowing burn to the right. The bothy was fenced-in. It was wooden, stained light brown – the size of a small family bungalow. It had a separate bedroom, flush toilet bathroom and kitchen – all electric; there was a large wood-burning stove in the main kitchen area. Table, chairs, easy chair – all this comfort in the middle of nowhere, all to myself. Blackaby took me on a tour of the site and explained the set-up.

There was a helluva lot to learn about fish farming. Blackaby showed me the source of the water supply, explained how it entered and left the site and how it circulated through the big fibre-glass fish tanks. He explained what to do if the water levels were too low or too high. He told me how to clean the filters and keep the supply free of debris, pointing out where all the tools and bags of fish feed were kept. He showed me my living quarters. The bedroom was small but clean and dry; the lamp cast soft shadows on the walls. It was so peaceful. I felt cured; felt truly human again. Freedom – sweet freedom! I slept that night as soundly as I ever have, the flowing water of the site lulling me to sleep.

Blackaby came every day that week and showed me something new daily. At first, it was hard work. The fish were the hardest. There were a few thousand in each tank and nearly fifty tanks of fish which were turning from golden-brown parr into silvery smolts – fish preparing for their natural seaward journey. The fish were all about six inches long; very quick and silvery. Blackaby explained how the fish rose up in columns – a kind of pecking order – and how they swam in the tanks. Only the sickest runts hovered over the filter screens, unable to assume their place in the column. He showed me how to tell healthy fish from unhealthy ones by the way they swam and dived. The routines became simple, monotonous. I looked in each tank through the fibreglass hatchways, removed any dead fish (later burned) and fed the fish only once a day, since salmon feed very little in cold water. The rest of the day was taken up with keeping the tanks clean, and free of algae and ice. That November I settled into the routines and kept diary from that time. I called the diary *Notes for a Painter.*

NOTES FOR A PAINTER "The fish swim around in circles. I float the food pellets around and they come up with a swirl and disappear again. They are getting to know me. I know how they feel. I was fed that way for three years so I try to give them peace. I am painting a lot. There are rats about the place. I hear them gnawing in the woodpile outside at night. However, stoats have discovered the rats. The stoats are white with black rings on their tails. Stoats rear up, sniff the air and pounce. They bite the rats behind the head and run away with them hanging from their jaws."

"Otters run along the burn. They dive and always come up with trout. They take the trout to a moss-covered rock in the middle of the burn. They strip the flesh from the wild trout and then float the fish skeletons back into the current. The otters slide on their rear ends back into the burn . . ."

"I see eagles every day. I thought I would not know the difference between an eagle and a high-flying buzzard. The difference is size. An eagle can disappear into the sky. Buzzards are afraid to fly that high."

"Blackaby came yesterday. Said the site is looking good . . . said the fish are in perfect health. Keep up the good work he said! . . ."

"The heron fly in at dusk in their jerky prehistoric way. They stand on the rim of the fish tanks at night, like ragged ghosts in the moonlight, try-ing to spear the fish. One day, I found a nearly-drowned heron in the tank. He let me fish him out. I stood him in the sunshine. He revived very slowly and finally began to waltz around the site, making choking noises. He shook the water free and flew away."

"Ben Ruachan is covered in a powder of snow. Silver clouds ring the top."

"I still hear voices at night, but not so often. They are more like singing now; a soft chanting. Most times I do not hear voices at all. Instead, I hear the wind and the rain and the croaking of herons and water running off the hill. Strangely, I can also 'hear' the silence. I would paint the silence azure; it is a restful silence. If a person could smell the beauty of this silence it would smell like fresh sheets that have hung in the wind and sun all day."

I kept a *Colour Diary* too. Highland colours never appear singly but mix and blend. However, in order to get any colour right in its blend and mix-ture, I tried to get the essence of each colour. For me, black and white were colours of the most powerful kind, despite what colour experts say.

MY COLOUR DIARY

"SILVER" The purity of the silver salmon scales left in my small green fish net. Pure silver; universes reflected in that silver.

"BLACK" I saw the eyes of a living stoat. He did not see me. Stoat eyes define black. There is nothing blacker.

"BLUE" which blue am I talking about here? The nearly-drowned heron had some blue in its delicate hieroglyph of soft feathers. It was so blue it wasn't blue if you know what I mean. I shouldn't put too many colours in this diary; it takes time to get each one right.

"GREEN" The green moss sends its long fingers out into the burn. The green rises and ebbs with the flow of the water. All green is living. Green must live on the canvas the same way."

My dreams at night were mostly peaceful. I dreamt of a long street of soft blue, lime or pink houses. There was a cafe on the street. Old men sat there in crisp white shirts with rolled-up sleeves. They drank cold beer. Some dozed in the sun like sated lizards. Children skipped rope and sang. Trees overhead were ripe with fruits of purple and yellow. That was my recurrent dream throughout the long winter. Sunshine, brightness, warmth. I loved the job. I managed my routines in half a day. Blackaby said that was OK. Also, I only had to give the site a quick check on Saturday morning and Sunday night but otherwise, had the weekend to myself. I could walk the hills, read, sit in front of the stove, chop firewood, drink endless cups of tea. I could paint. Typical Saturdays: slept late, got up, filled the stove with wood, lit the fire. Went out to the site, looked things over. Came back in. Made a big percolator of coffee and set it on the stove. Fried up ham, eggs mushrooms and bread. (Wait, a quick diversion on cuisine.) The trout I caught from the burn were small and golden brown. I fried them in butter and oatmeal. One day, a gamekeeper gave me a bag of venison which I cut into slivers with onions and leeks and baked it in a Dutch oven in the stove ash box, adding spuds and carrots. It was ready by tea time, cooked in its own juices. That was freedom, cooking my own food. Laugh if you want. 'Inside', we were fed the same way the small salmon are fed. In three years I wasn't allowed to even chop a carrot. They wouldn't trust us with sharp knives. I used to lie awake at night aching to chop a carrot or an onion; yearning to watch the small bits taking form in a pile, then scraping them deftly into a hot frying pan. (we also weren't allowed near flame or heat.).

Saturdays, I'd stand in front of the window and paint. Watching clouds, buzzards and herons gave me ideas. In case you think this is too precious I would actually have my old paint-spattered radio plugged in and listen to Saturday afternoon football. I sometimes imagined myself playing for A C Milan in front of seventy thousand people in their great Stadium – the San Siro. And I dreamed again of five thousand pounds and of lying in the sun in a forgotten village, surrounded by small dark children laughing and singing under Mediterranean skies.

So, the fish had their routines and I had mine. Christmas came and went. Blackaby brought me a turkey with all the veggies to go with it. I baked it in the wood stove and it was beautiful. Had leftovers for days. I garnished it with some magic mushrooms I'd found growing in a sheltered place on the hill. On Christmas Eve, there was heavy snow. I went out Christmas morning and saw the most delicate heron footprints all over the tanks and around the site. I had never seen anything so beautifully fragile. The exquisite heron footprints made me somehow think of the poet Basho.

The fish grew. I kept dreaming. The winter passed slowly. I heard no voices as Spring came to the land. Snow melted. Marsh marigolds appeared on the burn bank. Pale yellow primroses, the colour of the moon, appeared magically on the hillside. The bracken turned hard green and the whole world outside was burbling and jumping about. The fish were hungry and I was even busier feeding them. Each night, I would go to bed thinking about the five thousand pounds and how I would spend it.

Meanwhile, Blackaby had set the date for fish transport: the 1st of May. The helicopter had already been hired. The fish would be flown in special tanks to the sea pens on that day.

"Good work, Brown, Damn good work. You can work for us anytime." I had imagined that very day for six months. It would be a dazzlingly bright May day. I would see the fish off and then go into the bothy for a few days, potter around, pack up my things then up the hill I'd go. Free. I'd leave my paintings until a friend could fetch them.

However, that day never happened. I don't know what happened. But that day never happened. Maybe it was never meant to.

Some time, a few days before the big day, I awoke from dreaming of Italian chestnut trees. I looked out into the site yard, through my window. There was a bright moon – the sky was clear and light. I saw a huge heron standing in the back of the site, like a silent ghost. I pulled on my clothes and went out. The heron did not move. He stood there like a priest. I walked toward him He was tall and gaunt against the barbed wire fence where mist swirled up from the burn. I thought I was still asleep or dreaming. It wasn't a heron nor was it a man. Maybe it was a ghost. No, it wasn't a heron; but it seemed more spectre than man. He spoke in a whisper, exactly like the voices I used to hear. He told me of a plan. It was simple. I helped him put the plan into effect. His plan was freedom but he said it would set us both free. We prised up each of the screens at the bottom of the tanks. We lowered the stand pipes which controlled the water levels and flows in each tank. The fish swarmed out of the tanks, down the lowered stand pipes, into the raceways and out into the burn, where we saw their silver backs glistening in the moonlight. The young salmon could now follow their instincts to the sea, whence voices in their heads commanded them. The same voices would also one day bring them home again to spawn and die. I shook hands with the man and waved goodbye. He smiled sadly then faded into the colours of the cold dawn, into the fiery pinks and reds of that May sunrise. That is my whole story.

I had to leave at once. I didn't even have time to pack. I threw all of my paintings into the burn, watching their colours merge with the foaming water. I saw entire Italian villages bleed into the frothing snowmelt; children, women, watermelons and bright flowers all blending and vanishing into the cold Highland stream. I imagined the colours all following the salmon in their life-journey to the sea. I then trudged up the hill with my whole life in a very small rucksack. I walked away from it all.

I don't seek sunshine now. I have grown to love the silver, black and gold of the Scottish winter. I will paint Highland landscape one day now that the voices have finally stopped. You see, the voices in my head stopped for good the night all those silver salmon gained their freedom. I still don't know who that man was. I wonder if he too heard voices in his head. I wonder if he hears them now.

La Guerre

Tom Bryan

Our neighbour kept bees. They flew into the light of summer, to fields of clover and honeysuckle but always came home to feed on the thick brown sugar he put out for them in the early Spring. He said very little and usually spoke only about bees. I can remember the first thing he said to me: "In the hot Summer of 1936, I baited a throw line with a dead chicken and threw it into the river below the old trestle bridge at Gosport. I left it two nights and on the third night, I tied the rope to a mule and pulled out a catfish bigger than a pig. It was longer than I am tall." I learned later it was true.

The next time he spoke to me was more frightening.

My friend Danny was throwing stones at a huge maple tree across the street, and a few minutes later the old neighbour appeared at our door. He was about five feet tall and stooped over. He was dressed entirely in khaki. His eyes were blazing. The veins stood out from his wrinkled neck like red bleeding scars. He frightened Danny away with a walking stick. He was shouting in the breathless way of old people. "I saw men die in the trenches from less than a stone being thrown. Never let me see you or your friend fighting in the trenches again." He hobbled away, shaking his fist.

We lived across the alley and I could see his light on at night. We could see him rocking back and forth in his rocking chair. He would also walk for hours around the perimeter of his land. Weeds began to over-run the place and he began to burn the weeds, rather than pull them out of his garden. He was also building a barricade of some sort, out of piles of wood and corrugated tin. I saw him cut down the post which supported the nesting house for his beloved purple martins. He threw the post on the bonfire as well as the nesting boxes. He rocked away on his porch. He had yet to say the final thing to me or anyone else.

He lit small fires that we extinguished for him, but he'd return to light more fires. The birds began to flee from the garden – the first refugees. On a clear night in late summer, he torched the beehives and brood boxes. Thousands of bees perished. Some went into the luscious fields of clover to watch their home destroyed by the same hand who had tended them so lovingly for so long. They fled to surrounding forests of maple and poplar.

The firemen could do little except watch the flames lick up around the old man's sad grey face. The next day he was on his porch with a small battered suitcase. I think he had some medals pinned to his khaki overcoat. He walked into the shade of the maple which bounded our ground.

"Son," he said, "don't worry about the bees. Their Queen has just gone away for a while, but once Armistice is declared, she'll return home again."

He got into a long blue car and looked straight ahead as it pulled away. I never saw him again.

Ian McDonough

No Mad Men

The New Statistical Account of the parish of Clyne reports that in the year of 1840 there are five mad women and no mad men.

Clynemilton burn in spate – brown gobs of foam
race downwards to the Autumn sea. Leaves turn
on trees: it is so late, and still daft Katie lies in bed.
Her cow bleats like a bairn, hens frenzy at the sun –
Reverend Mackay is told. Something must be done.

Magga counts her blessings – ends before she starts,
as ghosts of sickly children croup and huddle round
an icy hearth. Married into strangers in this strangers'
strath, husband gone to serve the Queen, she walks
her agonies along the shore: a whispering starts.

Jeannie Mhor, fat Jeannie, fecund, grimed with soot,
gathers a happy, swarming brood and dances round
the stones of her domain. Whisky in her veins, and all
her world is gay, obliterating memory of childhood
beatings, rape. A passing neighbour watches, waits.

The study of the manse is running damp. He hunkers
on his knees – Lord purify the soul that countenances
thoughts like these. The tacksman of Kilbraur arrives
scarlet with tales of shame. Tonight the minister will
dream of women dancing, naked, sodden in the rain.

Euphemia Gordon, widow of Ascoile, heavy of purse
and light of sense, removes the corpses of the starlings
from the lawn. Eyes everywhere, she slaughters anything
that dares to spy on her affairs. The minister brings
sympathy, takes sugared tea and lingers on till dawn.

Dollina mends a net of souls and sings at stars – black
visions burn the pupils of her eyes. The wind's boat
ploughs a furrow through the muddy skies – men of
the cloth lie hidden in the grass, the women's skirts
are high. Blood roars inside her ears in swelling tides.

Clynemilton burn in spate – brown gobs of foam
race downwards to the Winter sea. The unbewildered
men allow restraint, arrange four women's transport
through the poorhouse door. The minister and widow
lift their cups, express the measure of their sympathy.

The Highland Railway Reaches Caithness

Metal, wood, stone hauled across the sodden moor
Hammered into arteries which pump the outside in.

Hammered into arteries which pump the outside in
Stone, wood, metal beating paths to every door.

Stone, wood, metal beating paths to every door
Harbingers of tongues which run at different speeds.

Harbingers of tongues which run at different speeds
Wood, metal, stone running faster than the deer.

Wood, metal, stone running faster than the deer
Ploughing up the bog, driving roads into the heart.

Ploughing up the bog, driving roads into the heart
Metal, stone, wood laying all the country bare.

Metal, stone, wood laying all the country bare
Carrying a spark that will flame into a fire.

Carrying a spark that will flame into a fire
Stone, metal, wood singing more, more, more.

Stone, metal, wood singing more, more, more
Holding up a mirror that will bend us to its view.

Holding up a mirror that will bend us to its view
Wood, stone, metal burning up the keening air.

Wood, stone, metal burning up the keening air
Hammered into arteries which pump the outside in.

Hammered into arteries which pump the outside in
Metal, wood, stone hauled across the sodden moor.

Holburn Head, Caithness

What has this to do with nations?
With the culture branded
like a laceration on our skin?
These cliffs do not aspire from
nor fall into the sea, and neither
do they poison children with their songs
of gallantry in death. The wind does not
howl like a banshee on Culloden moor,
but forms its sound by beating up the air;
the air, where gulls fly white as sheets
against a blue Atlantic, signalling
a saltire for the first and last of states.

Columba in the North

Straths curl like tapeworm through
the big-boned hills. No guiding light
among the paths that weave dark spells
beyond the reach of ordinary sight.
Hovels perch like carrion
beneath a filthy moon which soaks
the land with bestial longings of the night.
Strengthen my arm to flay this land
into a revelation of the Word.
Fill their huts with terror
at the many-coloured raiments of the Lord.

After the sea-crossing, marching north,
my soul stretched out like skin. Visions
of grace dissolved into strange ardours,
shameless in their wild profanity.
Last night I dreamed The Lamb had rent
this land asunder with his sword, then
cursed its spilling blood as he consumed
the flesh. Each day I test my mettle
on a heathen dawn, cutting a swathe
through stinging thistles to my God.

The Sea's Invitation to Its Dance

Come, you with such warm blood
throbbing gently in your temples,
can you not see me shiver?
It is an ancient coldness in my veins.

Do you not hear me beat my heart
to pieces on the shore?
I have such a story to reveal,
let me dance, dance with you.
The wind will whip us into feeling.

Later we will lie below the light,
saturated, bloated with our love.
Give me your hand, your hand my dear,
soon we will begin to waltz.

Reviews

The Human Face

The Human Face, Iain Crichton Smith, Carcanet, £7.95; *Good Girls Don't Cry*, Margaret Fulton Cook, Chapman Publishing, £5.95; *sweet, sour and serious*, Survivors' Press Scotland, £6.95; *Tracts*, Dave Ward, Headland, £6.95; *Dark Whistle*, Tom Watson, Akros.

Iain Crichton Smith's long poem *The Human Face* seemed to me to have a strong theological focus. Ending with a vision of a godless universe, at its heart is an intense struggle with the idea of God.

Moving examples are given of "Man's inhumanity to man": "But conscious man will kill and smash/ frail secret envelopes of the flesh". All are shown to be caused by people holding "blood-red ideas of kin and creed". But one creed, the idea of God dominates this poem. I read fascinated to find out whether a *good* God was going to emerge from behind the callous God the poet addresses directly as: "O God, who chose one not the other/ and has set brother against brother/ as Cain and Abel ..."

However, the poem derives much of its energy from its rebuttal of God. The tone is impassioned, beyond irony, as the poet says "The holocaust is a sign hung out by God."

Fiercely anti-dogma, the poem begs each person to make entirely "human decisions". Without reference to abstractions like 'honour', 'order', 'just war' the poet believes people will at last see each other.

> . . . That twisted face
> contorted by your ethics is
> your human brother, not a prize
> for your revolver.
> See how his scared uncertain eyes
> fearfully waver.
> See him, see him, as he is . . .

Whether this vision is possible, it's not entirely bleak for man is still part of nature. Some of the most memorable passages are the loving descriptions of this "dear landscape":

> . . . let's jot
> no final message
> but like the apple or the pear
> a ripple in the atmosphere
> a dappled leaf, a corn's late ear,
> austerely fall,
> though in the forest we can hear

no sound at all.

I have two criticisms only. There is a tendency to repeat ideas, most marked in the first half of the poem. Also, I didn't like how the verse form, Burns' most celebrated poetic form, Standard Habbie, was broken open. Far too often the last line of a stanza was part of a sentence carried over into the next stanza and even beyond. Consequently, the last rhyme of that line felt devalued as it wasn't conclusive.

More of Man's inhumanity in Margaret Fulton Cook's *Good Girls Don't Cry* – literally, as a large number of the poems show women being the victims of male abuse or male indifference.

Short, spare lines represent the degree of utterance possible in the terrible situation evoked as in 'Once' describing an unhappy father/daughter relationship: "I slit/ my tongue/ for you / cut/ it into/ halves/ and/ quarters/ so/ only/ the smallest/ of peeps/ could/ emit . . ."

I worked my way through this collection and found it difficult to read, at one point poem followed poem on domestic violence or incest. I did wonder if they could have been placed differently?

I most enjoyed the excellent sequence 'The Hill' about the poet's childhood, graphic, brooding, but shot through with humour. Here is 'Sometimes', the complete poem:

> during the day
> I could hear
> the mice
> scurrying
> in the cupboard
> where
> my pyjamas
> were keeping warm
> till night fall

I also appreciated those poems where I could take something away from the appalling situation described – some perspective, some image as in 'Once' where the father finally takes his daughter on a treat "to market/ to show me/ the happy Christmas turkey/ being strangled."

sweet, sour and serious is an illustrated anthology of poetry and prose by Survivors' Poetry Scotland. It contains the work of over fifty 'survivor' poets, those who have not only survived mental illness, or substance abuse, or sexual abuse but have, in many cases, survived the mental health system itself.

It's an upbeat book, hope coming out of collective sharing of some dreadful experiences as in 'In the Ward' by Gordon T Delaney where medication is forced upon a patient.

Judicious editing has given us poems of humour; 'The Flea' by Eddie Flanagan about a flea moving upmarket from the Gorbals as well as poems of sadness such as Wallace MacBain's 'Skippered' about a drunk living on the streets. A particularly wise poem is 'The Quiet Moment Late at Night' by Ruth Dunster. It struggles to discover where home is. The speaker is watching someone die, finding it unbearable he should leave the speaker or be dragged away "from this significant street of turnings". She hears "the winter geese/ calling across the dark/ following a pattern of stars" and thinks "they are going home/ which, north or south?". As creatures who migrate between places, the possibility dawns on the speaker "whether home might not be equally/ somewhere out there". I think for her and the person about to die home is in both places.

Iain Crichton Smith stresses human decisions we all must make. Dave Ward in *Tracts* lays stress on human actions and the power of the human imagination to transform an impoverished urban environment.

In spite of a landscape blighted with "smashed glass", where "above the chip shop door,/ the lopsided lettering/ recites the names of all the drugs/ the kids have/ heard of"; in spite of echoing spaces between the tower blocks "where lone dogs hunt and snarl", somehow people come together – two boys fighting each other, joined in sweat; people making love; and especially children through their games remaking the world they live in:

Two girls march
    their morris steps
    in the fallen leaves.
No music but
    the dusk's shy birdsong
    and the beat of plimsolled feet.

In Iain Crichton Smith's work, where nature *is*, is sanity whereas in Ward's work nature has been reduced to a flower which "grows/ with the smell/ of chemicals that smell/of the smell of powdered bones."

Lack of space forces me to focus on the poems written in English in Tom Watson's collection *Dark Whistle* as they are the greatest challenge to the reader. The fourteen poems in Scots are immediately accessible.

The simplest of the poems in English are about creatures, such as 'Deer', 'Gulls', 'Owls' and my favourite 'Ruminant': "The large and heavy pewter cow/ Playing bookend to her kine/ Lay down."

Image predominates in Watson's poetry and it's a mistake to search, as I did at first, for linear meaning. In 'Folk Dance' it's better to treat the "words as mirrors" (This is a quote from 'Reflections'). Just as in a mirror all is seen at once, so in this poem each stanza visits, as if from a Tardis, events oddly non-specific, yet typical historically. Like "the dancers turning, spinning" we whirl from "black guns" to "The ancient unsealed roads were dark as vandals/ Sacked two thousand years of greed" to "Old wheels were precious, walled in ghettos" and up to the present day.

Sometimes, I think Watson risks being obscure. He pares his language down to images that may not mean to his readers what they mean to him. In 'Black Canticle' will "the wires still sing their song" make people think of the wires of extermination camps, which, in an interview in *ZED₂O* he said they were. Are the clues sufficient – "cows with their crowns/ Of edelweiss"; a speaker talking to "My Clara" and how "You hardly heard the whistle/ Of the trains"?

As might be expected from an actor/poet, shifts in emotion communicate much. The poem ends on a note of unbearable grief, moving from the first version of a refrain:

Within the stone a frog,
Within a frog the blood,

to its final version:

Within the stone a stone
Within the frog bare bone
And the cows with their crowns
All shorn . . .

And again, the question about why there is human cruelty is asked:

The song is always – why?
Always the song is – why?

Maureen Sangster

Gumption

The Witching Tree, Alison Prince, Allison & Busby, £8.99; *Langwheeple*, Mercedes Clarasó, Black Ace Books, £14.95; *Empty Footsteps*, Lorn Macintyre, Black Ace £14.95.

Common sense used to dictate that 'here and now' was easily distinguished from 'there and then'. On the brink of the millennium perhaps we are not so sure. These novels in their different ways seek to show the inter-connectedness of events separated by time and distance, the flimsiness of the veil between past and present, reality and unreality.

Alison Prince is best known as a children's writer and *The Witching Tree* is her first adult novel. Mary McGuire believes herself to be a latter-day witch – a woman for whom intuition and coincidence work together to her advantage. She can make things happen. Although Mary does not know it, she is the descendant of a Scottish woman condemned to death as a witch leaving a young daughter also with witch-like powers. The life stories of these women, although separated by 400 years, run strangely parallel. The narrative flows backwards and forwards through the centuries as each woman has to defend herself against the prejudices and cruelties of her own time.

Alison Prince has a lyrical gift for description of the countryside and there are passages of great beauty in this book. She is also a skilful observer of character and behaviour. She has taken care to get the historic details right and paints a vivid picture of the daily life of the farmers and tinkers of 17th century Scotland. Similarly, her portrayal of wartime and post-war Britain has a wry authenticity about it. Her description of the treatment meted out to young women in an Edinburgh Home for Unmarried Mothers in the 1940s reminds us that we do not have to go far back in time for evidence of bigotry and inhumanity.

Prince conveys in an original way the familiar feminist message that women can possess a wisdom and strength denied to men. Perhaps inevitably her male characters are portrayed too simplistically as threats or hindrances to a woman of independent mind. But she has another message: in this mechanistic age men and women can best hope to survive by responding to the natural world, following their own intuition and creativity. This is a poetic and thought-provoking book.

Langwheeple is Mercedes Clarasó's fourth novel. Clarasó is of Scottish-Catalan descent and sets the book in the Borders, Edinburgh and South America. It is the story of Andrew, a shepherd's son, an introspective boy who from childhood has felt his destiny to become a minister. As an earnest young theology student in Edinburgh he becomes disillusioned with the perceived worldliness of his teachers and flings up his University course to pursue an unlikely career as a gaucho in Argentina.

His action has unforeseen repercussions – notably on Sandie, the daughter of his professor, who sees Andrew's rebellion as a noble and romantic act and becomes infatuated with him or rather the idea of him. As a result she is expelled from school and her life is irrevocably influenced by the episode. Andrew, meanwhile, is largely unaware of the havoc he has left behind. Their separate life-stories are chronicled more or less in parallel, although with some confusing time shifts and flashbacks. The excitement which triggered the whole thing off is followed for both of them by a humdrum and lonely existence. Disappointingly, Andrew finds the life of a gaucho boring, takes to teaching English and eventually returns to his native village of Langwheeple to live a life of quiet detachment, writing the occasional poem and ruminating on the past.

Mercedes Clarasó has a wonderful gift of characterisation and can also be very funny. The contrast between the serious-minded Andrew and the wayward Sandie could not be greater. For me Sandie is the more engaging character. The episodes featuring Sandie are spirited and amusing while those featuring Andrew are not. It is as if the first grand gesture of his life drained all the gumption out of him, leaving him self-absorbed and passive.

Like an uneventful life itself, this book is slow-moving with many a backward look, and some descriptive passages, especially of the hero's state of mind, are excessively long-drawn-out. But it demonstrates strikingly how settled plans can be deflected by merest chance with life-long consequences, and how there are few human activities that are without their effect on others for good or ill.

Lorn Macintyre's novel *Empty Footsteps* is

a solid achievement. It is the third in his *Chronicles of Invernevis* cycle – a highly researched series about the death of the old way of life in the Highlands. In *Empty Footsteps* the painful transition from feudalism to democracy (of a sort) is accelerated by the cataclysm of the First World War. Macintyre has astonishing descriptive powers, whether writing of the horrors of trench warfare or the tranquillity of a Highland glen. He is also a master of dialogue and the use of a single word or phrase can unerringly portray a mood or a personality.

Although some of the characters could be said to be archetypes – the old woman, the penniless laird, the loyal housekeeper and so on – we know that these people had an existence in the real world; they are brilliantly drawn and we care what happens to them.

The story charts the experience of a battalion of territorials attached to the 51st Highland Division who are torn from their occupations in a peaceful Highland village and flung into the carnage of the First World War. Simultaneously it is the story of families and friends they leave behind, and of the breaking down of social barriers and class taboos in a generalised tide of suffering and loss. The book is pervaded with Gaelic culture and includes songs and poetry. The "empty footsteps" are taken from a prophetic poem which foresaw the First World War. A strand of the supernatural runs through the book – an element of Gaelic magic realism which accepts that there are certain sights and experiences which transcend time and space, and that there can be a knowledge which has nothing to do with rationality.

The novel is concerned with time and change, but also with tradition and timelessness. Hector Macdonald pipes his comrades into the Battle of the Somme with the same heirloom pipes that had been played at Culloden. Clearly Lorn Macintyre is passionately involved with his subject and has a thorough understanding of the social and psychological forces which bring about change. A feature of the book is the compassion he has for all his characters, even the least sympathetic ones.

In spite of its tragic inevitability, this is a hugely enjoyable novel with moments of high comedy, and one is gripped by the story throughout. It is a fine achievement and I urge you to read it.   *Heather Scott*

Gaelic Tradition and the Individual Talent

Clann Iseabail, Màiri NicGumaraid, Acair, £6.99; *Bàrbachd Mhurchaidh Mhoireasdain*, Murchadh Moireasdan, Acair, £4.95; *Aotromachd agus Dàin Eile/Lightness and Other Poems*, Meg Bateman, Polygon, £6.95; *Fax and Other Poems*, Rody Gorman, Polygon, £6.95; *Oideachadh Ceart agus Dàin Eile/A Proper Schooling and Other Poems*, aonghas macneacail, Polygon, £6.95.

There are precious few novels available in the Gaelic language, which is one reason to welcome the arrival of Màiri NicGumaraid's *Clann Iseabail*. This sharply observed novel, would however hold its own against many recent English-language publications. At times it reminded me of the classic novel *The House With the Green Shutters*. We recognise all too readily the claustrophobic nature of a small Scottish community where the fine line between taking a healthy interest in somebody's affairs can blur dizzily with the urge to know where so-and-so is going, why they are going there and what time they will be back for a nice cup of tea and an interrogation.

The narrator, Ciorstaidh, and the Iseabail of the title are this short novel's most fully realised characters. NicGumaraid has a wonderful eye for evoking character through drawing our attention to the most telling of tiny details (e.g. nothing taller than a cup sits on the kitchen window-sill in order that Iseabail can see all that is going on in her outside world.) The dialogue is, for the most part, extremely realistic and the characters' relationships convincing.

NicGumaraid writes in a spare, enviably crisp Gaelic which suits the mood of this brief novel in which the local often represents the universal. She is not afraid to raise difficult questions regarding political and cultural issues. Ciorstaidh, for example, has a limited amount of sympathy for Scotty, a soldier who is killed while on duty in Ireland. (*"Gàidheal a' cogadh ri Gàidheal, Annag. Droch rud."* "A Gael fighting a Gael, Annag. A bad thing.") This is a novel as much about cultural identity and political difference as it is about personal relationships and petty prejudices. It is a short, stimulating read and is recommended to learners as well as native Gaelic speakers.

Bàrdachd Mhurchaidh Mhoireasdain (na

Hearadh) is another worthwhile read. The Harris-born poet's work is by turns irreverent, solemn, graceful and slight. Moireasdan's themes are traditional (love, faith, homesickness, humorous local events, etc.). Though the poems are varied, they are all very traditional in flavour. Morag NicLeòid's introduction is informative and adds much to the reader's enjoyment of the collection as a whole. She quotes Moireasdan's explanation of how one of his best-loved poems, '*A' Gheugag Fhraoich*' was inspired by catching sight of a piece of heather on a cold Glasgow street. He picked it up and by the time he'd reached his lodgings, the poem had composed itself. Elsewhere the poet recounts the tragedy of some ceilidh-bound singers who get stuck in a lift. Comic, grave, graceful, inherently musical, these poems consciously belong to a tradition which comes most alive in recitation or song and as such this book deserves to be read aloud!

In Meg Bateman's *Aotromachd agus Dàin Eile/Lightness and Other Poems* the poems appear "*gu ire mhòr san òrdugh san deach an sgrìobhadh*", "more or less in the order in which they were written". And the book gets off to a fantastic start. '*Gàrradh Moray Place, an Dun Eideann*', 'Moray Place Gardens, Edinburgh' is a superb poem. Vivid in its sensations and imagery; "*coire thaighean drùidhteach*", "a cauldron of imposing houses" and tangible atmosphere and movement, this is Bateman at her best. The following poem, too, '*A chionn 's gu robh mi measail air*', 'Because I was so fond of him' is a very fine one. It is brief, resonant and convincing. The title repeats mantra-like throughout the poem and yet its final meaning is something of a shock and stays poignantly with the reader. Bateman *can* be a most evocative and economical writer.

In the same way, however, that Bateman has commented that some of Anne Frater's poetry is too derivative of Derick Thomson, so I couldn't help thinking that Bateman's poetry is, at times, too derivative of Sorley MacLean. '*Dè 'm math dhòmhsa*', 'What good is it to me' and '*An e seo an cridhe?*', 'Is this the heart?' read, to me, like random stanzas from Sorley.

One of the problems I have with Bateman's work is that she tells us without showing, without proving. She ends a poem called '*Sìoladh na Gàidhlig*', 'The Decline of

Gaelic' with the following:

> *... nist tha mi a' faicinn nad shùilean*
> *briseadh-cridhe na cùise.*
> ... now I learn from your eyes
> the heart-break of the matter.

Even taking into account the repetition of the lovely long 'u' sound in the Gaelic version, this is not a strong ending for a poem. Surely a subject as important as Gaelic's decline deserves something more profound?

Like most readers, I like, expect a poem to end memorably. This is, after all, the juncture at which the poem ceases, where the poet-reader interaction comes, at least temporarily, to a close. I like, then, to be gifted something more than vague abstraction: and too many of the poems in this collection end with cloudy abstractions. '*Dealachadh*', 'Separation' ends:

> *. . . is ged nach robh dòigh eile ann,*
> *cha b' e idir nach robh de ghaol ann.*
> . . . and though there was nothing else for it,
> by no means was it that there was no love.

And? Often I felt cheated by anti-climactic last lines in these poems. Another irritation is Bateman's reliance on sentiment which doesn't always convince. '*Do Leanabh gun Bhreith*', 'To an Unborn Child' contains these lines, which are not meant ironically:

> A naoidhein, air ar saoghal dèan tròcair,
> gabh ort cor mìn-bhreòite nan daoine.
> Child, pity our world,
> Take on mankind's fair frailty.

Elsewhere she says:

> Fhir luraich 's fhir àlainn,
> thug thu dàn gu mo bhilean.
> O bonnie man, lovely man,
> You've brought a song to my lips.

Poetry rooted in tradition need not be old-fashioned. Although Bateman's collection is not short, I found it rather claustrophobic, both thematically and stylistically. Most of the poems are love poems addressed to a lover/ex-lover/would-be-lover or to her child. The poet's tone grew somewhat cloying by the end of the book. Although Bateman can write well, this is a disappointing collection. Great poetry does not merely expose the writer's feelings but demands a corresponding emotional response from the reader.

Rody Gorman's *Fax and other Poems* rep-

190

resents the nearest and most explorable star in the droll galaxy of his literature. He has amassed more than two thousand poems to date and, by the time you read this, probably three thousand. A Dubliner, he learned Scottish Gaelic in order, I suspect, to inject some humour into end-of-the-century Gaelic literature. His writing – strongly influenced by Iain Crichton Smith and Arthur Guinness – is often sardonic and thought-provoking, but it can also be rewardingly subtle. Some people have sniped at the simplicity of Gorman's work and in doing so have utterly missed the richness of his (very *Gàidhealach*) humour and the multi-textured honesty of his observations. Many of Gorman's poems say more than they seem to say. This he has in common with a number of the wily old Zen bards who occupied their time with bad wine, good living, and lasting poetry.

'*Ri Taobh Linne Shlèite*', 'Beside the Sound of Sleat' is a powerful, delicately-balanced love poem which leaves us with an aching, poignant image:

. . . a' ghealach
A' tuiteam an cridhe na beinne,
Fann agus sgàinte.
. . . the moon
Falling in the heart of the mountain,
Faint and rent.

One of the most moving poems in this debut collection was a brief poem called '*Mo Chuid Aodaich*', 'My Clothes'. There is so much going on in and after this short piece (the six little lines of which constitute a single sentence) that I can only urge the reader to seek out the poem and read it until the full meaning is absorbed. (Iain Crichton Smith and Donald MacAulay have both written magnificent poems about clothes/washing lines – I wonder whether a new Highland theme – to displace the Clearances – is emerging!) '*Naidheachd*', 'News', is another fine poem. Gaelic poetry – and (why not?) Gaelic broadcasting – need more poets jumping through their TV screens to declare their passion. Gorman is not afraid to take risks, imaginative leaps in public.

Some of the poems – '*Snugadair an t-Sean-chaidh*', 'The Storyteller's Snotrag' is a good example – are clearly more suited to public performances that the quiet communion between reader and page.

Perhaps one problem (if problem it is) with

Gorman's work is that much of the humour is lost on those who don't have Gaelic. For example, I would argue that '*Oran an Fhir-Chathrach*', 'The Chairman's Song' really does require some knowledge not just of present day Gaelic culture but also of the language itself in order to be best appreciated. The same goes for the untranslateable pun which concludes '*Na Glinn*', 'The Glens'.

Rody Gorman is very much a modern writer. He is not content with cosy images or archaic phrasings and so he takes risks with language, theme and style. He does not rely on tradition alone to carry his poetry into the magazines or bookshops. His is an honest voice, by turns exuberant, witty and sensitive.

In aonghas 'dubh' macneacail we have a truly international poet. His latest collection *Oideachadh Ceart agus Dàin Eile/A Proper Schooling and Other Poems* includes poems which have been variously published in journals and anthologies in Scotland, Ireland, Australia, Switzerland, Italy, Finland, America, Belgium, Croatia and Israel, which in itself is something of a triumph for a Gaelic poet.

In reading macneacail's work one might perceive a variety of influences – Pablo Neruda, Sorley MacLean, Native American literature as well as Shamanistic and Oriental writers – but aonghas dubh unequivocally has a voice of his own. He is a passionate as well as a compassionate writer and in late 20th century literature I, for one, admire these qualities very much. In '*beul beag*', 'little mouth', macneacail says to his son:

a bheòil bhig
an seinn thu dhomh
nad chànan ùr
na h-òrain òg
a thòisich tim
little mouth,
sing to me
in your new language
the young songs
that started time

macneacail frequently uses images of nature (trees, seasons, animals etc) and culture (*dè danaan*, Marilyn Monroe) in a uniquely personal way and perhaps more than any other poet in Scotland, macneacail knows how to use the metaphor. The sheer craft behind his writing makes the lack of logic (or, if you prefer, the nebulous presence of a dream-like logic) in his poetry intense and magically credible. In '*Samhla*', 'Appearance', macneacail announces:

> . . . *tha mise (sùil d' fhaileis) an seo . . .*
> . . . *mar phasgadh de shoillse reòit ann an linne cèir . . .*
> . . . i (your shadow's eye) am present . . .
> . . . like a folding of light in a pool of wax . . .

The title poem reminds us that the "proper schooling" is the one received outside of the classroom, the one passed down orally in the community:

> cha b' e eachdraidh ach cuimhne
> long nan daoine
> seòladh a-mach
> tro cheathach sgeòil . . .
>
> it wasn't history but memory
> the emigrant ships
> sailing out
> through a fog of stories . . .

aonghas dubh has his own identifiable voice. I like the fact that he is keen to develop (rather than rely on) the Gaelic tradition, and that he does this with an imagination which seems to have unleashed itself with a physical force.

macneacail dedicates his book "*Do gach bàrd aithnichte is neo-aithnichte a sheinn a' Ghàidhlig riamh*", "To every bard, known and anonymous, who ever made the Gaelic language sing". I think for a good many years to come bàrds, Gaelic and otherwise, will be citing aonghas macneacail as an influence. His writing is not just imaginative, it is *important*. (And how many writers do we have who are important – genuinely important – to our culture? Precious few.)

By dint of this, aonghas macneacail is Sorley MacLean's true heir. It is appropriate to end this review with the final stanza from the relatively short but inherently epic '*salm an fhearainn*', 'psalm of the land':

> trì ràithean dhut is ràith an tàimh
> ràith cur is fàs is buain
> bi cùramach mun talamh chrìon
> tha aighear anns an fhàs.
>
> three active seasons one of rest
> you sow you grow and reap
> be careful of the fragile earth
> for there is joy in growth

Kevin MacNeil

Offshore Lives

For the Islands I Sing. An Autobiography, George Mackay Brown, John Murray £16; *Selected Poems 1954-1992*, George Mackay Brown, John Murray £8.99; *Foresterhill*, George Mackay Brown, Babel Verlag, Postfach 1231, D-86938 Schondorf, Germany £9; *Dove-Marks on Stone: Poems for George Mackay Brown*, ed K A Perryman, Babel Verlag, Germany £25; *On the Rigs: Images of a Life Offshore*, George Gunn & Allan Wright, Keepdate Publishing, £19.95; *Sea Monster Tattoo and other stories*, Ruth Thomas, Polygon £7.99; *Wittgenstein's Web: Stories*, Sheena Blackhall, GKB Books £5.99

Why should a poet whose oeuvre had won acclamation as a testimonial to individual and communal experience decide in his mid-sixties to undertake that most authorised of personal histories, the autobiography? In the accedence of the modern writer to the demand for verifiable facts, George Mackay Brown had espied "the enemy of the creative imagination", and as a man who disliked talking about himself anyway, he must have been sensible of a contradiction: "Over the past four centuries there has been too much emphasis on the life and personality of authors – great streams of reminiscence, biography and autobiography", he complains, not far into this volume. Indeed, only a year before sitting down to write *For the Islands I Sing*, in an interview conducted in 1984 and recently collected in Isobel Murray and Bob Tait's *Scottish Writers Talking*, the idea of swelling those "great streams" with an account of his own life must still have seemed anathema:

> IM: Had you ever thought yourself of writing anything autobiographical? GMB: No, no fear. Oh no. [. . .]
> IM: So you're fairly determined to keep your own self as tucked away as the ballad maker or the skald, or whatever.
> GMB: Yes. I won't be writing any autobiographies.

The harnessing of antilogous tension is an ancient and honourable motor to thought, and GMB, whose poems instinctively retreat from closure, had a penchant – in his rare and unwilling excursions to the territory of logical argument – for the open syllogism. In one passage appended to the book in 1993, for instance, he meditates on the international scene: "There will never be a good society, there are too many flaws in human nature . . . But the idea of the good society ought always to be in our minds". And half way through the book he writes: "One of the great experiences of most lives never happened to me – I never fell in love with anybody", a statement seemingly irreconcilable with a later passage in which he recalls the "confused happiness and pain" he felt during the early sixties in the company of Stella Cartwright, whose death in 1985 may have prompted the writing of the book. A dutiful urgency enters the writing at this point:

> If I celebrate here, in plain prose, a young beautiful woman who lived in Edinburgh at this time, it is because she deserves to be remembered, and there is a danger that she may be inadequately dealt with if someone comes to write about the Scottish literary scene in the decade round 1960.

Though this passage of the book in particular has (possibly) licensed more sensationalist accounts (e.g. Gillian Harris, *Scotland on Sunday*, March 30, 1997) than GMB's and since the book's appearance, there has been some 'off-stage' muttering to the tune that "Of course this is not the whole story", there is also a sense in which it is just that: the story as GMB needed to tell it. GMB's 'life' unfolds as a series of anecdotes and reflections whose pace and phrasing, unworried by the structural demands of investigative prose, are those of the practised raconteur. If this autobiography does not contain 'the whole story', then that has been less the product of its author's desire to conceal the truth than of his manner of telling stories. It is, after all, 'for the islands' he sings, his narrative voice remaining accountable to a reading community whose sense of decorum and suspicion of individualism the Orcadian writer had himself helped establish, and it is this rather than the measure of the poet's confessional zeal that carries conviction.

For the poet Deborah Randall, too, the bardic/skaldic anonymity of GMB's writing has less to do with idiosyncrasy than with the place the poet inhabited within the continuities of Orcadian life:

> By staying and being, you kept the faith,
> The art to be still, blended into the background,
> You became invisible, your words failed

To single you out from the elements.

I cite these lines from an elegy of graceful sobriety entitled 'George Mackay Brown', one of a garland of poems intended for the late poet's 75th birthday: *Dove-Marks on Stone*. As "a gesture of celebration rather than sadness" this lovingly produced anthology achieves its aim admirably, collecting sensitive tributes by Catherine Fisher, Seamus Heaney, Christopher Jenkin-Jones, K A Perryman, Sheenagh Pugh, Deborah Randall and R S Thomas, as well as a poem entitled 'Carol' by GMB himself.

The latter work may have come too late to have been included in the new, enlarged paperback edition of the *Selected Poems*. To the previous edition of this book GMB has added one poem each from the collections *Voyages* and *The Wreck of the Archangel*, as well as three new sequences originally published as separate books: 'Tryst on Egilsay' celebrating the meeting of Earls Magnus Erlendson and Hakon Paulson on Easter Monday AD 1117; 'Foresterhill', imagining "a medieval monastic beginning for Foresterhill, the Aberdeen Royal Infirmary", and 'Brodgar Poems' which envisages the construction of the Neolithic stone circle at Brodgar over several generations. Though GMB's preface to the new *Selected*, written only two months before his death, states that all the poems in the book were written on the Orkney Islands, he tells us in a short introduction to 'Foresterhill' that this sequence – first published and still available in a handsome limited edition by Babel – was begun while GMB was a patient at Aberdeen Royal Infirmary and was "trying to express some gratitude . . . to the surgeons, doctors and nursing staff". With the aural acuity of a northern Lorca – "Moon never fails, the shifting silver of the plate/ A-jostle with fish" ('A Scroll') the sequence combines a stark visual simplicity reminiscent of seasonal miniatures in a medieval Book of Hours: "Three axemen from the woodyard. They mark/ A tree here and there. Snow/ Comes shivering from black branches." ('Lux Perpetua') The work is a paean to asylum – medical and spiritual – wrenched from conditions of extreme affliction, an asylum pledged to serve friend and foe, rich and poor, aware that recklessness and ill-guided politics can render such generosity, if not meaningless, then practically useless: "At Foresters' Hill is no provision/ For a festival of wounds." ('Lowlanders').

To GMB, the roaring flare-stack of the Flotta oil terminal would undoubtedly have fallen among those symbols of "material progress, which ... would end by ruining the life of Orkney as we know it, and all the other unique lonely places of the world beside". To the poet George Gunn, however, one of a generation of "residual working class males" from the Highlands to whom 'life offshore' for all its hardships made sound economic sense, the oil rig remains a more ambivalent point of orientation. *On the Rigs*, with 72 colour photographs by one-time 'roustabout' Allan Wright and 13 poems of welcome lexical density by George Gunn, as well as an informative introduction by the poet, is dedicated "to all those who know the true price of oil". The poems address that 'true price' – broadly speaking, the cost to life and limb – at two levels, and the book generously rewards enquiry into each. Firstly, the book's documentary pitch tells us much about the darker side of an industry that has remained strangely exotic for all the central role it plays in the economy of these islands:

When I look back to those times of the seventies I see the youth of a nation almost as though it had gone to war. We suck the hydrocarbon deposits from the Orcadian basin of the North Sea and choppers go down and boats sink. Rigs break their anchors and drift. The *Ekofisk* has happened, the *Alexander Kielland* has happened. The *Piper Alpha* is a grim reality that could happen again.

Secondly, these poems strain beyond documentary specificity and beyond a condition that "shuts you down, hems you in, makes it hard to speak from inside" to find a potent cipher for life as lived in our times – life offshore, unhinged, yet dependent on the double-edged instruments of modern technological progress: hanging "un-voiced from a greasy spar/ Shoreless" ('Greasy Spar') we – the reader too – are "digging, digging/ into the formation where the thing/ that will finally hold us is waiting" ('The Derrickman').

Quotidian lives unhinged, groping for epiphany against the disconcerting backdrop of the hyper-ordinary fill the pages of Ruth Thomas's first collection *Sea-Monster Tattoo*. Her characters have an acquired modesty, though usually one grown of disappointment. Fulfilment is a foreign word, and the certainty of its absence is the most positive thing that can be expected from the end of an evening: "We don't kiss; we just shuffle" ('Gloves'). Loneliness, the inability to translate oneself or be translated into the web of another's life is what these stories are about: "None of us really knows each other, we're all part of a collective dream. You forget conversations as soon as you walk out the door" ('Strange Birds'). Ruth Thomas's extraordinary eye for the telling detail and grasp of atmosphere have been highly praised, and rightly so. It is obvious that more than one publisher will be eager to see her using longer fictional forms. If I feel any qualm about the prospect, it stems from the structural repetitiveness of the Thomas recipe: the emptiness, the hypocrisies, the single or half sentence – usually the last – redeeming a glimmer of lost hope, celebrating the evanescent. As I have suggested, absence is a telling presence here: " ... running away from them, away from the houses, something bright and good." ('Beautiful Fox'); "Part of her wanted to rush in and rescue him, but something was gone already." ('Broadcast'); "Then it's just me and this bag of apples. For some stupid reason, I feel lonely" ('Therapeutic').

Translation is the central concern of Sheena Blackhall's *Wittgenstein's Web*, which contains, besides thirteen Doric tales of her own making, her 'owersettin' into Doric of stories by Italo Svevo, Alberto Moravia and Italo Calvino. In her forceful introduction, a literary-linguistic manifesto asserting her right to "eese Doric tae screive on the mappamound", taking in the full gamut of "politics, philosophy an current affairs", Blackhall writes: "As a Scots screiver, I sit in the mids o ma culture, like a wyver in her wab". The spider's artful entrapment of foreign sustenance suggests the writer's awareness that the survival of a language may be more dependent on what is gained in translation than on regrets over what has been lost. Sheena Blackhall was "brocht up bilingual", learning Doric from her "bluid kin" and hearing "Inglis on the wireless" and at school. She was also aware of the "echoes o anither leid", the Gaelic of the Deeside folk who had named "maist o the howes and knowes aboot the place". It is not surprising then that Blackhall's stories tend to play along the edges of cultural and linguistic divides. Translation, in these stories, can be seen as a threat: "There's be nae furreign bluid inower *her* kailyard waa. Deeside they'd be, in bluid, in cast, in spikk." ('Spikk') Or trapped in our own language web, we may be blind to alterity and therefore to the potential humour of our mis-translations: "Fin ma Granny Ross tuckit me inno bed the nicht, she said Ma wis a '*Fast Piece*'. Bit Ma aye takks ages tae spreid a piece. Sae I ken yon's a lee" ('The Diary'). Perhaps the most ambitious act of translation here is her transferral of the effect of the Hiroshima atomic bomb explosion to Aberdeen, putting eye-witness accounts into the mouths of contemporary Aberdonians, subverting the couthiest of childhood memories: "Deid bodies chokit the shore, bobbin up an doun in the puils like Halloween aipples". I think my favourite in this collection was 'The Cox's Pippin', a longer piece whose wisdom and compassion helps make this, like all the books reviewed here, thoroughly recommendable reading.

Iain Galbraith

The Body Politic

Politics and Society in Scotland, Alice Brown, David McCrone and Lindsay Paterson, Macmillan Press, £12.99; Strategies for Self-Government: The Campaigns for a Scottish Parliament, James Mitchell, Polygon; Welsh Europeans, John Osmond, Seren, £6.95; Scotland: An Unwon Cause, PH Scott, Canongate, £9.99.

My first reaction after the YES/YES vote on September 11th 1997 must have been quite widely shared – suddenly, arguments which one had doggedly employed over and over again through three decades were no longer needed. The Scottish people had shown that they were not afraid of proportional representation, of dominance of Scotland by Strathclyde or even of potentially higher taxation. A large area of controversy remains. Should Scotland accept a position resembling that of Catalans and Basques within the overall Spanish state, or should we not rather move on to match the independence of countries of comparable size, Denmark and Portugal, within the European Union? But friends in England, I noticed, assumed that through the Referendum vote Scotland had regained 'independence' and, within severe limitations, so we have. We enter the 1998 World Cup Finals as a manifestly distinct nation.

Does this mean that Paul Scott's anthology, *Scotland: An Unwon Cause*, is now out of date? Not in the least. It is an erudite and invaluable compilation of writings and statements, from Tacitus to Alex Salmond, bearing on questions of national freedom and identity. Here, in an inexpensive book, one can find the texts of the Declaration of Arbroath, 1320, and the Fourth Claim of Right for Scotland, 1989, of the National Covenant of 1638, the Treaty of Union of 1707 – and Tom Nairn on Scottish 'self-emasculation', 1977. One paradoxical point emerging is that Fletcher of Saltoun's position on self-government seems tortuous and cautious set alongside (for instance) the wish that Scots language should be taught in schools voiced by Henry Cockburn who was a convinced unionist. Scottish national *feeling*, sustained with consistent strength since 1707, has attached itself to church doctrines, to literature and music, to landscape and football, often so powerfully that the existence of a Parliament would have made no difference one way or the other: a consideration voiced by Fletcher when he said that if he could make the nation's ballads, he didn't mind who made the nation's laws.

The authors of *Politics and Society in Scotland* as political scientists are committed to definition of terms which are discussed 'theoretically'. Such discussion can seem excruciatingly pointless to non-academics, but Brown, McCrone and Paterson make theirs useful. Their discrimination between 'state', 'society', and 'nation' illuminates Fletcher's comment. 'Laws' are produced within state structures to regulate societies which exist within certain geographical borders. 'Nations' sing on regardless. Nationalism is not the expression of objective differences , but the mobilisation of those differences which actors believe to be salient. The "nation", then, is not a primordial form of social organisation, but an idea, an aspiration. It should be considered not so much as "place" but as "process".

After 1707 Scotland retained not only a 'national' church which was a focus for pride and contention of intensity such as we can hardly imagine now, but its distinctive laws and legal system. This would have been enough in itself to ensure that Scottish 'society' under an umbrella 'Great British' state which took Scotland in and out of its wars retained a distinctive character. If the Liberals who dominated Scottish political life for nearly a century after the Reform Act of 1832 at first brought Scotland closer and closer to the English model, it was because that was what Scottish voters wanted. But the creation of the post of Scottish Secretary in the Cabinet in 1885 – a response to nationalistic stirrings at a time when Irish Home Rule was the dominant issue in British politics – marked movement back towards distinctiveness. The arrival of a large – devolved – Scottish Office in the centre of Edinburgh in the 1930s may eventually be seen as a more fundamental development than the recreation of a Scottish Parliament in the year 2000. (I hope not. I will come back to this point later.) It ensured that a multitudinous Scotland-based bureaucracy ran most of what might be called 'Scottish civil society' in coorie-close cooperation with Scottish elites – professional and entrepreneurial. The Quango-Scotland of the 1990s was prefigured as the former Clydeside Socialist and Home Ruler, Tom Johnston, as Secretary of State in Churchill's 1939-1945 coalition, mobilised elites towards the creation of Scotland's own Welfare State. The ostensible and admirable logic of Labour's policy of devolution for Scotland is that the large powers and budgets of the Scottish Office should be subject to direct democratic control. But the drive of New Labourism is towards a situation where Blair-clones dominating a Scottish Parliament will ideally ensure that Scotland marches precisely in step with England.

John Osmond in his valuable *Welsh Europeans* writes incisively about the politics of Labourism in his own country, and what he says has all-too-much application to Scotland. These politics involve "a kind of nationalisation or incorporation of the radical impulses of democracy and socialism into a British safety standard of inactivism . . ." Westminster-orientated Labour culture is "essentially demobilising, instinctively paternalistic, bred on patronage, and unused and unsympathetic to the democratic impulse." This could well describe the Scottish Labour Party which from 1945 to the 1980s returned scores of deservedly forgotten hack MPs to Westminster, leaving the democratic agenda, and the aspirations of the 'nation' to persons hopping and swithering between the Communist Party, the Campaign for Nuclear Disarmament, Liberalism and a Scottish National Party which itself did not quite know how to cope with experimental radicalism.

James Mitchell's *Strategies for Self-Government* was completed in an anxious, even agonised spirit after Roseanna Cunningham's victory for the SNP in the Perth and Kinross by-election of 1995 but before the definitive Tory wipe-out in May 1997 and the subsequent united front of SNP and SLD with Labour and the Referendum Campaign. The tales he has to tell make that blink of harmony seem both explicable and uncanny. All three parties had at different times led the movement towards 'home rule' after 1885. And Mitchell reminds us that there was a tradition of Conservative Nationalism too, making the National Party in early days quite fairly vulnerable to jibes about 'Tartan Toryism'. The SNP did not clarify its position as a left-of-centre party till the 1980s.

In the 1920s, when 'Red Clydeside' Labour MPs tried, with complete sincerity, several times to push Home Rule bills through a Conservative-dominated Commons, the 'idea', the 'aspiration' of 'national' feeling had double thrusts. For Maxton and Buchanan it was primarily involved with Scottish traditions of social concern and democratic vision. But people well to the right of such men envisaged Scotland as an equal partner with England in an Empire which was evolving into a Commonwealth. By the 1930s, the effectual independence of the 'white Dominions' would be confirmed, and even such a radical as MacDiarmid for a time settled at 'Dominion' status for Scotland. It was good that Nationalism did not develop, in the 1930s such a hideous face as it acquired in Germany, Croatia, Hungary and so on. Mosley's impact North of the Border was negligible. But so was the electoral presence of the National Party in a country subjected to Tory paternalism and, in Glasgow, Labour immobilisation.

The continuous survival of the SNP, as Mitchell tells the story, becomes quite mysterious. After the charismatic literary men – Mackenzie, MacDiarmid, Linklater – who gave it early public salience dropped away, and the exuberant John McCormick debunked to flirt with every other party in his wondrously ineffectual Convention movement, the doggedness of such persons as Robert McIntyre and Arthur Donaldson kept it going till it was galvanised during the Springtime of Nations in the post-imperial Sixties. The fretful and damaging behaviour of its large parliamentary representation in 1974-79 derived partly from the absence of sufficient viable tradition, as did the incapacity of the Old Guard either to accommodate or expunge the mild radicalism of the socialist 79 Group. It belonged to the dreamworld of 'nation' and fumbled to connect itself realistically to 'state' or even with 'society'. What restored the SNP's credibility was the growing realisation that there was a definable, secure place for an independent Scotland within the European Union. "It's Scotland's Oil" was the slogan of happy-go-lucky opportunists; 'Scotland in Europe' is an idea which embodies resolved constitutional thought.

But as Osmond's book reminds us, Europe is an arena where big 'nation states' with their 'big nationalisms' are dissolving increasingly into regions. Lisbon now fears that North Portugal might throw in its lot with Galicia. Chunks of Germany with no autonomous 'national' tradition now function successfully as 'regions'. An ironic outcome of all our fuss and anguish aimed at reviving the Scottish Parliament might be that such a body would face demands not only from Shetland but from Grampian for autonomy within a 'Europe of the Regions' – which, as it happens, would represent a modern version of Fletcher of Saltoun's vision of a Europe of City States in which Inverness would rank with Edinburgh.

The paradoxes of Welsh 'identity' were exhibited on that nailbiting night when Ron Davies secured by the narrowest of majorities a vote for Labour's proposed Assembly.

Reader's of John Osmond's book will be surprised to find Davies who seemed so shifty and blunder-prone during the Welsh Referendum campaign, presented as a hero. If the two great late Socialist Williams's, the novelist and critic Raymond and the historian Gwyn, emerge as the appropriate intellectual mentors for the Welsh which Osmond wants, Davies secures his commendation as the first prominent Labourite ever to stake his career on the concept of democratic Welsh Home Rule.

The historical differences between Wales and Scotland are enormous. Though the armies of Edward I and Oliver Cromwell briefly occupied Scotland, our country has never been wholly 'conquered', let alone 'colonised'. Wales was conquered in the Middle Ages, brutishly united to England in 1536, and allowed to retain such distinctiveness as its national language and customs afforded simply because it was economically and politically so peripheral and ignorable. The Industrial Revolution made Wales important. English and Scottish capital as managers, and workers poured in to colonise the valleys, rip out coal and forge steel. As Osmond observes, Welsh national feeling is based on traditions of defeat – Llewellyn the Last and Owen Glendower were beaten down like the miners of the 1920 and the 1980s. Patriotic Welshmen associate themselves with two ill-assorted phenomena – an ancient and threatened language and a tradition of working class, Methodist-inspired, English-speaking militancy rather inconsequentially involved with memories of magnificent rugby teams. Between them these two factors just outweighed, in the referendum vote, Pembroke's ancient status as Little England, the natural gravitation of the eastern marchlands towards Liverpool, Birmingham and Bristol and the immobilising Labourism and Toryism of Quango-happy Cardiff. Meanwhile, rancour within the Welsh Labour Party and woeful prophesying by mindless Tory businessmen recalled, and even perhaps exceeded in disgrace, the ghastly Scottish Referendum 'debate' of 1979.

Thank whatever Gods may be that such debates are now over. The struggle now will be to ensure that the new Scottish Parliament and the new Welsh Assembly are not dominated by the local elites which have sorted out affairs in our two countries to their own satisfaction and advantage under Labour and Tory alike since the Second World War in close cahoots with Whitehall and the Party Whips. My own slogan at the moment is 'abolish all Quangos'. ALL of them. Reorganise on a 'level playing field' so that democratically elected representatives actually control what happens in our 'societies' and that whatever status our nations establish for themselves in Europe is negotiated in the interests of all of us, not those of entrenched sectional interests always poised to rush off to plot with Big Brother Blair's anti-democratic acolytes. In short, we must democratise 'the state', or at least as much of it as we can get our mitts on.

Angus Calder

Lyrical Vein

The Hand in the Well, Sebastian Barker, Enitharmon, £6.95; *On a Deserted Shore*, Kathleen Raine, Agenda Editions, £6.00; *Scanning the Forth Bridge*, Robin Bell, Peterloo Poets, £5.95; *Vestiges*, William Cookson, Agenda Editions, £6.00.

Sebastian Barker's *The Hand in the Well* is in six sections. The most interesting is 'Tinkering with the Fine Tuning', which is bookended by two sonnets; the first an injunction to speak out against lies in an intensely heightened language ("new words on the high wire"); the latter a valedictory dismissal, encouraging the sequence to "inscribe in kingdom come/ What ruin is, lies ruined, to blind and death and dumb." Both attempt a lyrical intensity of Parnassian proportions, which they almost achieve. The poems strain under a level of artifice which at once makes them beautiful and self-conscious articulations of a desire to express 'the truth'. In the light of the plainer title-poem, this high degree of artificiality seems to be deliberate. Its narrator joins a group of people who with scalpels, pipettes and other instruments are tinkering with the fine-tuning:

> By now I am irritated.
> Why did they ask me to come?
> So I stroll over and put the boot in
> the fine tuning, demanding to know
> What they think they are doing?
> We were on the verge, they have the
> audacity to say,

Of tuning in to the human heart,
Until you came along. Read this, I say.
The poem successfully criticises over-precious aesthetics, both through its message and its medium. It is, however, boasting a great deal about what follows.

These include pieces dealing with the torture and murder of helpless innocents, narrated by the perpetrators. Sentences are short, syntactically straightforward, unadorned by artifice. The tone is rational and impassive. As each speaker records his crime there is no admittance of guilt or regret. One of the speakers admits he now lives a comfortable suburban life. Extreme violence is not explained as a rogue transgression of the rational values of our 'civilised' society. It is generated by, and accommodated within that society

The sequence argues that to make an *object d'art* out of such uncomfortable realities is to trivialise their seriousness. Prettification is the artist's gratification of an egoistic desire to assert his/her personality on the material. This is the "tinkering with the fine tuning" which Barker wishes to bypass. The sequence's disclaimer pre-empts criticism that it does not innovate, that its language is not highly charged. "Device is irrelevant, we're telling it how it is" state these poems.

My criticism is that they don't go far enough. Why for instance are 'A Simple Twist of Fate' and 'Kristel' written in quatrains? The stanzas exercise (rightly in this instance) little formal control over the material, so why bother? Is there a feeling that the semblance of such an established organising device will confer the authority of tradition on a piece and therefore legitimise its claim to our attention? Such a choice undermines Barker's purpose. Furthermore, the appeal to objective reality is unfair. All writing mediates and manipulates. There may be no pretty ornamentation, but there is plenty of artifice here. The authenticity of the speakers' voices for example is not entirely convincing. They sound *too* rational and *too* in control. Their apparent honesty, the lack of desire either to cover up or to self-aggrandise strikes a false chord. In particular the last stanza of 'A Simple Twist of Fate' is forced and unsubtle.

If there is a partial failure here, it is a noble one. The strain in these poems is, in part, due to a very real tension between what certain notions of 'tradition' acknowledge as legitimate and what others, operating outside those notions, find necessary.

The rest of the book displays skill at handling a variety of poems. There are jubilant celebrations of spontaneity and playful debunking of portentousness. Section VI consists of mainly elegiac poems, some of which rise admirably to the challenge of tradition and some of which sink under the burden. The poems in 'A Love Song for Eros' tend to objectify their woman/muse figure; some will find this section discomforting.

At its simplest, Kathleen Raine's *On a Deserted Shore*, a sequence of 130 short poems, is an elegy for a departed lover. But for Raine there is more to reality than the simple presence/absence of materialism ("The language of the flesh/ Too faintly cries:"). The elegy is also a starting point for meditations on the relationship of the individual to a transcendental, universal whole:

If many, how lonely,
Even in requited love how far
Each heart from other;
But if one the whole, and we
Leaves on that great tree,
And weary time a flow in starry veins,
Nourished from hidden roots, and blossoming boughs
Where birds of heaven rest,
Then no love lost.

As the narrator walks along a beach, grieving for her lover, the sea assumes symbolic significance. It is both barrier and bridge between worlds. It is the great unknown, beyond which are the souls of the departed. It represents memory, throwing up litter from the past, and the deepest fears of the subconscious.

Poems often link tangentially rather than directly. Reading the sequence, one gradually becomes aware of a pattern. Some poems weave mythic elements into the fabric (Eurydice, the tree of life), others the vocabulary of Platonism and the mysteries of Christianity. Rhyme and assonance frequently chime through a poem and are then picked up, echoed and subtly amplified throughout the sequence. The careful ear begins to identify a music underpinning the whole work. In some ways this is curiously like H D's later poetry.

Raine *could* win readers back to poetry more than the trendy Maxwell and Armitage are ever likely to, for all their idle boasting about "the new rock 'n' roll". Hers is the kind of writing that many casual readers of poetry, fed a diet of Romanticism at school, would recognise as having the authoritative voice of 'poetry'. This book does perhaps only some of the things which poetry can do, but it does them well.

The title poem of Robin Bell's *Scanning the Forth Bridge* is a *tour-de-force*. It demonstrates the acoustic effects that classical metres have and vividly presents the Bridge and its traffic with playful wit. It shows how traditional forms can be purposefully used not to merely imitate or justify meaning, but to allow meaning to arise from form itself.

The bridge is wide. The Forth is deep.
Iambic trains are made for sleep.

Trochee trains are bright achievers,
sparkling through the cantilevers.

As a title poem though, it is a little misleading. There is quite a homogenous body of work in this book, but it is very unlike 'Scanning the Forth Bridge'. The sense of playfulness is much less evident elsewhere and the technical choices sometimes seem beside the point.

Which is rather ungracious. If one bridges the disparity between the opening poem and the others, there are some good pieces here. 'Ruchill Linn' assumes an organic shape so that the free verse movement is at one with the development of thought. It is a beautiful nature lyric, but offers more than pretty description. There is a way in which the curlew "freeing itself from fear/ with one clear call" and the waterfall which "was to itself a waterfall" are 'selving' themselves in Hopkins' sense of that word. They stress both their uniqueness and their belonging to the landscape. Some of the vocabulary (swirling), sound patterning (clear/call, seek/slake) and even the compounding of the verb 'hung over' into "overhung" also recall Hopkins. The performative sense in which the curlew announces itself in the night can be a metaphor for the defining acts by which any of us relate to our environment.

A few of Bell's poems sound like workshop pieces – meditations on objects of past significance, nostalgic childhood recollections. 'Mercator's Projection' attempts to force too much significance out of a number of metaphors which could have been unpacked a little more subtly. Judged by the best pieces here though, Bell has valuable talent.

William Cookson's *Vestiges* collects 13 poems written between 1955 and 1995. Ezra Pound is everywhere present. This is superficially most obvious in the typography. Brief, evocative phrases are laid on the page in small, isolated clusters, often indented and surrounded by swathes of white space. The poems are haunted by an atmosphere of melancholy and loss which is visually echoed by the lonely-looking lines. Typography apart, the influences come from both the very visual but slightly static Pound of his imagist phase, as well as the fragmentary, beautiful 'Drafts and Fragments' of the last Cantos. There is more to this book than Pound though. In the ending of 'Local Epiphanies' for example, there is something Shakespearean both in the cadence and the bitter-sweet sentiment:

The mind should hold
moments like these
until
in the end
from the long dream of the years
we awake to death

Considering that they have been written over forty years these poems are remarkably consistent in tone and style. There are numerous epigrammatic presentations of nature in freeze-frame. These hint at emotions or thoughts not explicitly stated. One might criticise that too many of these come at the reader successively, dulling their intensity. Alone they have a suggestive power that they do not in sequence. In Pound's later poetry, these kind of images are broken up with more conversational elements so that such compact, jewel-like phrases shine out more brightly. A book based solely on such a method takes on an almost fragile preciousness. On the other hand, fragility is an essential quality of the subject of this book. Cookson is precious about beauty and love (not only romantic, but also paternal) because they are fragile. With an almost Anglo-Saxon, elegiac acceptance of the mutability and transience of life Cookson both laments and rejoices simultaneously.

The title comes from Pound's Canto 74 ("no vestige save in the air") written at a time when Paradise was only visible to him in fragments; "unexpected excellent sausage/ the smell of mint, for example,/ Ladro the night cat". Cookson's vestiges are garnered from half a lifetime of memories, loves, visions and reading. If I call this book a modest achievement I hope the author might not be offended. He will recall Pound's comment that it is "better to present one Image in a lifetime than to produce voluminous works." Cookson has presented a few memorable images and not cluttered our shelves with pages of flaccid, flabby poetry. Would that more poets did the same.

Chris Jones

Pamphleteer

Welsh publishers Seren (2 Wyndham Street, Bridgend, Wales, CF31 1EF) have four poetry books up for review here, each priced £6.95 and the author of each being either Welsh by birth or by having adopted Wales as their homeland. *Animaculture* is the latest effort by Hilary Llewellyn-Williams and her third to be published by Seren. One of the most notable qualities of the poems in this collection is the immediacy of the text, cleverly coupled with an almost laid-back inclusion of mythology and pagan energies. The first is the titular poem, which contains a crossover of religious ideas. There are Christianity's angels complete with haloes involved in tending to the world in its need, but with a more pagan, 'natural' idea introduced by the symbolism of the world as a garden which needs cultivating – these are, in fact, 'gardening angels'! "Each one/ has hoe and sickle, spade and watering-can/ and wings, and a small patch/ to care for."

The oneness and unity of everything in existence is displayed with the narrative voice explaining how, having been tended all 'her'(?) life,

The gardening angels prune and propagate
moving in secret through the soul's acres;
have I called on mine too late?
Whistling, she strolls in from long ago,
and she hands me the rake and hoe –
Your turn, she says; and I feel my wings stir.

The message is to give back to the earth and the universe the attention and care one receives from them.

Similarly, 'Ursa' has a naturalistic ambience which is both peaceful and energetic at the same time. The former because of the quality of the description of the surroundings – "warm slabs of sun"; "all the forest/ hushed in frost"; the latter for the more basically animal elements interspersed throughout – "I eat. Blood in my mouth,/ sweet salmon flesh"; "My claws and teeth gleam". There is always the sense of the dualistic character of nature, on the one hand serenity and sleepiness, on the other, primitive violence and vitality.

The best of Llewellyn-Williams' poems contain these elements to some degree or other, but above all, the reader feels that here is someone who has accepted that nature and history, mankind and the future are all interconnected at some deep inescapable level and who wants to celebrate that fact in her writing.

Sheenagh Pugh's collection, *ID'S HOSPIT* is more down to earth, concerning itself more with the mundane, everyday things of life. From 'Snowman', with it's child's-eye point-of-view through 'Territories' with the parent versus child scenario to 'ID'S HOSPIT' looking to the past, Pugh manages to present the reader with a multitude of subjects to consider and reconsider in the light of the fresh view given. A more realistic and prosaic writer than Llewellyn-Williams, she nevertheless manages to re-kindle fantasy by way of poems such as 'The Embarkation of the Pigs' (on hearing that British publishers no longer welcome pig characters in children's books), reminding people of their childhood by way of Piglet, the Three Little Pigs, Pooh and Rupert. This poem also serves as a reminder that there is a place for everyone where they will be accepted, "where the Piggywig stands; where the round moon/ will countenance their portly, tolerant curves./ This is where the outlaws dance. Shine on; shine on".

'Booklifting' and 'Fellow-Feeling' are also worth mentioning, the first because every bibliophile will recognise the temptation outlined in the impecunious narrator's justification in stealing books, and the second for managing to convey approximately the right accent with "He was South Efrican, with that eccent/ you can't mistake". Pugh's poems may be slightly less accessible than Llewellyn-Williams' at the outset, but are definitely worth pursuing.

John Davies has an interesting assortment in *Dirt Roads* where the mining elements of Wales and also America are among the subjects he covers. Again a sense of landscape and history are prominent, heritage being important. In 'Braveheart', "Doug from Carolina" is of "Welsh and Scots ancestry", and can't decide which to follow up, and so watches the film *Braveheart* to help him decide, then plumps for Scots. This poem notes quite well the basic need to have roots, and to establish oneself, and Americans, with what many regard as the lack of their own history seem to feel this more than most. Coming at the issue from the other end, if you like, are the poems which deal with those who sought to establish themselves and their families in America, and one of these in particular, 'Sheriff' is very evocative with the opening lines "When silver was found, a few of the boys/ got married in the excitement,/ wiped out the last Indian/ then named the town after him". Again, I found the Wales-based poems quite peaceful with many references to nature.

Useful by Peter Finch is again more prosaic in subject and language. Old age, a writer's class of irritating students who "all seem to have/ been coming here for/ decades and no one/ ever improves", a break-up of a relationship –may seem depressing subjects, but the poems do not sink into dull, morbid self-pity, but instead present situations which, while often sad, are similar to experiences of any person's life. As Finch writes, in 'All I need is Three Plums (apologies to William Carlos Williams)', "these things just happen". Not all the poems are serious, though, with 'Summer School' and its stereotypes that anyone who has been to a writing class will recognise, and also 'Useful', where the narrator has bought "an ackers kit" for a son, who intends to use it to speak to someone in the Pentagon and blow up ships, but the narrator explains "lots of typing bloody brilliant/ stops im nickin cars it does/ an setting fire to animals".

Porpoises on the Moray Firth (Redbeck Press, 24 Aireville Road, Frizinghall, Bradford BD9 4HH, £3.95) is by West Lothian author Billy Watt. Quite a thin book, it is nicely presented and is inexpensive for what you get. Anyone who knows the isle of Bute well will love 'Day Trip to Bute', with its six parts entitled 'Rothesay Bay', St Blane on the Rocks', 'Easy. Easy. (Ettrick Bay)', 'The Sleeping

Warrior (by the Sound of Bute)', 'Cross and Cromlech (Dunagoil)' and 'Ferry Terminal'. Rothesay is drawn well, with the "preening, jostling for position" seafront houses and the "grander houses, withdrawn uphill" which "have tucked a helm of trees around them", and Arran gets its mention, along with Glasgow families and, of course, the rain. Other poems are written in dialect, like 'Video. Double Period', which details classroom activities, and the author, being a teacher, obviously knows his stuff. Others deal with parents, both from the point of view of having parents, and being one. The mention of names such as the Clyde, Glasgow and the Black Isle ground the majority of the poems in Scotland, and are hence very accessible for readers acquainted with Scotland.

Craigmillar Writer's Group have a collection out, *Do You Think You Know Me?* (Craigmillar Festival Society, 63 Niddrie Mains Terrace, Edinburgh EH16 4NX, £2.00), which contains work from a variety of the members of the group, who cover many topics amongst them, including discrimination, self-mutilation, drugs, prostitution, George Armstrong Custer and also has a new take on Mary, of 'Mary had a little Lamb' fame. Because of the variety of people in the group, the work is equally diverse and should therefore contain something of interest for everyone. One writer, Sandra, who wrote the poem 'Look Again' (the first line of which gives the collection its name) uses some particularly hard-hitting material. All proceeds from the book go back to the group for future projects, so have a look.

New Millennium (292 Kennington Road, London SE11 4LD) have published a new work, *O Didaskalos* by Michael James Cook, author of four other books, at £7.95, which is very reasonable given the size and content. The subject-matter is wide-ranging and again should appeal to most people in some way. Some poems are witty, especially those written with reference to celebrities such as Roger Taylor or George Best. Others are more thoughtful, more introspective, while yet others are investigative of people in their various shapes and sizes, all of which adds up to a pretty impressive collection.

The poems in *Darker Earlier* by Will Stone (Prozac Press, Old Wool Shop, Yoxford, Suffolk IP17 3EP £3.00) are rather melancholic, often dealing with death in some way which may turn some people off, but would probably appeal to those who still fondly drag out their old Cure and Smiths albums every now and then. Which, yes, does include myself.

Various other collections are available which are also worth a look: David Perman's *The Building* (Acumen Publications, 6 The Mount, Higher Furzeham, Brixham, South Devon, TQ5 8QY) covers a wide range of subjects and ideas well; Peter Loney in *London Idylls* (The Causeway Press, 14 Christchurch Road, London N8 9QL) not surprisingly is based largely in London, and deals with the city's different types of areas, and its associations for the author, and different rooms the author has inhabited there. *Bang*, by Carrie Hanson (Spout Publications, The Word Hoard, 46/47 Byram Arcade, Huddersfield HD1 1ND) has more hard-hitting material with poems like 'Unreported', and 'Step two three, one two three', which deal with rape and child abuse respectively, and 'What You Know' concerns the accurate and inaccurate knowledge a child has of a father who has left home. Fans of Robert Roberts will be glad to know he has another collection out, *Fourth Selection* (Pikestaff Press, Ellon House, Harpford, Sidmouth, Devon EX10 0NH) which is full of his usual skill and honesty and is sure to be popular. And for anyone who likes to access work by new poets, *Five Leaves Left* (Neruda Press, 51 Allison Street, Glasgow) is a collection of work by five authors, all Scottish and previously unpublished. Nick E Melville's poems from *Post Off* are especially worth investigating.

Was Your Mother's Name Jocasta? by Kath Hardie (Rookbook Publications, 16 Angle Park Terrace, Edinburgh EH11 2JX) is a great collection of poems and stories, the latter of which are set in Ballanogue, a fictional Irish location. The stories in particular are well-written and sharp, portraying well the idiosyncrasies of human nature, and there's a real flow to the writing which makes the reading of it a treat. Lastly, *The Skye Bridge: an Unfinished Story* by Robert Danskin, is funded by the Skye Bridge Appeal Group and is a chronicle of the bridge and the various issues surrounding it. Included in the work are the brief specifications for the bridge before it was built, a chronological sequence of events, information on the Appeal Group itself – reasons for its having arisen, and its agenda, among other things – and also discussion of the tolls levied, and an interesting selection of quotations regarding the bridge from a fair variety of people, including various MPs and reporters. All in all it's well worth looking at even if just to skim over, to get an idea of what exactly the bridge has meant to the people it concerns most – the ones that have to use it.

C J Lindsay

Catalogue

Scottish writers and writing are featured in most of the books in this catalogue. New from Thistle Publishing are John Buchan's *Complete Short Stories* in three volumes (£20 each) edited by Andrew Lowrie. This really is the definitive Buchan collection – some of the stories are appearing in book form for the first time and others have been out of print for almost a century. The stories are in chronological order, taking us, in the first volume, from the young student writing tales inspired by the countryside and people of Upper Tweedsdale, to the final volume with work more obviously by the author of *The Thirty-Nine Steps*. Any fan of Buchan would find these a delightful read. Included is an informative introduction and a glossary, and although the books are expensive, they are beautifully bound hardbacks and well worth the pennies.

Edinburgh Uni Press has reprinted another neglected work – James Hogg's *Lay Sermons* (£25), edited by Gillian Hughes and Douglas Mack. Published for the first time since 1834, Hogg's sermons on 'Good Principles and Good Breeding' were a response to the Victorian demand for religious and improving literature and may give the reader some new insights into the author of *The Confessions of a Justified Sinner*. Recommended more for those with an academic interest in Hogg – it hardly makes for light bedtime reading.

If your knowledge of Buchan, Hogg or any other Scottish writer is less than sketchy, pick up a copy of *Discovering Scottish Writers* (Scottish Cultural Press; £7.95), edited by Alan Reid and Brian D Osborne. Eighty Scottish writers from the 14th to the 20th century are briefly outlined by various academics and writers which makes for lively and enthusiastic entries from the likes of Owen Dudley Edwards and Iain Crichton Smith.

The oral tradition of the North-East is carefully preserved in *North-East Song and Story* (Scottish Cultural Press; £9.99), edited and introduced by Willian Morrice Wilson. The work includes some old, neglected writers that have been out of print for many years, as well as more famous names like John Barbour. A valiant attempt to keep the oral storytelling tradition alive or at least in print.

We continue the North-East connections with *Anither Dash O' Doric* (Canongate; £5.99), by Norman Harper and Robbie Shepherd. Following up the success of *A Dash O' Doric* they bring to you another collection of anecdotes, illustrating the particularly droll humour of the North-East. This might appeal to an older generation of readers, I did find the humour a bit too much like the 'funny' stories that appear on the Reader's Page of *The Sunday Post*. ('Last week, my granddaughter said . . . ') However, I'm sure your Granny would like it. For those with a more serious, academic interest in the dialect of the North-East, *A Doric Dictionary* (Scottish Cultural Press; £5.99) would be a good investment.

Moving further south, *An Arran Anthology* (Mercat Press; £9.99), edited by Hamish Whyte, brings together a host of writers in a "celebration and revelation of Arran's enduring appeal". A book of traveller's tales and holiday reminiscences in the form of poetry, prose and fiction, there is much of interest in this book. The reader will find famous names such as Walter Scott, William Wordsworth, Robert Browning and Iain Banks among the contributors. If the last time you went to Arran was in knee-high socks, this would be a nice little book to remind you of those halcyon days.

At the Sign of the Cleikum (avail. from Jean Moffat, 40 Damside, Innerleithen EH44 6HR; £7.95) is a collection of reminiscences of the Peebleshire town of Innerleithen between 1926 and 1932. First written by John A Anderson in a local newspaper column and compiled and edited by the author's daughter,

Olive M W Russell, the book records local legends and the history and traditions of the old weaving town. The book would probably appeal to locals more than those who know nothing of the town – it's not particularly accessible as a document of social history. Memories of a more harrowing kind can be found in Joe Pieri's *Isle of the Displaced* (Neil Wilson Publishing; £12.99), memoirs of an Italian-Scot's internment during the Second World War. Pieri's account of his arrest in his home town of Glasgow, his imprisonment on a Canadian river-island prison camp for three years and final release in 1943 are written in a lucid and commendably balanced way. His story is important in reminding us of the atrocities perpetrated by our own government during this time. Many Italian (and German) born Britons suffered under the government's Emergency Powers Bill of 1939, which permitted the arrest of innocent people.

On a lighter note, a new publication from Watergaw (Penninghame Schoolhouse, Newton Stewart DG8 6HD) is *A Braw Brew – Stories in Scots for Young Folk*, (£6.99) edited by Liz Niven and Pete Fortune with a foreword by Janet Paisley. This book is a treat – not only because of the entertaining, modern stories but because it attempts to help kids get to grips with the confusing disparity between the language most Scots speak and the language we read and write. Including writers like Sheena Blackhall and Anne Donovan, it's nice to see a book in the vernacular for children.

A book for Scottish history buffs, *Scottish Historical Documents* (£14.99) by the late Prof Gordon Donaldson, is republished by Neil Wilson Publishing. The source material in this book would be of particular use to students – it covers 1000 years and includes extracts from Bede's Ecclesiastical History, the 1295 Treaty with France, the 1320 Declaration of Arbroath, and concludes with the 1707 Articles of Union. It's interesting and informative, but a basic knowledge of Scottish history is needed, since the book doesn't include a historical narrative.

Land ownership reform has always been an urgent ecological and political issue in Scotland. This is what makes Andy Wightman's *Who Owns Scotland* (Canongate; £14.99) such a timely and important work. This is the second edition of the book that makes available crucial information about who actually owns the land in Scotland, and it manages to be factual and comprehensive without being inaccessible. Wightman clearly brings across the need for imminent reform in the law which bears more resemblance to the old feudal system than the law of a modern country.

If you're thinking of doing a bit of island hopping this summer, *The Scottish Islands* (£25) by Hamish Haswell-Smith, also from Canongate, is "a comprehensive guide to every Scottish island". It includes history, geology, wildlife and places of interest, but being a hefty hardback, it's hardly a pocket guide.

From travel to poetry with *Summoning The Sea – An Anthology of Contemporary Poetry and Prose* edited by Wolfgang Gortschacher and Glyn Pursglove (University of Salzburg Press). This is a 'literary festschrift' for James Hogg; no, not that Scottish novelist again, but a retired Prof of English Studies and the editor/funder of the the University of Salzburg Press. The book is a tribute from poets and academics for the professor's support of mainly British poetry. This really is a mixed bag, but worth a look because of the haunting poetry of Jenny Johnson and the enlightening essay by James Kirkup about phallic worship. The reader will never look at a prize leek or a crimson letter box in the same way again.

Less down to earth is *Earth Ascending – An Anthology of Living Poetry* edited by Jay Ramsay (Stride Publications; £9.50). This is an environmental poetry book taking the view that, "there are things which must be said , and the poet is often the only person capable of saying them". It's a shame that the lofty, new age-type language of the introduction is so pretentious; in a world over-run with capitalism and consumerism this book is a nice concept. It's also a shame because some of the poetry is good and includes work from Valerie Gillies and Ted Hughes. A cynic would call it spiritual nonsense, but no, man, poetry will save the world!

A more historical insight into spirituality can be found in Homer Sykes' *Celtic Britain* (Weidenfeld & Nicolson; £14.99). It's an attractive book covering the history and culture of the elusive Celts and contains some beautiful photography of standing stones, from Shetland to Cornwall.

The culture of modern Britain is laid bare in *British Cultural Identities* (Routledge; £13.99) edited by Mike Storry and Peter Childs. It's a comprehensive and informative book, aimed particularly at overseas students, but useful to anyone who wants to get to grips with what it means to be British in the 1990s. The chapter on youth culture is particularly good; it is very well informed and avoids sweeping statements, presenting balanced views on drugs, sex and the enduring appeal of the Doc Marten boot. The book also avoids anglocentricity, giving fair coverage to the Scottish and Welsh experience. This is cutting-edge stuff – a sharp evaluation of the society of the twentieth century as we approach the millennium.

A Guide to Welsh Literature c.1530-1700 (University of Wales Press; £14.95) is a weighty and academic text, the third in a series of books outlining the history and development of Welsh literature. Edited by R Geraint Gruffydd, the book includes essays on free-metre poetry, Welsh humanist learning and Bible translations. Less highbrow is *Gulliver and Beyond* (Channel Four TV; £4.95), edited by Paul Barker. Inspired by Channel Four's 1996 adaptation of Swift's novel, a group of contemporary writers including Gerald Kaufman and Polly Toynbee compare the satire of Swift's time to modern politics and society. Although contributors such as ex-Tory MP Julian Critchley fail to mention the book at all (typical politician), other writers who have actually read the novel make sharp comparisons between Swift's world and our own.

Anyone with an interest in science fiction and fantasy writing may enjoy *The Third Alternative*, a magazine of fiction, features and spooky-looking artwork. Available from TTA Press, 5 Martins Lane, Witcham, Ely, Cambs. CB6 2LB. Finally, from the Glasgow University (School of Scottish Studies, 9 Uni. Gardens, Glasgow G12 8QH) comes *Skinklin Star*, a biannual poetry and graphic art broadsheet. The third issue features Gaelic poetry with an optional English translation. The illustrations are elegant, but the size of the broadsheet makes for an interesting map-folding reading experience. A magazine we hope flourishes.
Emma Pitcairn

Stevenson Catalogue

PIANO MUSIC

Grade Guide for all piano works listed

a – advanced;

m – moderately difficult;

e – easy

Computer Printed scores –

Piano Transcriptions from Purcell:

The Queen's Dolour (e/m)

3 Grounds (m)

Toccata (a)

Hornpipe (m)

Little Variations on Purcell's Scotch Tune (m)

South Uist Folksong Suite (e/m)

Three Scots Fairy Tales (e)

Facsimile Photocopy scores

Symphonic Elegy for Liszt (a)

Norse Elegy (a)

Fugue on a Fragment of Chopin (a)

Three Elizabethan Pieces after John Bull (a)

A 20th Century Music Diary (m)

A Scottish Triptych (a)

Three Scottish Ballads (m)

Sonatina Serenissima (m)

Recitative and Air (m)

Motus Perpetuus (a)

Passacaglia on DSCH (a)

Pensées sur des Préludes de Chopin (a)

Also available from the Society

Prelude, Fugue and Fantasy (Novello) (a)

Peter Grimes Fantasy (Boosey & Hawkes) (a)

Hebridean Seascape (Roberton) (a)

Ella Savourna's Notebook (Roberton) (e)

Young Pianist's Grainger (Schott) (e/m)

Sounding Strings (UMP) (e/m)

SOLO SONGS with PIANO

Nine Haiku: cycle for high voice (23pp)

Eight Selected Soutar Songs for medium voice (28pp)

Hills of Home (R L Stevenson cycle) for baritone (19pp)

A Child's Garden of Verses (R L Stevenson cycle) for 1 or 2 high voices (80pp)

Border Boyhood for tenor
Selected MacDiarmid Songs, Vol 1 for medium/high voice (19pp)
Selected MacDiarmid Songs, Vol 2 for medium/high voice (34pp)
Selected MacDiarmid Songs, Vol 3 for baritone (41pp)
Two Tagore Songs for soprano (22pp)
Four Morgenstern Songs for medium/high voice (20pp)

CHORAL MUSIC

Computer-printed scores

Peace Motets – SATB a capella (Bible texts)
Canticle to the Sun – SATB, also for soprano and mezzo or alto a capella (text: St Francis of Assisi)
No Coward Soul is Mine – SSAA and harp or piano (text: Emily Bronte)

Facsimile photocopy scores

Medieval Scottish Triptych – SATB a capella
Choral Recitative and Psalm 23 – SATB a capella (Bible texts: Lorimer/Montgomerie)
Twelve-Part Motet In Memoriam Robert Carver – 4-part women's chorus, 4-part men's chorus and 4-part mixed choir a capella or with organ (text: James Reid Baxter)

CHAMBER MUSIC

Computer-printed scores

Recitative and Air in memoriam Dmitri Shostakovich for string quartet
Recitative and Air in memoriam Dmitri Shostakovich for violin and piano. Also available for viola and piano; cello and piano.
Golden Song (ed Ralph Holmes) for violin and piano
Homage to John Field for clarinet and piano
Bergstimmung for horn and piano

Facsimile photocopy scores

Voces Vagabundae for string quartet
Alma Alba for piano and string quartet
Four Meditations for string quartet
Scots Suite for solo violin
Don Quixote and Sancho Panza for guitar duo
Two Cambrian Cantos for harp
Duo Sonata for harp or piano

Fantasia polifonica for harp

ORCHESTRAL MUSIC

Please contact the RSS for full details

RECORDINGS ON CDs

Stevenson plays Stevenson piano works. – Passacaglia, Recitative & Air, Prelude, Fugue and Fantasy. ALTARUS 9091– 2cds
Salute to Scotland. Stevenson plays Grainger. Ronald Stevenson. ALTARUS 9040
Cathedrals in Sound. Chopin, Marek, McDowell, Stevenson, Bach-Busoni. Ronald Stevenson. ALTARUS 9043
Stevenson piano music. Fugue on a fragment of Chopin, A 20th Century Music Diary, Symphonic Elegy for Liszt, Motus Perpetuus. Joe Banowetz. ALTARUS 9089
Taken into the Mountains. Stevenson piano music. Ballad after Grieg, Norse Elegy, Beltane Bonfire. Donna Amato. ALTARUS 9021
Piano Concertos 1 & 2. Murray McLachlan, piano and Chetham's Symphony Orchestra, cond Julian Clayton. OLYMPIA 429
Piano Music from Scotland. Includes FG Scott transcriptions by Stevenson, Beltane Bonfire, Three Scottish Ballads. Murray McLachlan. OLYMPIA 261
The Essence of Busoni. Ronald Stevenson. ALTARUS 9041
Twentieth-Century Operatic Fantasias. Ronald Stevenson, piano. ALTARUS 9042
Busoni for two pianos. Ronald Stevenson and Joe Banowetz. ALTARUS 9044
In memoriam John Ogdon. Includes Stevenson's Prelude and Fugue on a theme of Liszt, Kevin Bowyer, organ, and Piano Sonatina no 1, Ronald Stevenson. ALTARUS 9063
Essentially Scottish. Includes South Uist Folksong Suite, A Wheen Tunes for Bairns tae Spiel, Three Scottish Ballads. Ronald Brautigam. KOCH-SCHWANN 3 1590 2

Available from other sources –

In memoriam Benjamin Britten. Includes Sonatina Serenissima. Anthony Goldstone. GAMUT CLASSICS 526
Passacaglia on DSCH. Raymond Clarke. MARCO POLO 8.223545

Eurocantica. Includes Calbharaigh/Calvary. Choral setting of Sorley MacLean. Sung in Gaelic. SAIN 2047

Twentieth Century Scottish Choral Music. Includes 12-part motet in memoriam Robert Carver (text: James Reid Baxter). Capella Nova. LINN RECORDS 014

Books –

Western Music: a brief introduction, Kahn and Averill, London 1971

ed *Bernhard Ziehn: Canonical Studies,* Kahn and Averill, London, 1976.

ed *Time Remembered, a symposium for the 80th birthday of Alan Bush,* Ventura 1981

The Paderewski Paradox, Klavar Music Foundation, GB and Société Paderewski 1992.

Biography –

Ronald Stevenson, a musical biography, Malcolm MacDonald, The National Library of Scotland 1989.

Critical articles by Ronald Stevenson, mainly literary:

'MacDiarmid, Joyce and Busoni', eds K D Duval and Sydney Goodsir Smith. *Hugh MacDiarmid: a festschrift.* K D Duval 1962.

'K H Sorabji', Hugh MacDiarmid. *The Company I've Kept.* Hutchison. 1966.

'The Emergence of Scottish Music', ed Karl Miller. *Memoirs of a Modern Scotland.* Faber 1970.

'MacDiarmid's Muses', eds P H Scott and A C Davis. *The Age of MacDiarmid: Essays on Hugh MacDiarmid.* Mainstream 1980.

'Byron', *Byron* ed Alan Bold.

'Wilfred Owen's 'Strange Meeting'', ed John Blackburn. *Hardy to Heaney.* Oliver & Boyd 1986.

'MacLean: musician manqué (and a composer's collaboration)', eds Raymond J Ross and Joy Hendry. *Sorley MacLean: Critical Essays.* Scottish Academic Press 1986.

There is of course a massive number of musicological articles by Stevenson, which are currently being collated.

Prices available on application to the RSS.

Notes on Contributors

Martin Anderson publishes books on music as Toccata Press and writes on music and economics. He has been Editor of *Economic Affairs* and *The OECD Observer.*

Louis Aragon (1897-1982). One of the most prolific writers in 20th century French. The title of the Centenary Conference at Manchester University, 'From Surrealism to Socialist Realism', gives a fair over-view.

Jamie Reid Baxter: from Banffshire and now lives and works in Scotland (which he enjoys) and Luxembourg (which he enjoys less).

Ven Begamudré: born in South India, was the 1995-6 Canada Scotland Exchange Writer-In-Residence. His contribution is from his new book, *Laterna Magika.*

John Bellany's paintings are in collections throughout the world. Forthcoming solo exhibition – Beaux Arts Gallery, London.

Martin Bennett has had work in *Poetry Ireland Review*, *Lines Review*, *West Africa* and elsewhere. *West African Trickster Tales* was published by Oxford University Press 1994.

Hamish Brown has written/edited over 20 books/anthologies and contributed stories to many publications. *The Bothy Brew and other stories* was published in 1993 (Luath Press).

Tom Bryan: widely published poet and fiction writer. Freelance journalist. Story collection and two novels under consideration. At 48, feels he deserves a big break in '98! Former fish farmer.

Angus Calder published a collection of poetry *Waking in Waikato* (diehard) this year.

Alastair Chisholm is Director of Music at the Cathedral of the Isles, Millport. He has written and broadcast on various musical figures including Bernard van Dieren.

Victoria Crowe: Painter and printmaker, part-time lecturer at Edinburgh College of Art. Exhibits widely in UK and Europe, work in major public and private collections.

Angus Dunn: writes fiction and poetry. 1995 RLS/Christian Salvesen Award Winner. Currently Writer in Residence for Aberdeenshire and working on a novel. Lives in Ross-shire.

Mark Tyler Edwards was born in 1970. He lives and works in East Sussex and is currently seeking a publisher for his first novel.

Geoffrey Elborn has written biographies of Edith Sitwell and Francis Stuart. He is a reviewer for *The Guardian*, a contributor to *Contemporary Novelists* and *The New Dictionary of National Biography.*

Pete Fortune: a widely published fiction writer. Bogged down in a novel of late.

Peter France has published many translations from French and Russian, most recently the *Selected Poems, 1954-94* of Gennady Aygi (Angel Books, 1997). He is editing the *Oxford Guide to Literature in English Translation.*

Iain Galbraith's recent publications include editions of Stevenson's *Treasure Island* and *Travels with a Donkey*, and an adaptation of *Trainspotting* for the German stage.

Robin Hamilton was educated at the University of Glasgow and now teaches English at Loughborough University. His collected poems *The Lost Jockey* was published in 1985.

Tom Hubbard is currently a visiting professor of literature and language at the Univ. of North Carolina at Asheville. His most recent book is *The Integrative Vision: Poetry and the Visual Arts in Baudelaire, Rilke and MacDiarmid.*

Philip Hutton studied Gray's School of Art, Aberdeen. He taught art in Border primary schools for many years. He now works as a freelance artist.

Chris Jones: born in Wales, lives just outside St Andrews. Has performed his poetry in Berlin, London and Oxford. His translations from German have appeared in *Oasis.*

C J Lindsay: Scary and Ginger more than Sporty, Posh or Baby, which suits both work and writing purrfectly – Spice Up Your Life!.

Malcolm MacDonald: lives in Gloucestershire, edits *Tempo, the Quarterly Review of Modern Music*. His books include a musical biography of Ronald Stevenson and the Brahms and Schoenberg volume in the *Master Musicians* series (OUP).

Eddie McGuire is a composer and the flautist with the Scottish music group Whistlebinkies. He has been a member of the Communist Party of Britain (Marxist-Leninist) since 1970.

Menzies McKillop is a retired schoolteacher and will blow the gaff on the seamy underbelly of the educational system if offered an advance by a newspaper magnate.

Wilson McLeod is a postgraduate student in the Dept. of Celtic, University of Edinburgh.

Aonghas MacNeacail: Stakis Scottish Writer of the Year. Has written *Sgathach*, with Alasdair Nicholson, *An Turas* with William Sweeney and song lyrics for Donald Shaw-Phil Cunningham.

Rob MacNeacail is a loyal Hibernian supporter and Blackburn Rovers fan. Other interests: tennis, roller-blading, ice-hockey, shinty, drawing, Roald Dahl, chanter and piano, taught by Ronald.

Kevin MacNeil was born and raised on the Isle of Lewis. A widely published writer of poetry, drama and prose, his debut collection, *Love and Zen in the Outer Hebrides*, is published by Canongate.

John Manson: retired teacher. Writes critical essay on Scottish literature and translates from mainly from the French and Spanish.

Alexander Moffat is Head of Painting at Glasgow School or Art. His paintings of Hugh MacDiarmid, Norman MacCaig, Sorley MacLean and Muriel Spark are in the collection of the Scottish National Portrait Gallery.

Thom Nairn's first collection *The Sand Garden* was published in 1994 (*Dionysia Press*) and his new collection *Chagall Takes a Fall* is due in 1998 (Scottish Cultural Press).

Emma Pitcairn is an unemployed graduate who stays sane by volunteering at *Chapman*. Open to job offers.

John Purser: author of *Scotland's Music* and has published three books of poetry and a number of radio plays including *The Secret Commonwealth*. As a composer his works cover everything from opera to solo guitar.

Joanna Ramsey has lived in Orkney since 1988. She has appeared in *Orkney Arts Review, The New Shetlander* and other publications. She is currently completing a collection of short stories.

Alan Riach, b. Lanarkshire 1957. Senior lecturer in English, Uni of Waikato, New Zealand. Author of Hugh MacDiarmid's *Epic Poetry* (EUP) and editor of MacDiarmid's *Collected Works*. Poetry collections; *Folding Map, An Open Return, First and Last Songs*.

Dilys Rose lives in Edinburgh. Previous publications include *Madame Doubtfire's Dilemma, Our Lady of the Pickpockets* and *Red Tides*. The stories in this issue are from *War Dolls* due out in August 1998.

Virginia Rounding, poet, translator, book and concert reviewer has had poems published in most of the literary journals in the UK. She is currently working on a poetry collection *A Century of Women*.

Maureen Sangster: born Aberdeen 1954. Lives in Edinburgh. Her first poetry collection *Out of the Urn* was published by Scottish Cultural Press in 1997.

Heather Scott born London 1935. Married poet Tom Scott 1963. Has occasionally contributed poetry and prose to magazines.

Robert Dawson Scott is Arts Editor of *The Scotsman*, just. Previously he was arts editor for *Scotland on Sunday*. He has also broadcast extensively on radio and television.

Colin Scott-Sutherland was born 1930 in Fife, the son of an artist. Author of *Arnold Bax* (Dent), *John Ireland* (Triad Press), *Elizabeth Mary Watt* (Patten Press).

Ian Shearer: born in the West Midlands. Contributes book reviews to the London Magazine and poetry in several magazines.

Judy Steel: founded the Borders festival in 1985 and currently runs the James Hogg Exhibition at Aikwood Tower and the Rowan Tree Company which specialises in the performances of the stories and songs of the Borders.

Arseny Tarkovsky (1907-1989) A friend of Ahkmatova and Tsvetayeva, he was the most respected of the older generation of poets who lived to see the era of 'glasnost'.

Derick Tulloch: Fae Yell in Shetland. Used tae hae a croft and sheep. Poetry published in *New Shetlander, Shetland Life, Northwords*.

Gael Turnbull's most recent collections are *For Whose Delight* (Mariscat) and *A Rattle of Scree* (Akros).

George Vafopoulos (1903-1996): poet, editor and critic, (not to mention 5 volumes of autobiography). A translation of his *Collected Poems* is due out 1998 from Dionysia Press.

Derek Watson is a composer, pianist, writer and bookseller. Among his output are books on Bruckner, Liszt and Wagner. He has worked as musical director with most Scottish theatre companies.

Kenneth White: born on the West Coast of Scotland, currently lives in Brittany. Books include *The Bird Path, The Blue Road* and *Pilgrim of the Void*.

Ruzena Wood is a freelance musician and journalist, author of *The Palace of the Moon*, André Deutsch, London, 1981.

D Zeranou grew up in Athens, but has lived in Scotland for the last 20 years. She is editor, poet and playwright. Her first full collection of poems was *The Stone Moon* (1997).